Django JavaScript Integration: AJAX and jQuery

Develop AJAX applications using Django and jQuery

Jonathan Hayward

[PACKT] open source *
community experience distilled

PUBLISHING

BIRMINGHAM - MUMBAI

Django JavaScript Integration: AJAX and jQuery

Copyright © 2010 Packt Publishing

All rights reserved. No part of this book may be reproduced, stored in a retrieval system, or transmitted in any form or by any means, without the prior written permission of the publisher, except in the case of brief quotations embedded in critical articles or reviews.

Every effort has been made in the preparation of this book to ensure the accuracy of the information presented. However, the information contained in this book is sold without warranty, either express or implied. Neither the author, nor Packt Publishing, and its dealers and distributors will be held liable for any damages caused or alleged to be caused directly or indirectly by this book.

Packt Publishing has endeavored to provide trademark information about all of the companies and products mentioned in this book by the appropriate use of capitals. However, Packt Publishing cannot guarantee the accuracy of this information.

First published: January 2011

Production Reference: 1291210

Published by Packt Publishing Ltd.
32 Lincoln Road
Olton
Birmingham, B27 6PA, UK.

ISBN 978-1-849510-34-9

www.packtpub.com

Cover Image by Vinayak Chittar (vinayak.chittar@gmail.com)

Credits

Author
Jonathan Hayward

Reviewers
Jake Kronika
Michael Szul

Acquisition Editor
Steven Wilding

Development Editor
Maitreya Bhakal

Technical Editors
Vanjeet D'souza
Conrad Sardinha

Indexers
Hemangini Bari
Monica Ajmera Mehta

Editorial Team Leader
Akshara Aware

Project Team Leader
Ashwin Shetty

Project Coordinator
Joel Goveya

Proofreader
Sandra Hopper

Production Coordinator
Aparna Bhagat

Cover Work
Aparna Bhagat

Foreword

In this book, we will be exploring Django JavaScript integration and build an Ajax application using jQuery. We will build a Web 2.0 intranet employee directory, and we will aim for a solution that is Pythonic in more ways than one.

Web development that is more "Pythonic" than just Python

This book is intended to be a book about how to do web development in the spirit of **Python++**.

The term "Python++" as we use it here is **not** the usual "Python is great," even if that may also be our opinion, but a more direct analogy to C++. When the effort was made to improve the C language, the basic kind of improvement attempted was to expand and broaden the core language. It is no accident that Stroustrup's *The C++ Programming Language* is far longer than Kernigan and Ritchie's *The C Programming Language*. The latter is a small book describing a small core language, while the former is a large book made large by the large core language it describes. The analogy intended by Python++ is somewhat loose here, and specifically does *not* include a large, or even a small, expansion of the core language. It is possible to tinker with the core language—`easy_extend` lets you extend Python to include a do-while loop (where the test condition is first evaluated at the end, not the beginning)—or add primitive syntax so you can do things like `if remote_ip in 10.0.0.0:`, but this is almost beside the point.

The real possibilities for expanding Python do not need to radically expand the core language, or change the core language at all. Django (`http://www.djangoproject.com/`) is not a general purpose enhancement to Python: if you are automating system administration tasks, for instance, you very probably have no reason to use Django. But for a limited problem domain, namely certain kinds of web development, *Django is more Pythonic than Python*. Python's `cgi` module is good for some kinds of small and simple tasks, but if you are going to make a serious, large-scale web application with many standard functions, using *Python core language + Python standard library + Django* is a fundamentally more Pythonic approach than just *Python core language + Python standard library* alone.

On StackOverflow, someone asked the question, "Have you considered using Django and found good reasons not to?" There were various answers, but the answer with the most "up" votes by far said, "I am an honest guy, and the client wanted to charge by the hour. There was no way Django was going to make me enough money."

Django itself is not the limit to Python++. Pinax (`http://pinaxproject.com/`) is built on top of Django and offers a "more Django than Django" platform to build a social network. Satchmo (`http://satchmoproject.com/`) is also "more Django than Django" for another narrower focus: e-commerce webshops. And there are other platforms built on Django; it is time well spent to search the Python Package Index (`http://pypi.python.org/pypi`) for Django to see what is already available. In this text we will often use "Django" as a shorthand for either basic Django or any of the many good tools built on top of Django.

Depending on what you are trying to do, it may be that the bulk of the Python work in Django is resolved surprisingly quickly: you can build and brand a Pinax social network by doing little more than overriding the CSS and adding images. This book will address the Python side and try to give a solid basis for programming Python for Django, working with the templates, and so on, but that problem can often be solved so cleanly that most of the work that remains is styling and Ajax.

Django and its templating engine

Before further exploring technical details, it would be worth taking a look at the opinions and philosophy behind the Django templating language, because an understandable approach of, "Oh, it's a general purpose programming language very slightly adapted for templating," is a recipe for needless frustration and pain. The Django developers themselves acknowledge that their opinions in the templating language are one just opinion in an area where different people have different opinions, and you are welcome to disagree with them if you want. If you don't like the templating system that Django comes with, Django is designed to let you use another. But it is worth understanding what exactly the philosophy behind the templating language is; even if this is not the only philosophy one could use, it is carefully thought out.

The Django templating language is intended to foster the separation of presentation and logic. In its design decisions, both large and small, the Django's templating engine is optimized primarily for designers to use for designing, rather than programmers to use for programming, and its limitations are almost as carefully chosen as the features it provides. Unlike ASP, JSP, and PHP, it is not a programming language interspersed with HTML. It provides enough power for presentation, is intended *not* to provide enough power to do serious programming work where it doesn't belong (in the Django opinion), and is simple enough that some non-programmers can pick it up in a day. For a programmer, the difficulty of learning the templating basics is comparable to the difficulty of simple HTML or SQL: it is simple, and a good bit easier to learn than wrapping your arms around a regular programming language. It is likely that there are a number of Django programmers out there who started by asking, "Why doesn't the templating language just let you mix Python and HTML?" and after playing with it, found themselves saying, "This isn't what I would have come up with myself, but I really, really like it."

Additional benefits include it being *fast* (most of the work is done by a single regular expression call, and the founders talk about disabling caching because it couldn't keep up with the template rendering engine's speed), *secure* (it is designed so that it can be used by untrusted designers without allowing a malicious designer to execute arbitrary code), and *versatile* enough to generate whatever text format you want: plain text, HTML, XML, XHTML, JSON, JavaScript, CSV, ReStructuredText, and so on. We will be using it to generate web pages and JSON, but Django's templating language is a general-purpose text templating solution.

What we will do in this book—building a Web 2.0 intranet employee photo directory

Many books will teach you a new technology by walking through a sample project. This book is no different, but the sample project is not a toy: it is a walk through making a real, live Web 2.0 intranet employee photo directory that you can customize to your organization's needs. This is something that is both useful, and will give us a tour of the potential for developing Ajax applications using Django on the server side and jQuery on the client side.

- Jonathan Hayward

About the Author

Jonathan Hayward as a child ranked 7th in a nationwide math contest, and later programmed a video game on his calculator. He holds master's degrees in bridging mathematics and computer science (UIUC), and philosophy and theology (Cambridge). Jonathan has lived in the U.S., Malaysia, France, and England, and has studied well over a dozen dialects and languages. He wears the hats of author, philosopher, theologian, artist, poet, wayfarer, philologist, inventor, and a skilled web developer who holds a deep interest in the human side of computing. He has a website showcasing his works at `http://JonathansCorner.com` and can be reached via e-mail at `jonathan.hayward@pobox.com`.

> I would like to thank my parents, John and Linda, who love learning and taught me faith, my brothers, Matthew, Kirk and Joe, my parish, St. Innocent of Moscow, for a wealth of support. I would also like to thank the editorial team at Packt: Steven Wilding, who helped me come up with the book idea in the first place, Ved Prakash Jha, who helped see it to completion, and Joel Goyeva, who helped me with innumerable logistics along the way. And, of course, the reviewers Jake Kronika and Michael Szul, who offered an invaluable sharpening. The Django list, `django-users@googlegroups.com`, is worth its weight in gold. I would like to thank Daniel Roseman, Alex Robbins, Dan Harris, Karen Tracey, Oleg Lokalma, Mark Linsey, Jeff Green, Elijah Rutschman, Brian Neal, Euan Goddard, Sævar Öfjörð, "Ringemup", Ben Atkin, Tom Evans, Sam Lai, and Preston Holmes.
>
> Authors have to leave somebody out who deserves to be mentioned; that's just part of the territory. But I would like to thank one person in particular: the reader. You're really the reason the book is here, and you've chosen to invest some money in a book and some time in fascinating technologies and let me help you along the way. Thank you so much.

About the Reviewers

Jake Kronika, a web designer and developer with over fifteen years of experience, brings to this book a strong background in frontend development with JavaScript and AJAX, as well as exposure to the Django framework.

Having earned a Bachelors of Science degree in Computer Science from Illinois Wesleyan University in 2005, with a minor in Business Administration, Jake went on to become Senior User Interface (UI) Specialist for Imaginary Landscape, LLC, a small web development firm in Ravenswood, on the north side of Chicago. In this role, the foundations of his strengths in Cascading Style Sheets (CSS) and JavaScript (JS) were built, as well as extensive use of Python and the Django Framework.

From there, Jake went on to work for the Sun-Times News Group, owner of the Chicago Sun-Times and numerous suburban newspapers in Chicagoland. It was in this role that he was initially exposed and rapidly became an expert with the jQuery framework for JS.

Following an intermediate position as Technology Consultant with Objective Arts, Inc, Jake has worked as UI Prototyper for JP Morgan Chase since February 2010. Since 1999, he has also operated Gridline Design & Development, a sole proprietorship for web design, development, and administration.

> I would like to thank my wife, Veronica, for her ongoing support. She and my twin children Mykaela and Kaden provide all the joy I could want in this world.

Michael Szul has designed and developed software applications for Fortune 500 companies, including AIG and Praxair, since 1998. Later, he served as a senior software engineer for the technology division of Performance Media Group, contributing to their fast growth and success, including placement on the Inc. 5000.

Szul's expertise in social software development led to a lateral move within the company to become the director of development for their travel social network. He even built successful social software for companies such as Apple Vacations and Conde Naste's Gourmet Magazine.

As a partner at Barbella Digital, Inc., he currently designs and develops enterprise-level workflow systems and mobile applications for educational institutions.

www.PacktPub.com

Support files, eBooks, discount offers and more

You might want to visit `www.PacktPub.com` for support files and downloads related to your book.

Did you know that Packt offers eBook versions of every book published, with PDF and ePub files available? You can upgrade to the eBook version at `www.PacktPub.com` and as a print book customer, you are entitled to a discount on the eBook copy. Get in touch with us at `service@packtpub.com` for more details.

At `www.PacktPub.com`, you can also read a collection of free technical articles, sign up for a range of free newsletters and receive exclusive discounts and offers on Packt books and eBooks.

PACKTLIB

`http://PacktLib.PacktPub.com`

Do you need instant solutions to your IT questions? PacktLib is Packt's online digital book library. Here, you can access, read and search across Packt's entire library of books.

Why Subscribe?

- Fully searchable across every book published by Packt
- Copy and paste, print and bookmark content
- On demand and accessible via web browser

Free Access for Packt account holders

If you have an account with Packt at `www.PacktPub.com`, you can use this to access PacktLib today and view nine entirely free books. Simply use your login credentials for immediate access.

Table of Contents

Preface	**1**
Chapter 1: jQuery and Ajax Integration in Django	**7**
Ajax and the XMLHttpRequest object	**8**
Human speech: An overlaid function	8
Ajax: Another overlaid function	8
The technologies Ajax is overlaid on	9
JavaScript	9
XMLHttpRequest	14
Methods	14
Properties	15
HTML/XHTML	17
XML	18
JSON	18
CSS	19
The DOM	19
iframes and other Ajax variations	20
JavaScript/Ajax Libraries	21
Server-side technologies	21
A look at Django	**21**
Django templating kickstart	22
A more complete glimpse at Django templating	23
Setting JavaScript and other static content in place	**32**
Summary	**33**
Chapter 2: jQuery—the Most Common JavaScript Framework	**35**
jQuery and basic Ajax	**36**
jQuery Ajax facilities	**39**
$.ajax()	39
context	40
data	42

dataFilter	43
dataType	43
error(XMLHttpRequest, textStatus, errorThrown)	44
success(data, textStatus, XMLHttpRequest)	44
type	44
url	44
$.aj0axSetup()	**45**
Sample invocation	45
$.get() and $.post()	45
.load()	46
jQuery as a virtual higher-level language	**48**
The selectors	48
A closure-based example to measure clock skew	**52**
Case study: A more in-depth application	**56**
Chapter 3: Validating Form Input on the Server Side	56
Chapter 4: Server-side Database Search with Ajax	56
Chapter 5: Signing Up and Logging into a Website Using Ajax	57
Chapter 6: jQuery In-place Editing Using Ajax	57
Chapter 7: Using jQuery UI Autocomplete in Django Templates	57
Chapter 8: Django ModelForm: a CSS Makeover	57
Chapter 9: Database and Search Handling	57
Chapter 10: Tinkering Around: Bugfixes, Friendlier Password Input, and a Directory That Tells Local Time	58
Chapter 11: Usability for Hackers	58
Appendix: Debugging Hard JavaScript Bugs	58
Summary	**58**
Chapter 3: Validating Form Input on the Server Side	**61**
The standard lecture: low-level validation	**62**
Matching regular expressions	62
You cannot guarantee absolutely valid data	63
Validating can detect (some) malicious input	63
The Django way of validation	**64**
Django gives you some things for free	64
The steps in Django's validation	65
A more sensible and cruelty-free approach to validation	66
Things get murkier	67
The zero-one-infinity rule: a cardinal rule of thumb in usability	68
An improvement on Django's advertised approach	68
A validation example: GPS coordinates	70
Avoiding error messages that point fingers and say, "You're wrong!"	71

Validation as demanding that assumptions be met	**72**
Old-school: conform to our U.S.-based assumptions!	72
Adding the wrong kind of band-aid	74
Making assumptions and demanding that users conform	**76**
At least names are simple, right?	76
Even in ASCII, things keep getting murkier	77
Better validation may be less validation	**78**
Caveat: English is something of a lingua franca	79
We don't have to negotiate with pistols	80
Doing our best to solve the wrong problem: a story	81
It really does apply to validation	82
Facebook and LinkedIn know something better	83
Summary	**83**
Chapter 4: Server-side Database Search with Ajax	**85**
Searching on the client side and server side	86
Handling databases through Django models	86
Models for an intranet employee photo directory	87
Searching our database	95
A tour of Django persistence facilities	100
Summary	103
Chapter 5: Signing Up and Logging into a Website Using Ajax	**105**
admin.py: administrative functions called once	107
functions.py: project-specific functions, including our @ajax_login_required decorator	107
views.py: functions that render web pages	108
style.css: basic styling for usability	113
search.html: a template for client-side Ajax	114
The Django admin interface	122
Summary	124
Chapter 6: jQuery In-place Editing Using Ajax	**125**
Including a plugin	127
How to make pages more responsive	127
A template handling the client-side requirements	128
The bulk of the profile	132
Whitespace and delivery	133
Page-specific JavaScript	136
Support on the server side	137
Summary	139

Chapter 7: Using jQuery UI Autocomplete in Django Templates — 141
Adding autocomplete: first attempt — 142
Progressive enhancement, a best practice — 142
A real-world workaround — 146
"Interest-based negotiation": a power tool for problem solving when plan A doesn't work — 146
A first workaround — 148
Boilerplate code from jQuery UI documentation — 154
Turning on Ajax behavior (or trying to) — 156
Code on the server side — 156
Refining our solution further — 159
Summary — 163

Chapter 8: Django ModelForm: a CSS Makeover — 165
"Hello, world!" in ModelForm — 165
Expanding and customizing the example — 168
Customizing ModelForm pages' appearance — 170
Going under ModelForm's hood — 182
An excellent "stupid" question: where's the e-mail slot? — 184
Summary — 187

Chapter 9: Database and Search Handling — 189
Moving forward to an AHAH solution — 189
Django templates for simple AHAH — 192
Templating for a list of search results — 192
Template for an individual profile — 195
Views on the server side — 202
Telling if the user is logged in — 202
A view to support deletion — 202
The AHAH view to load profiles — 203
Helper functions for the AHAH view for searching — 204
An updated model — 206
An AHAH server-side search function — 207
Handling the client-side: A template for the main page — 209
CSS for styling the directory — 232
Our updated urlpatterns — 241
Summary — 241

Chapter 10: Tinkering Around: Bugfixes, Friendlier Password Input, and a Directory That Tells Local Time — 243
Minor tweaks and bugfixes — 243
Setting a default name of "(Insert name here)" — 244
Eliminating Borg behavior — 244

Confusing jQuery's load() with html()	245
Preventing display of deleted instances	246
Adding a favicon.ico	249
Handling password input in a slightly different way	**250**
A directory that includes local timekeeping	**252**
Summary	**260**
Chapter 11: Usability for Hackers	**261**
Usability begins with anthropology… and Django hackers have a good start on anthropology	**262**
Anthropological usability techniques	**263**
An introductory example: card sorting	263
Focus groups: cargo cult research for usability	**265**
Anthropological observation: the bedrock of usability	**265**
More than one way to see the same situation	266
Applying this foundation to usability	**268**
It's just like (hard) debugging	**271**
Lessons from other areas	**272**
Live cross-cultural encounters	272
History	273
Old books and literature	274
The last other area: whatever you have	277
Understanding the user	**278**
A lesson from optimization	278
What's wrong with scratching an itch, or you are not your user	279
Worst practices from the jargon file	279
Python and usability	**280**
It's not all about the computer!	280
What to do in the concrete	**282**
Further reading	**283**
Summary	**284**
Appendix: Debugging Hard JavaScript Bugs	**285**
"Just fiddling with Firebug" is considered harmful	**285**
Cargo cult debugging at your fingertips	285
The scientific method of debugging	286
Exhausting yourself by barking up the wrong tree	287
The humble debugger	289
The value of taking a break	289
Two major benefits to asking for help	290

Firebug and Chrome developer tools	**290**
The basics across browsers	290
Zeroing in on Chrome	293
Summary	**298**
Index	**299**

Preface

You want to create an AJAX application. Why would you use Django? Why would you use jQuery? Why would you use both together? Enter Django JavaScript Integration: AJAX and jQuery—your comprehensive answer to all these questions and the only extensive, practical, and hands-on guide to developing any AJAX application with Django and jQuery.

Gone are the days when you used to lament over the lack of official documentation on AJAX with Django. This book will teach you exactly why Django is called The web framework for perfectionists with deadlines, how jQuery—the "write less do more" JavaScript library—is practically a virtual higher-level language, and why they both deserve to be integrated with AJAX.

This hands-on-guide shows you how to put Django and jQuery together in the process of creating an AJAX application. In this book, they are brought together in a real-world scenario, with attention to usability, to build and develop an AJAX application.

The first two chapters provide a short and necessary introduction to the world of Django, jQuery, and AJAX; the remaining chapters are based on a case study that will make you realize the immense potential and benefits of integrating Django and jQuery with your AJAX application.

By the time you are done with this book, you'll be developing your AJAX applications with Django and jQuery in less time than you can say "integrate".

You will cover the basics of AJAX; use jQuery, the most common JavaScript library, on the client side, and learn form validation with an eye towards usability, build things with Django on the server side, handle login and authentication via Django-based AJAX, and then dip into the rich jQuery plugin ecosystem to build in-place editing into your pages.

You will add auto-complete functionality courtesy of jQuery UI, easily build forms with Django ModelForm, and then look at a client-side search implementation that can look things up without network access after initial download. You will learn to implement a simple, expandable undo system, and offer more full-blooded account management, tinker, fix some bugs, offer a more usable way to handle password input, add local time support for people who are not in your time zone, look at usability, and finally take a look at debugging.

After working through this book, you will have both an AJAX application: a Web 2.0 employee intranet photo directory, and with it a deep understanding that you can use to customize, extend, and further develop it in your organization.

What this book covers

This book covers Django JavaScript integration and building an Ajax application with Django on the server side and jQuery on the client side. It provides first an overview, then a first Ajax application, and introduces jQuery; discusses form validation, server-side database search; Ajax login facilities; jQuery in-place editing and autocomplete, Django Modelform, and how to give auto-generated forms a transformational CSS makeover. It also discusses client-side functionality, customization, and further development with tinkering and added features, before a grand finale exploring usability, and an appendix on debugging hard JavaScript bugs.

Chapter 1, jQuery and Ajax Integration in Django lays a solid foundation and introduces you to the working pieces of Django Ajax to be explored in the rest of the book.

Chapter 2, jQuery – the Most Common JavaScript Framework explores the "higher-level" way of doing things in jQuery. You will learn how jQuery is not Python and does not look like Python, but how there is something "Pythonic in spirit" about how it works.

Chapter 3, Validating Form Input on the Server Side will teach you how to send an Ajax request to the server via jQuery, and validate it on the server side based on the principle that all input is guilty until proven innocent of being malicious, malformed, incomplete, or otherwise invalid.

Chapter 4, Server-side Database Search with Ajax looks both at the merits of handling searching and other backend functions with the full power of a backend environment, and explores why, on the client side, you should work hard to be as lazy as possible in doing network-related work.

Chapter 5, Signing-up and Logging into a Website Using Ajax introduces Django authentication facilities and account management and includes both server-side and client-side code.

Chapter 6, jQuery In-place Editing Using Ajax goes from a basic foundation to a continuing practical application. It will show a way to use jQuery to make an in-place replacement of a table that allows in-place editing, which communicates with the server in the background, adding persistence to changes.

Chapter 7, Using jQuery UI Autocomplete in Django Templates tells you what you need on the client side and server side to get autocomplete working with jQuery UI. It also includes creative problem solving when something goes wrong. This chapter will tell you why it is not uncommon for programmers to write plugins their first day doing jQuery.

Chapter 8, Django ModelForm: a CSS Makeover explores Django ModelForm and how to use it.

Chapter 9, Database and Search Handling covers all the bases for a simple, AHAH solution. In addition to showing "lazy" best practices, it also showcases a JavaScript in-memory database, with an application designed, at the developer's preference, to either always perform lazy handling of search and other requests, or start loading an in-memory database and falling back to lazy handling until the in-memory database is available.

Chapter 10, Tinkering Around: Bugfixes, Friendlier Password Input, and a Directory That Tells Local Time covers some tinkering and tweaks, and bugfixes along the way

Chapter 11, Usability for Hackers steps back from your application and takes a look at usability and the bedrock competencies hackers can leverage to do usability.

Appendix, Debugging Hard JavaScript Bugs looks at the state of mind that is needed to debug difficult bugs.

What you need for this book

This book assumes a broad technical maturity and an ability to learn and integrate different skills. It helps to be a Pythonista with the usual strengths that come with Python, and knowledge of the Web. A basic understanding of, or the ability to learn, Django and JavaScript will be helpful.

If you're a good generalist programmer who wants to learn Django JavaScript integration, this book is for you.

Who this book is for

This book is for people looking to integrate AJAX / JavaScript functionality into their web applications. It is for Django users who are looking to easily integrate AJAX features into their applications. Conversely, it will also be a priceless companion for users familiar with Django and jQuery who are looking to integrate them in their AJAX applications. A working knowledge of Django and basic familiarity with AJAX and jQuery are assumed.

Conventions

In this book, you will find a number of styles of text that distinguish between different kinds of information. Here are some examples of these styles, and an explanation of their meaning.

Code words in text are shown as follows: "You can override the empty string by setting TEMPLATE_STRING_IF_INVALID in your settings.py file".

A block of code is set as follows:

```
function outer()
    {
    result = 0;
    for(i = 0; i < 100; ++i)
        {
        result += inner(i);
        }
    return result
    }
```

When we wish to draw your attention to a particular part of a code block, the relevant lines or items are set in bold:

```
def ajax_profile(request, id):
    entity = directory.models.Entity.objects.filter(id = int(id))[0]
    if entity.is_invisible:
        return HttpResponse(u'<h2>People, etc.</h2>')
```

New terms and **important words** are shown in bold. Words that you see on the screen, in menus or dialog boxes for example, appear in the text like this: "We can then click on **Entity** (or **Locations**), and add an entity".

[Warnings or important notes appear in a box like this.]

Reader feedback

Feedback from our readers is always welcome. Let us know what you think about this book—what you liked or may have disliked. Reader feedback is important for us to develop titles that you really get the most out of.

To send us general feedback, simply send an e-mail to feedback@packtpub.com, and mention the book title via the subject of your message.

If there is a book that you need and would like to see us publish, please send us a note in the **SUGGEST A TITLE** form on www.packtpub.com or e-mail suggest@packtpub.com.

If there is a topic that you have expertise in and you are interested in either writing or contributing to a book, see our author guide on www.packtpub.com/authors.

Customer support

Now that you are the proud owner of a Packt book, we have a number of things to help you to get the most from your purchase.

> **Downloading the example code for the book**
>
> You can download the example code files for all Packt books you have purchased from your account at http://www.PacktPub.com. If you purchased this book elsewhere, you can visit http://www.PacktPub.com/support and register to have the files e-mailed directly to you.

Errata

Although we have taken every care to ensure the accuracy of our content, mistakes do happen. If you find a mistake in one of our books—maybe a mistake in the text or the code—we would be grateful if you would report this to us. By doing so, you can save other readers from frustration and help us improve subsequent versions of this book. If you find any errata, please report them by visiting http://www.packtpub.com/support, selecting your book, clicking on the **errata submission form** link, and entering the details of your errata. Once your errata are verified, your submission will be accepted and the errata will be uploaded on our website, or added to any list of existing errata, under the Errata section of that title. Any existing errata can be viewed by selecting your title from http://www.packtpub.com/support.

Piracy

Piracy of copyright material on the Internet is an ongoing problem across all media. At Packt, we take the protection of our copyright and licenses very seriously. If you come across any illegal copies of our works, in any form, on the Internet, please provide us with the location address or website name immediately so that we can pursue a remedy.

Please contact us at copyright@packtpub.com with a link to the suspected pirated material.

We appreciate your help in protecting our authors, and our ability to bring you valuable content.

Questions

You can contact us at questions@packtpub.com if you are having a problem with any aspect of the book, and we will do our best to address it.

1
jQuery and Ajax Integration in Django

We will be working with the leading Python web framework, Django, on the server side, and jQuery-powered Ajax on the client side. During the course of this book, we will cover the basic technologies and then see them come together in an employee intranet photo directory that shares some Web 2.0 strengths.

There is more than one good JavaScript library; we will be working with jQuery, which has reached acceptance as a standard lightweight JavaScript library. It might be suggested that Pythonistas may find much to like in jQuery: jQuery, like Python, was carefully designed to enable the developer to get powerful results easily.

In this chapter, we will:

- Discuss Ajax as not a single technology but a technique which is overlaid on other technologies
- Cover the basic technologies used in Ajax JavaScript
- Cover "Hello, world!" in a Django kickstart
- Introduce the Django templating engine
- Cover how to serve up static content in Django

Overall, what we will be doing is laying a solid foundation and introducing the working pieces of Django Ajax to be explored in this book.

Ajax and the XMLHttpRequest object

Ajax is not a technology like JavaScript or CSS, but is more like an overlaid function. So, what exactly is that?

Human speech: An overlaid function

Human speech is an **overlaid function**. What is meant by this is reflected in the answer to a question: "What part of the human body has the basic job of speech?" The tongue, for one answer, is used in speech, but it also tastes food and helps us swallow. The lungs and diaphragm, for another answer, perform the essential task of breathing. The brain cannot be overlooked, but it also does a great many other jobs. All of these parts of the body do something more essential than speech and, for that matter, all of these can be found among animals that cannot talk. Speech is something that is *overlaid* over organs that are there in the first place because of something other than speech.

Something similar to this is true for **Ajax**, which is not a technology in itself, but something **overlaid** on top of other technologies. Ajax, some people say, stands for **Asynchronous JavaScript and XML**, but that was a retroactive expansion. JavaScript was introduced almost a decade before people began seriously talking about Ajax. Not only is it technically possible to use Ajax without JavaScript (one can substitute VBScript at the expense of browser compatibility), but there are quite a few substantial reasons to use **JavaScript Object Notation (JSON)** in lieu of heavy-on-the-wire **eXtensible Markup Language** (XML). Performing the *overlaid function* of Ajax with JSON replacing XML is just as eligible to be considered full-fledged Ajax as a solution incorporating XML.

Ajax: Another overlaid function

What exactly is this overlaid function?

Ajax is a way of using client-side technologies to talk with a server and perform partial page updates. Updates may be to all or part of the page, or simply to data handled behind the scenes. It is an alternative to the older paradigm of having a whole page replaced by a new page loaded when someone clicks on a link or submits a form. Partial page updates, in Ajax, are associated with **Web 2.0**, while whole page updates are associated with **Web 1.0**; it is important to note that "Web 2.0" and "Ajax" are not interchangeable. Web 2.0 includes more decentralized control and contributions besides Ajax, and for some objectives it may make perfect sense to develop an e-commerce site that uses Ajax but does not open the door to the same kind of community contributions as Web 2.0.

Some of the key features common in Web 2.0 include:

- Partial page updates with JavaScript communicating with a server and rendering to a page
- An emphasis on user-centered design
- Enabling community participation to update the website
- Enabling information sharing as core to what this communication allows

The concept of "partial page updates" may not sound very big, but part of its significance may be seen in an unintended effect. The original expectation of partial page updates was that it would enable web applications that were more responsive. The expectation was that if submitting a form would only change a small area of a page, using Ajax to just load the change would be faster than reloading the entire page for every minor change. That much was true, but once programmers began exploring, what they used Ajax for was not simply minor page updates, but making client-side applications that took on challenges more like those one would expect a desktop program to do, and the more interesting Ajax applications usually became slower. Again, this was not because you could not fetch part of the page and update it faster, but because programmers were trying to do things on the client side that simply were not possible under the older way of doing things, and were pushing the envelope on the concept of a web application and what web applications can do.

The technologies Ajax is overlaid on

Now let us look at some of the technologies where Ajax may be said to be *overlaid*.

JavaScript

JavaScript deserves pride of place, and while it is possible to use VBScript for Internet Explorer as much more than a proof of concept, for now if you are doing Ajax, it will almost certainly be Ajax running JavaScript as its engine. Your application will have JavaScript working with `XMLHttpRequest`, JavaScript working with HTML, XHTML, or HTML5; JavaScript working with the DOM, JavaScript working with CSS, JavaScript working with XML or JSON, and perhaps JavaScript working with other things.

While addressing a group of Django developers or Pythonistas, it would seem appropriate to open with, "I share your enthusiasm." On the other hand, while addressing a group of JavaScript programmers, in a few ways it is more appropriate to say, "I feel your pain." JavaScript is a language that has been discovered as a gem, but its warts were enough for it to be largely unappreciated for a long time. "Ajax is the gateway drug to JavaScript," as it has been said—however, JavaScript needs a gateway drug before people get hooked on it. JavaScript is an excellent language and a terrible language rolled into one.

Before discussing some of the strengths of JavaScript—and the language does have some truly deep strengths—I would like to say "I feel your pain" and discuss two quite distinct types of pain in the JavaScript language.

The first source of pain is some of the language decisions in JavaScript:

- The Wikipedia article says it was designed to resemble Java but be easier for non-programmers, a decision reminiscent of SQL and COBOL.
- The Java programmer who finds the C-family idiom of `for(i = 0; i < 100; ++i)` available will be astonished to find that the functions are clobbering each other's assignments to `i` until they are explicitly declared local to the function by declaring the variables with `var`. There is more pain where that came from.

The following two functions will not perform the naively expected mathematical calculation correctly; the assignments to `i` and the result will clobber each other:

```
function outer()
    {
    result = 0;
    for(i = 0; i < 100; ++i)
        {
        result += inner(i);
        }
    return result
    }

function inner(limit)
    {
    result = 0;
    for(i = 0; i < limit; ++i)
        {
        result += i;
        }
    return result;
    }
```

The second source of pain is quite different. It is a pain of inconsistent implementation: the pain of, "Write once, debug everywhere." Strictly speaking, this is not JavaScript's fault; browsers are inconsistent. And it need not be a pain in the server-side use of JavaScript or other non-browser uses. However, it comes along for the ride for people who wish to use JavaScript to do Ajax. Cross-browser testing is a foundational practice in web development of any stripe; a good web page with semantic markup and good CSS styling that is developed on Firefox will usually look sane on Internet Explorer (or vice versa), even if not quite pixel-perfect. But program directly for the JavaScript implementation on one version of a browser, and you stand rather sharp odds of your application not working at all on another browser. The most important object by far for Ajax is the `XMLHttpRequest` and not only is it not the case that you may have to do different things to get an XMLHttpRequest in different browsers or sometimes different (common) versions of the same browser, and, even when you have code that will get an `XMLHttpRequest` object, the objects you have can be incompatible so that code that works on one will show strange bugs for another. Just because you have done the work of getting an `XMLHttpRequest` object in all of the major browsers, it doesn't mean you're home free.

Before discussing some of the strengths of the JavaScript language itself, it would be worth pointing out that a good library significantly reduces the second source of pain. Almost any sane library will provide a single, consistent way to get `XMLHttpRequest` functionality, and consistent behavior for the access it provides. In other words, one of the services provided by a good JavaScript library is a much more uniform behavior, so that you are programming for only one model, or as close as it can manage, and not, for instance, pasting conditional boilerplate code to do simple things that are handled differently by different browser versions, often rendering surprisingly different interpretations of JavaScript. We will be using the jQuery library in this book as a standard, well-designed, lightweight library. Many of the things we will see done well as we explore jQuery are also done well in other libraries.

We previously said that JavaScript is an excellent language and a terrible language rolled into one; what is to be said in favor of JavaScript? The list of faults is hardly all that is wrong with JavaScript, and saying that libraries can dull the pain is not itself a great compliment. But in fact, something much stronger can be said for JavaScript: *If you can figure out why Python is a good language, you can figure out why JavaScript is a good language.*

I remember, when I was chasing pointer errors in what became 60,000 lines of C, teasing a fellow student for using Perl instead of a real language. It was clear in my mind that there were interpreted scripting languages, such as the bash scripting that I used for minor convenience scripts, and then there were *real* languages, which were compiled to machine code. I was sure that a real language was identified with being compiled, among other things, and that power in a language was the sort of thing C traded in. (I wonder why he didn't ask me if he wasn't a real programmer because he didn't spend half his time chasing pointer errors.) Within the past year or so I've been asked if "Python is a real programming language or is just used for scripting," and something similar to the attitude shift I needed to appreciate Perl and Python is needed to properly appreciate JavaScript.

The name "JavaScript" is unfortunate; like calling Python "Assembler Kit", it's a way to ask people not to see its real strengths. (Someone looking for tools for working on an assembler would be rather disgusted to buy an "Assembler Kit" and find Python inside. People looking for Java's strengths in JavaScript will almost certainly be disappointed.)

JavaScript code may look like Java in an editor, but the resemblance is a façade; besides Mocha, which had been renamed LiveScript, being renamed to JavaScript just when Netscape was announcing Java support in web browsers, it is has been described as being descended from NewtonScript, Self, Smalltalk, and Lisp, as well as being influenced by Scheme, Perl, Python, C, and Java. What's under the Java façade is pretty interesting. And, in the sense of the simplifying "façade" design pattern, JavaScript was marketed in a way almost guaranteed not to communicate its strengths to programmers. It was marketed as something that nontechnical people could add snippets of, in order to achieve minor, and usually annoying, effects on their web pages. It may not have been a toy language, but it sure was dressed up like one.

Python may not have functions clobbering each other's variables (at least not unless they are explicitly declared global), but Python and JavaScript are both multiparadigm languages that support object-oriented programming, and their versions of "object-oriented" have a lot in common, particularly as compared to (for instance) Java. In Java, an object's class defines its methods and the type of its fields, and this much is set in stone. In Python, an object's class defines what an object starts off as, but methods and fields can be attached and detached at will. In JavaScript, classes as such do not exist (unless simulated by a library such as Prototype), but an object can inherit from another object, making a prototype and by implication a prototype chain, and like Python it is dynamic in that fields can be attached and detached at will. In Java, the `instanceof` keyword is important, as are class casts, associated with strong, static typing; Python doesn't have casts, and its `isinstance()` function is seen by some as a mistake, hence the blog posting "`isinstance()` considered harmful" at http://www.canonical.org/~kragen/isinstance/.

The concern is that Python, like JavaScript, is a duck-typing language: *If it looks like a duck, and it quacks like a duck, it's a duck!* In a duck-typing language, if you write a program that polls weather data, and there's a `ForecastFromScreenscraper` object that is several years old and screenscrapes an HTML page, you should be able to write a `ForecastFromRSS` object that gets the same information much more cleanly from an RSS feed. You should be able to use it as a drop-in replacement as long as you have the interface right. That is different from Java; at least if it were a `ForecastFromScreenscraper` object, code would break immediately if you handed it a `ForecastFromRSS` object. Now, in fairness to Java, the "best practices" Java way to do it would probably separate out an `IForecast` interface, which would be implemented by both `ForecastFromScreenscraper` and later `ForecastFromRSS`, and Java has ways of allowing drop-in replacements *if* they have been explicitly foreseen and planned for. However, in duck-typed languages, the reality goes beyond the fact that if the people in charge designed things carefully and used an interface for a particular role played by an object, you can make a drop-in replacement. In a duck-typed language, you can make a drop-in replacement for things that the original developers never imagined you would want to replace.

JavaScript's reputation is changing. More and more people are recognizing that there's more to the language than design flaws. More and more people are looking past the fact that JavaScript is packaged like Java, like packaging a hammer to give the impression that it is basically like a wrench. More and more people are looking past the silly "toy language" Halloween costume that JavaScript was stuffed into as a kid.

One of the ways good programmers grow is by learning new languages, and JavaScript is not just the gateway to mainstream Ajax; it is an interesting language in itself. With that much stated, we will be making a carefully chosen, selective use of JavaScript, and not make a language lover's exploration of the JavaScript language, overall. Much of our work will be with the jQuery library; if you have just programmed a little "bare JavaScript", discovering jQuery is a bit like discovering Python, in terms of a tool that cuts like a hot knife through butter. It takes learning, but it yields power and interesting results soon as well as having some room to grow.

XMLHttpRequest

The `XMLHttpRequest` object is the reason why the kind of games that can be implemented with Ajax technologies do not stop at clones of Tetris and other games that do not know or care if they are attached to a network. They include massive multiplayer online role-playing games where the network is the computer. Without having something like `XMLHttpRequest`, "Ajax chess" would probably mean a game of chess against a chess engine running in your browser's JavaScript engine; with `XMLHttpRequest`, "Ajax chess" is more likely man-to-man chess against another human player connected via the network. The `XMLHttpRequest` object is the object that lets Gmail, Google Maps, Bing Maps, Facebook, and many less famous Ajax applications deliver on Sun's promise: the network *is* the computer.

There are differences and some incompatibilities between different versions of `XMLHttpRequest`, and efforts are underway to advance "level-2-compliant" `XMLHttpRequest` implementations, featuring everything that is expected of an `XMLHttpRequest` object today and providing further functionality in addition, somewhat in the spirit of level 2 or level 3 CSS compliance. We will not be looking at level 2 efforts, but we will look at the baseline of what is expected as standard in most `XMLHttpRequest` objects.

The basic way that an `XMLHttpRequest` object is used is that the object is created or reused (the preferred practice usually being to reuse rather than create and discard a large number), a callback event handler is specified, the connection is opened, the data is sent, and then when the network operation completes, the callback handler retrieves the response from `XMLHttpRequest` and takes an appropriate action.

A bare-bones `XMLHttpRequest` object can be expected to have the following methods and properties.

Methods

A bare-bones `XMLHttpRequest` object can be expected to have the following methods:

1. `XMLHttpRequest.abort()`

   This cancels any active request.

2. `XMLHttpRequest.getAllResponseHeaders()`

   This returns all HTTP response headers sent with the response.

3. `XMLHttpRequest.getResponseHeader(headerName)`

   This returns the requested header if available, or a browser-dependent false value if the header is not defined.

4. `XMLHttpRequest.open(method, URL)`,
   `XMLHttpRequest.open(method, URL, asynchronous)`,
   `XMLHttpRequest.open(method, URL, asynchronous, username)`,
   `XMLHttpRequest.open(method, URL, asynchronous, username, password)`

   The `method` is `GET`, `POST`, `HEAD`, or one of the other less frequently used methods defined for HTTP.

   The `URL` is the relative or absolute URL to fetch. As a security measure for JavaScript running in browsers on trusted internal networks, a **same origin policy** is in effect, prohibiting direct access to servers other than one the web page came from. Note that this is less restrictive than it sounds, as it is entirely permissible for the server to act as a proxy for any server it has access to: for developers willing to undertake the necessary chores, other sites on the public internet are "virtually accessible".

   The `asynchronous` variable defaults to `true`, meaning that the method call should return quickly in most cases, instead of waiting for the network operation to complete. Normally this default value should be preserved. Among other problems, setting it to `false` can lock up the visitor's browser.

   The last two arguments are the username and password as optionally specified in HTTP. If they are not specified, they default to any username and password defined for the web page.

5. `XMLHttpRequest.send(content)`

   Content can be a string or a reference to a document.

Properties

A bare-bones `XMLHttpRequest` object can be expected to have the following properties:

1. `XMLHttpRequest.onreadystatechange`,
   `XMLHttpRequest.readyState`

   In addition to the provided methods, the reference to one other method is supplied by the developer as a property, `XMLHttpRequest.onreadystatechange`, which is called without argument each time the ready state of `XMLHttpRequest` changes. An `XMLHttpRequest` object can have five ready states:

   ○ Uninitialized, meaning that `open()` has not been called.

   ○ Open, meaning that `open()` has been called but `send()` has not.

   ○ Sent, meaning that `send()` has been called, and headers and status are available, but the response is not yet available.

- Receiving, meaning that the response is being downloaded and `responseText` has the portion that is presently available.
- Loaded, meaning that the network operation has completed. If it has completed successfully (that is, the HTTP status stored in `XMLHttpRequest.status` is 200), this is when the web page would be updated based on the response.

2. `XMLHttpRequest.responseText, XMLHttpRequest.responseXML`

   The text of the response. It is important to note that while the name "*XML*HttpRequest" is now very well established, and it was originally envisioned as a tool to get *XML*, the job done today is quite often to get *text* that may or may not happen to be XML. While there have been problems encountered with using `XMLHttpRequest` to fetch raw binary data, the `XMLHttpRequest` object is commonly used to fetch not only XML but XHTML, HTML, plain text, and JSON, among others. If it were being named today, it would make excellent sense to name it "*Text*HttpRequest." Once the request reaches a ready state of 4 ("loaded"), the `responseText` field will contain the text that was served up, whether the specific text format is XML or anything else. In addition, if the format does turn out to be XML, the `responseXML` field will hold a parsed XML document.

3. `XMLHttpRequest.status, XMLHttpRequest.statusText`

   The `status` field contains the HTTP code, such as 200 for OK; the `statusText` field has a short text description, like OK. The callback event handler should ordinarily check `XMLHttpRequest.readyState` and wait before acting on server-provided data until the `readyState` is 4. In addition, because there could be a server error or a network error, the callback will check whether the status is 200 or something else: a code like 4xx or 5xx in particular needs to be treated as an error. If the server-response has been transmitted successfully, the `readyState` will be 4 and the `status` will be 200.

This is the basic work that needs to be done for the `XMLHttpRequest` side of Ajax. Other frameworks may simplify this and do much of the cross-browser debugging work for you; we will see in the next chapter how jQuery simplifies this work. But this kind of task is something you will need to have done with any library, and it's worth knowing what's behind the simplified interfaces that jQuery and other libraries provide.

HTML/XHTML

HTML and XHTML make up the bedrock markup language for the web. JavaScript and CSS were introduced in relation to HTML; perhaps some people are now saying that JavaScript is a very interesting language independent of web browsers and using standalone interpreters such as SpiderMonkey and Rhino. However, HTML was on the scene first and other players on the web exist in relation to HTML's story. Even when re-implemented as XHTML, to do HTML's job while potentially making much more sense to parsers, a very early web page, the beginning of the source at `http://www.w3.org/History/19921103-hypertext/hypertext/WWW/TheProject.html`, is still quite intelligible:

```
<HEADER>
<TITLE>The World Wide Web project</TITLE>
<NEXTID N="55">
</HEADER>
<BODY>
<H1>World Wide Web</H1>The WorldWideWeb (W3)
is a wide-area
<A NAME=0 HREF="WhatIs.html">
hypermedia</A> information retrieval
initiative aiming to give universal
access to a large universe of documents.<P>
Everything there is online about
W3 is linked directly or indirectly
to this document, including an
<A NAME=24 HREF="Summary.html">executive
summary</A> of the project,
<A NAME=29 HREF="Administration/Mailing/Overview.html">
Mailing lists</A> ,
<A NAME=30 HREF="Policy.html">Policy</A> , November's
<A NAME=34 HREF="News/9211.html">W3   news</A> ,
<A NAME=41 HREF="FAQ/List.html">Frequently Asked Questions
</A> .
<DL>
...
```

At the time of this writing, HTML 5 is taking shape but is not "out in the wild", and so there are no reports of how the shoe feels after the public has worn it for a while. Code in this book, where possible, will be written in XHTML 1.0 Strict. Depending on your situation, this may or may not be the right decision for you; if you are working with an existing project, the right HTML/XHTML is often the one that maintains consistency within the project.

XML

eXtensible Markup Language (XML) is tied to an attempt to clean up early HTML. At least in earliest forms, HTML was a black sheep among specific markup languages derived from the generalized and quite heavy **Standard Generalized Markup Language (SGML)**. Forgiving web browsers meant, in part, that early web hobbyists could write terrible markup and it would still display well in a browser. The amount of terrible markup on the web was not just an issue for purists; it meant that making a parser that could make sense of early "Wild West" web pages in general was a nearly impossible task. XML is vastly simplified from SGML, but it provides a generic space where an HTML variant, XHTML, could pick up the work done by HTML but not present parsers with unpredictable tag soup. XHTML could be described as HTML brought back into the fold, still good for doing web development, but without making machine interpretation such a hopeless cause. Where early HTML was developed with browsers that were meant to be forgiving, XML requested draconian error handling, and validated XML or XHTML documents are documents that can be parsed in a sensible way.

XML works for exchanging information, and it works where many of its predecessors had failed: it provides interoperability between different systems after a long history of failed attempts at automating B2B communication and failed attempts at automated conversion between text data formats. Notwithstanding this, it is a heavy and verbose solution, with a bureaucratic ambiance, compared in particular to a lean, mean JSON. XML-based approaches to data storage and communication are increasingly critiqued in discussions on the web. If you have a reasonable choice between XML and JSON, we suggest that you seriously consider JSON.

JSON

JavaScript Object Notation (JSON) is a brilliantly simple idea. While formats like XML, ReStructuredText, and so on share the assumption that "if you're going to parse this from your language, your language will need to have a parser added," JSON simply takes advantage of how an object would be specified in JavaScript, and clarifies a couple of minor points to make JSON conceptually simpler and cross-browser friendly. JSON is clear, simple, and concise enough that not only is it a format of choice for JavaScript, but it is gaining traction in other languages, and it is being used for communication between languages that need a (simple, added) parser to parse JSON. The other languages can't use `eval()` to simply run JSON, and in JavaScript you should have JSON checked to make sure it does not contain malicious JavaScript you should not `eval()`. However, JSON is turning out to have a much broader impact than the initial "in communicating with JavaScript, just give it code to declare the object being communicated that can simply be evaluated to construct the object."

CSS

Cascading Style Sheets (**CSS**) may have introduced some new possibilities for presentation, but quite a lot of presentation was already possible beforehand. CSS did not so much add styling capabilities, as it added good engineering *to* styling (good engineering is the essence of "separating presentation from content"), and make the combination of semantic markup *and* attractive appearance a far more attainable goal. It allows parlor tricks such as in-place rebranding of websites: making changes in images and changing one stylesheet is, at least in principle, enough to reskin an extensive website without touching a single character of its HTML/XHTML markup. In Ajax, as for the rest of the web, the preferred practice is to use semantic, structural markup, and then add styles in a stylesheet (not inline) so that a particular element, optionally belonging to the right class or given the right ID, will have the desired appearance. Tables are not deprecated but should be used for semantic presentation of tabular data where it makes sense to use not only a `td` but a `th` as well. What is discouraged is using the side effect that tables can position content that is not, semantically speaking, tabular data.

The DOM

As far as direct human browsing is concerned, HTML and associated technologies are vehicles to deliver a pickled **Document Object Model** (**DOM**), and nothing more. In this respect, HTML is a means to an end: the DOM is the "deserialized object," or better, the "live form" of what we really deliver to people. HTML may help provide a complete blueprint, and the "complete blueprint" is a means to the "fully realized building." This is why solving Ajax problems on the level of HTML text are like answering the wrong question, or at least solving a problem on the wrong level. It is like deciding that you want a painting hung on a wall of a building, and then going about getting it by adding the painting to the blueprint and asking construction personnel to implement the specified change. It may be better to hang the painting on the wall directly, as is done in Ajax DOM manipulations.

`document.write()` and `document.getElementById().innerHTML()` still have a place in web development. It is a sensible optimization to want a static, cacheable HTML/XHTML file include that will only be downloaded once in the usual multi-page visit. A JavaScript include with a series of `document.write()` may be the least Shanghaiing you can do to technologies and still achieve that goal. But this is *not* Ajax; it is barely JavaScript, and this is not where we should be getting our bearings. In Ajax, a serious alternative to this kind of solution for altering part of a web page is with the DOM.

As the book progresses, we will explore Ajax development that works with the DOM.

iframes and other Ajax variations

Ajax includes several variations; **Comet** for instance, is a variation on standard Ajax in which either an `XMLHttpRequest` object's connection to a server is kept open and streaming indefinitely, or a new connection is opened whenever an old one is closed, creating an Ajax environment in which the server as well as the client can push material. This is used, for instance, in some instant messaging implementations. One much more essential Ajax variation has to do with loading documents into seamlessly integrated iframes instead of making DOM manipulations to a single, frame-free web page.

If you click around on the page for a Gmail account, you will see partial page refreshes that look consistent with Ajax DOM manipulations: what happens when you click on **Compose Mail**, or a filter, or a message subject, looks very much like an Ajax update where the Gmail web application talks with the server if it needs to, and then updates the DOM in accordance with your clicks. However, there is one important difference between Gmail's behavior and a similar Ajax clone that updates the DOM for one frameless web page: what happens when you click the browser "Back" button. Normally, if you click on a link, you trigger an Ajax event but not a whole page refresh, and Ajax optionally communicates with a server and updates some part of the DOM. This does not register in the browser's history, and hitting the **Back** button would not simply reset the last Ajax partial page update. If you made an Ajax clone of Gmail that used DOM manipulations instead of seamlessly integrated iframes, there would be one important difference in using the clone: hitting **Back** would do far more than reverse the last DOM manipulation. *It would take you back to the login or load screen.* In Gmail, the browser's **Back** button works with surgical accuracy, and the reason it can do something much better than take you back to the login screen is that Gmail is carefully implemented with iframes, and every change that the **Back** button can undo is implemented by a fresh page load in one of the seamlessly integrated iframes. That creates browsing history.

For that matter, a proof of concept has been created for an Ajax application that does not use client-side scripting or programming, instead using, on the client side, a system of frames/iframes, targets, links, form submissions, and meta refresh tags in order to perform partial page updates. Whether this variant technique lends itself to creating graceful alternatives to standard Ajax implementations, or is only a curiosity merely lending itself to proofs of concept, it is in principle possible to make an Ajax application that loses nothing if a visitor's browser has turned off scripting completely.

Comet and iframes are two of many possible variations on the basic Ajax technique; what qualifies as Ajax is more a matter of Python- or JavaScript-style duck-typing than Java-style static typing. "Asynchronous JavaScript and XML" describes a reference example more than a strict definition, and it is not appropriate to say "if you replace XML with JSON then, by definition, it isn't really Ajax." This is a case of, "the proof of the pudding is in the eating," not what technologies or even techniques are in the kitchen.

JavaScript/Ajax Libraries

This book advocates taking advantage of libraries, and as a limitation of scope focuses on jQuery. If you only learn one library, or if you are starting with just one library, jQuery is a good choice, and it is widely used. It is powerful, but it is also a much easier environment to get started in than some other libraries; in that way, it is somewhat like Python. However, it is best not to ask, "Which one library is best?" but "Which library or libraries are the right tools for this job?", and it is common real-world practice to use more than one library, possibly several.

JavaScript libraries offer several advantages. They can reduce chores and boilerplate code, significantly lessening the pain of JavaScript, and provide a more uniform interface. They can also provide (for instance) ready-made widgets; we will be working with a jQuery slider later on in this book. And on a broad scale, they can let the JavaScript you write be higher-level and a little more Pythonic.

Server-side technologies

Many of the "usual suspects" in client-side technologies have been mentioned. The list of client-side technologies is generally constrained by what is available in common web browsers; the list of available server-side technologies is only constrained by what will work on the server, and any general-purpose programming language *can* do the job. The question on the server is not "What is available?" but "Which option would you choose?" Python and Django make an excellent choice of server-side technology, and we will work with them in this book.

A look at Django

Django's developers call it "the web framework for perfectionists with deadlines," and it is one of the most popular Python web frameworks, perhaps the most popular. In contrast to the MVC pattern, which separates concerns into Model, View, and Controller, it could be described as an MTV pattern, which separates concerns into Model, Template, and View. The **Model** is a class that ties into an ORM where instances correspond to rows in the table but act and feel like Python objects. The **Template** is a system designed to be easy for non-Python developers (though easy for Pythonistas too), and limits the extent to which HTML needs to be sprinkled throughout the Python source. The **View** is a function that renders, in most cases, from a template. Let's look at a kickstart example of Django in action.

Django templating kickstart

Let us briefly go through how to install Django, create a sample project, and create and use a basic template that can serve as a basis for further tinkering.

Django installation instructions are at `http://docs.djangoproject.com/en/dev/intro/install/`; for Ubuntu, for instance, you will want to run `sudo apt-get install python-django`.

Once you have Django installed, create a project named `sample`:

```
django-admin.py startproject sample
```

Go into the `sample` directory, and create the directory `templates`. Enter the `templates` directory.

Create a template file named `index.html` containing the following template:

```html
<!DOCTYPE html PUBLIC "-//W3C//DTD XHTML 1.0 Strict//EN" "http://www.
w3.org/TR/xhtml1/DTD/xhtml1-strict.dtd">
<html xmlns="http://www.w3.org/1999/xhtml" xml:lang="en-US"
lang="en-US">
  <head>
    <title>{% block title %}Hello, world!{% endblock title %}
    </title>
      <meta http-equiv="Content-Type" content="text/html;
          charset=UTF-8" />
  </head>
  <body>
    {% block body %}
      <h1>{% block heading %}Hello, world!
      {% endblock heading %}</h1>
      {% block content %}<p>Greetings from the Django
        templating engine!</p>{% endblock content %}
    {% endblock body %}
  </body>
</html>
```

Go up one level to the `sample` directory and edit the `urls.py` file so that the first line after `urlpatterns = patterns('',` is:

```
(r'^$', 'sample.views.home'),
```

Then create the `views.py` file containing the following:

```python
#!/usr/bin/python/

from django.shortcuts import import render_to_response

def home(request):
    return render_to_response(u'index.html')
```

Edit the `settings.py` file, and add:

```
os.path.join(os.path.dirname(__file__), "templates"),
```

right after:

```
TEMPLATE_DIRS = (
```

Then, from the command line, run:

```
python manage.py runserver
```

This makes the server accessible to your computer only by entering the URL `http://localhost:8080/` in your web browser.

If you are in a protected environment behind a firewall, appropriate NATting, or the like, you can make the development server available to the network by running:

```
python manage.py runserver 0.0.0.0:8080
```

There is one point of clarification we would like to make clear. Django is packaged with a minimal, single-threaded web server that is intended to be just enough to start exploring Django in a development environment. Django's creators are attempting to make a good, competitive web framework and not a good, competitive web server, and *the development server has never undergone a security audit.* The explicit advice from Django's creators is: when deploying, use a good, serious web server; they also provide instructions for doing this.

A more complete glimpse at Django templating

Before further exploring technical details, it would be worth taking a look at the opinions and philosophy behind the Django templating language, because an understandable approach of, "Oh, it's a general purpose programming language used for templating," is a recipe for needless frustration and pain. The Django developers themselves acknowledge that their opinions in the templating language are one just opinion in an area where different people have different opinions, and you are welcome to disagree with them if you want. If you don't like the templating system that Django comes with, Django is designed to let you use another. But it is worth understanding what exactly the philosophy is behind the templating language; even if this is not the only philosophy one could use, it is carefully thought out.

The Django templating language is intended to foster the separation of presentation and logic. In its design decisions, both large and small, Django's templating engine is optimized primarily for designers to use for designing, rather than programmers to use for programming, and its limitations are almost as carefully chosen as the features it provides. Unlike ASP, JSP, and PHP, it is not a programming language interspersed with HTML. It provides enough power for presentation, and is intended *not* to provide enough power to do serious programming work where it doesn't belong (in the Django opinion), and is simple enough that some non-programmers can pick it up in a day. For a programmer, the difficulty of learning the templating basics is comparable to the difficulty of simple HTML or SQL: it is simple, and a good bit easier to learn than wrapping your arms around a regular programming language. Some programmers like it immediately, but there are some who started by asking, "Why doesn't the templating language just let you mix Python and HTML?" and after playing with it, found themselves saying, "This isn't what I would have come up with myself, but I really, really like it."

Additional benefits include it being *fast* (most of the work is done by a single regular expression call, and the founders talk about disabling caching because it wasn't as fast as the template rendering), *secure* (it is designed so that it can be used by untrusted designers without allowing a malicious designer to execute arbitrary code), and *versatile* enough to generate whatever text format you want: plain text, HTML, XML, XHTML, JSON, JavaScript, CSV, ReStructuredText, and so on. We will be using it to generate web pages and JSON, but Django's templating language is a general-purpose text templating solution.

Following the Django site's lead, let us use a template intended as an example of how one might begin a base template for a site, then start to walk through its contents, and then look at some of how it could be used and parts overridden to create a specific document.

This renders as follows, if we strip out blank lines:

```
<!DOCTYPE html PUBLIC "-//W3C//DTD XHTML 1.0 Strict//EN" "http://www.
w3.org/TR/xhtml1/DTD/xhtml1-strict.dtd">
<html xmlns="http://www.w3.org/1999/xhtml" xml:lang="en-US"
lang="en-US">
  <head>
    <title></title>
    <link rel="icon" href="/static/favicon.ico"
          type="x-icon" />
    <link rel="shortcut icon" href="/static/favicon.ico"
          type="x-icon" />
    <meta http-equiv="Content-Type" content="text/html;
          charset=UTF-8" />
    <meta http-equiv="Content-Language" value="en-US" />
```

```
    <link rel="stylesheet" type="text/css"
          href="/static/css/style.css" />
  </head>
  <body>
    <div id="sidebar">
    </div>
    <div id="content">
      <div id="header">
        <h1></h1>
      </div>
    </div>
    <div id="footer">
    </div>
  </body>
    <script language="JavaScript" type="text/javascript"
            src="/static/js/jquery.js"></script>
</html>
```

Let us unwrap what is going on here; there is more to the template than how it renders to this page, but let us start with that much.

The `{% block dtd %}` style tags begin, or the case of `{% endblock dtd %}` end, a semantic block of text that can be left untouched or can be replaced. In the case of this one template, the effect is to strip them out like comments, but they will yield benefits later on, much like semantic HTML markup with CSS yields benefits later on.

Django templating reflects a choice to go with hooks rather than includes because hooks provide the more versatile solution. The "beginner's mistake" version of a header to include might be something like the following:

```
<!DOCTYPE html PUBLIC "-//W3C//DTD XHTML 1.0 Strict//EN" "http://www.
w3.org/TR/xhtml1/DTD/xhtml1-strict.dtd">
<html xmlns="http://www.w3.org/1999/xhtml" xml:lang="en-US"
lang="en-US">
  <head>
    <title>Welcome to my site!</title>
    <link rel="icon" href="/favicon.ico" type="x-icon" />
    <link rel="shortcut icon" href="/favicon.ico"
          type="x-icon" />
    <meta http-equiv="Content-Type" content="text/html;
          charset=UTF-8" />
    <meta http-equiv="Content-Language" value="en-US" />
    <link rel="stylesheet" type="text/css"
          href="/css/style.css" />
  </head>
  <body>
```

This solution could be continued by adding a sidebar, but there is a minor problem, or at least it seems minor at first: there are bits of this header that are not generic. For a serious site, having every page titled, "Welcome to my site!" would be an embarrassment. The language is declared to be "en-US", meaning U.S. English, which is wonderful if the entire site is in U.S. English, but if it expands to include more than U.S. English content, hardcoding "en-US" will be a problem. If the only concern is to accurately label British English, then the more expansive "en" could be substituted in, but hardcoding "en-US" and "en" are equally unhelpful if the site expands to feature a section in Russian. This header does not include other meta tags that might be desirable, such as "description", which is ideally written for a specific page and not done as site-wide boilerplate. Including the header verbatim solves a problem, but it doesn't provide a very flexible solution.

The previous example builds in hooks. It does specify:

```
{% block html_tag %}<html xmlns="http://www.w3.org/1999/xhtml" xml:lang="en-US" lang="en-US">{% endblock html_tag %}
```

If not overridden, this will render as:

```
<html xmlns="http://www.w3.org/1999/xhtml" xml:lang="en-US" lang="en-US">
```

However, in a template that extends this, by having `{% extends "base.html" %}` as its opening tag, if the base is loaded as `base.html`, then:

```
{% block html_tag %}<html xmlns="http://www.w3.org/1999/xhtml" xml:lang="en-GB" lang="en-GB">{% endblock html_tag %}
```

will render:

```
<html xmlns="http://www.w3.org/1999/xhtml" xml:lang="en-GB" lang="en-GB">
```

And Russian may be declared in the same way:

```
{% block html_tag %}<html xmlns="http://www.w3.org/1999/xhtml" xml:lang="ru-RU" lang="ru-RU">{% endblock html_tag %}
```

will render:

```
<html xmlns="http://www.w3.org/1999/xhtml" xml:lang="ru-RU" lang="ru-RU">
```

The template as given does specify "en-US" more than once, but each of these is inside a block that can be overridden to specify another language.

We define initial blocks. First, the DTD:

```
{% block dtd %}<!DOCTYPE html PUBLIC "-//W3C//DTD XHTML 1.0 Strict//
EN" "http://www.w3.org/TR/xhtml1/DTD/xhtml1-strict.dtd">
{% endblock dtd %}
```

Then, the HTML tag:

```
{% block html_tag %}<html xmlns="http://www.w3.org/1999/xhtml" xml:
lang="en-US" lang="en-US">{% endblock html_tag %}
```

Then we define the head, with the title and favicon:

```
{% block head %}<head>
  <title>{% block title %}{{ page.title }}
    {% endblock title %}</title>
  {% block head_favicon %}<link rel="icon"
    href="/static/favicon.ico" type="x-icon" />
  <link rel="shortcut icon" href="/static/favicon.ico"
    type="x-icon" />{% endblock head_favicon %}
```

Then we define hooks for meta tags in the head. We define a Content-Type of UTF-8; this is a basic point so that non-ASCII content will display correctly:

```
{% block head_meta %}
  {% block head_meta_author%}{% endblock head_meta_author %}
  {% block head_meta_charset %}
    <meta http-equiv="Content-Type" content="text/html;
      charset=UTF-8" />
  {% endblock head_meta_charset %}
  {% block head_meta_contentlanguage %}
    <meta http-equiv="Content-Language" value="en-US" />
  {% endblock head_meta_contentlanguage %}
  {% block head_meta_description %}
  {% endblock head_meta_description %}
  {% block head_meta_keywords %}
  {% endblock head_meta_keywords %}
  {% block head_meta_othertags %}
  {% endblock head_meta_othertags %}
  {% block head_meta_refresh %}
  {% endblock head_meta_refresh %}
  {% block head_meta_robots %}
  {% endblock head_meta_robots %}
{% endblock head_meta %}
```

We declare a block to specify an RSS feed for the page:

```
{% block head_rss %}{% endblock head_rss %}
```

We add hooks for CSS, both at the site level, and section, and page. This allows a fairly fine granularity of control:

```
{% block head_css %}
  {% block head_css_site %}
    <link rel="stylesheet" type="text/css"
          href="/static/css/style.css" />
  {% endblock head_css_site %}
  {% block head_css_section %}
  {% endblock head_css_section %}
  {% block head_css_page %}{% endblock head_css_page %}
{% endblock head_css %}
```

We add section- and page-specific header information:

```
{% block head_section %}{% endblock head_section %}
{% block head_page %}{% endblock head_page %}
```

Then we close the head and open the body:

```
</head>{% endblock head %}
  {% block body %}
  <body>
```

We define a sidebar block, with a hook to populate it:

```
<div id="sidebar">
  {% block body_sidebar %}{% endblock body_sidebar %}
</div>
```

We define a block for the main content area:

```
<div id="content">
{% block body_content %}
```

For the header of the main content area, we define a banner hook, and a header for the page's title, should such be provided. (If none is provided, there is no crash or error; the empty string is displayed for {{ page.title }}.)

```
<div id="header">
{% block body_header %}
  {% block body_header_banner %}
  {% endblock body_header_banner %}
  {% block body_header_title %}<h1>
    {{ page.title }}</h1>
  {% endblock body_header_title %}
```

We define a breadcrumb, which is one of many small usability touches that can be desirable:

```
{% block body_header_breadcrumb %}
  {{ page.breadcrumb }}
{% endblock body_header_breadcrumb %}
{% endblock body_header %}
</div>
```

We add a slot for announcements, then the body's main area, and then close the block and `div`:

```
{% block body_announcements %}
{% endblock body_announcements %}
{% block body_main %}{% endblock body_main %}
{% endblock body_content %}
</div>
```

We define a footer `div`, with a footer breadcrumb, and a hook for anything our company's lawyers asked us to put:

```
<div id="footer">
{% block body_footer %}
  {% block body_footer_breadcrumb %}
    {{ page.breadcrumb }}
  {% endblock body_footer_breadcrumb %}
  {% block body_footer_legal %}
  {% endblock body_footer_legal %}
{% endblock body_footer %}
```

Now we close that `div`, the body, and the body block:

```
</div>
</body>{% endblock body %}
```

We add a footer, with JavaScript blocks, again at the site/section/page level of hooks:

```
{% block footer %}
  {% block footer_javascript %}
    {% block footer_javascript_site %}
      <script language="JavaScript" type="text/javascript"
          src="/static/js/jquery.js"></script>
    {% endblock footer_javascript_site %}
    {% block footer_javascript_section %}
    {% endblock footer_javascript_section %}
    {% block footer_javascript_page %}
```

```
            {% endblock footer_javascript_page %}
        {% endblock footer_javascript %}
    {% endblock footer %}
</html>
```

And that's it.

You can make as many layers of templates as you want. One suggested approach is to make three layers: one base template for your entire site, then more specific templates for sections of your site (whatever they may be), and then individual templates for end use. The template given is a base template, and it provides hooks as narrow as a specific meta tag or as broad as the main content area.

For our extended example, if it is named \base.html, then we can create another template, russian.html, which will declare its content to be in the Russian language. (Ordinarily one would do more interesting things in overriding a template than merely replacing tags, but for illustration purposes we will do that, and only that:

```
{% extends "base.html" %}
{% block html_tag %}<html xmlns="http://www.w3.org/1999/xhtml" xml:lang="ru-RU" lang="ru-RU">{% endblock html_tag %}
{% block head_meta_contentlanguage %}<meta http-equiv="Content-Language" value="ru-RU" />{% endblock head_meta_contentlanguage %}
```

These block overrides may occur anywhere; while the {% extends "base.html" %} tag must be placed first, the two tags may be swapped. It would work just as well to create a language-agnostic base.html with only an empty hook:

```
        {% block head_meta_contentlanguage %}
        {% endblock head_meta_contentlanguage %}
```

and a default HTML tag of:

```
<html xmlns="http://www.w3.org/1999/xhtml">
```

And then create english.html and russian.html, or en-US.html and ru-RU.html, as base templates for those languages.

However, there are many other tags than those used for blocks and overriding. We will just barely sample them below, looking at how to display variables, and then other tags.

There are other tags that look like {% ... %}, but I would comment briefly on the variable tags such as {{ page.title }}. The Django templating language uses dotted references, but not in exactly the same way as Python's dotted references. Where Python requires a couple of different things to get values, dotted references provide one-stop shopping in Django's templating. When a reference to {{ page.title }} occurs, it will display page[u'title'] if page[u'title'] is available. If not, it will display page.title if page.title is available as an attribute, and if there is no such attribute, it will display page.title() if page.title() is available, and failing that, if the reference is a non-negative integer like 2, it will display page[2] if page.2 is requested. If all of these fail, then Django defaults to the empty string because it's not acceptable for a professional site to crash because a programming error has the template asking for something that is not available. You can override the empty string by setting TEMPLATE_STRING_IF_INVALID in your settings.py file, and *in development* it may make sense to set TEMPLATE_STRING_IF_INVALID to something like LOOKUP FAILED, but you will want to set it back to the empty string for deployment in any production environment.

At this point, while there are explicit hooks to pull in multiple JavaScript and CSS files, the preferred practice, per Steve Souders's ground rules for client-side optimizations for high performance websites, is: for each page to load initially, you should have one HTML/XHTML page, one CSS file included at the top, and one JavaScript file included at the bottom. The hooks are more flexible than that, but this is intended more as "development leeway" than what the tightened final product should be.

If-then, if-then-else statements, and for loops are straightforward, and else clauses are optional:

```
{% if results %}
  <ul>
    {% for result in results %}
      <li>{% result.title %}</li>
    {% endfor %}
  </ul>
{% else %}
  <p>There were no results.</p>
{% endif %}
```

There are a number of convenience features and minor variations available; these are several of the major features.

Setting JavaScript and other static content in place

For the development server, putting static content, including images, CSS, and static content, is straightforward. For production use, the recommended best practice is to use a different implementation, and Django users are advised to use a separate server if possible, optimized for serving static media, such as a *stripped-down* build of Apache, or nginx. However, for development use, the following steps will serve up static content:

1. Create a directory named `static` within your project. (Note that other names may be used, but do not use `media`, as that can collide with administrative tools.)
2. Edit the `settings.py` file, and add the following at the top, after `import os`:

    ```
    DIRNAME = os.path.abspath(os.path.dirname(__file__))
    ```
3. Change the settings of `MEDIA_ROOT` and `MEDIA_URL`:

    ```
    MEDIA_ROOT = os.path.join(DIRNAME, 'static/')
    ...
    MEDIA_URL = '/static/'
    ```
4. At the end of the `settings.py` file, add the following:

    ```
    if settings.DEBUG:
      urlpatterns += patterns('django.views.static',
        (r'^%s(?P<path>.*)$' % (settings.MEDIA_URL[1:],), 'serve', {
          'document_root': settings.MEDIA_ROOT,
          'show_indexes': True }),)
    ```

This will turn off static media service when `DEBUG` is turned off, so that this code does not need to be changed when your site is deployed live, but the subdirectory `static` within your project should now serve up static content, like a very simplified Apache. We suggest that you create three subdirectories of `static`: `static/css`, `static/images`, and `static/js`, for serving up CSS, image, and JavaScript static content.

Summary

Guido van Rossum, the creator of the Python programming language, for one project asked about different Python frameworks and chose the Django templating engine for his purposes (http://www.artima.com/weblogs/viewpost.jsp?thread=146606). This chapter has provided an overview of Ajax and then provided a kickstart introduction to the Django templating engine. There's more to Django than its templating engine, but this should be enough to start exploring and playing.

In learning a new technology, a crucial threshold has been passed when there is enough of a critical mass of things you can do with a technology to begin tinkering, and taking one step often invites the question: "What can we do to take this one step further?". In this chapter, we have provided a kickstart to begin working with the Django templating engine.

In this chapter, we have looked at the idea of Pythonic problem solving, discussed Django and jQuery in relation to Pythonic problem solving, and discussed Ajax as not a single technology, but an *overlaid function* or technique that is overlaid on top of existing technologies. We have taken an overview of what the "usual suspect" technologies are for Ajax; given a kickstart to the Django templating engine, introducing some of its beauty and power; and addressed a minor but important detail: putting static content in place for Django's development server.

This is meant to serve as a point of departure for further discussion of jQuery Ajax in the next chapter, and building our sample application. Interested readers who want to know more of what they can do can read the official documentation at http://docs.djangoproject.com/en/dev/topics/templates/.

In the next chapter, we will push further and aim for a critical mass of things we can do. We will explore jQuery, the most common JavaScript library, and begin to see how we can use it to reach the point of tinkering, of having something that works and wondering, "What if we try this?", "What if we try that?", and being able to do it.

2
jQuery—the Most Common JavaScript Framework

JavaScript frameworks can offer at least two kinds of advantages, as we have discussed earlier. Firstly, they can offer considerable facilities when compared to building from scratch. TurboGears and Django are both server-side web frameworks in Python and both offer major advantages compared to web application development in Python using only the standard library, even with the CGI module included. Secondly, they can offer a more uniform virtual programming interface compared to writing unadorned JavaScript with enough detection and conditional logic to directly conform to disparate JavaScript environments so that code written in one browser and debugged in another browser stands a fighting chance of working without crashing in every common browser.

As regards the question, "Which is best?" if you only learn one client-side JavaScript framework, jQuery is an excellent choice. It is one of the most popular JavaScript frameworks, partly because it is (like Python) gentle to newcomers. However, comparing jQuery to Dojo is like comparing a hammer to a wrench. (A general JavaScript framework comparison is at http://en.wikipedia.org/wiki/Comparison_of_JavaScript_frameworks.) Unlike server-side web development frameworks such as Django and TurboGears, you don't necessarily ask, "Which one will we use for this project?" as there might be good reasons to use more than one framework in a web application. jQuery's developers know it isn't the only thing out there. It only uses two names in the global namespace: $ and jQuery. Both do the same thing; you can always use jQuery() in lieu of $(), and if you call jQuery.noconflict(), jQuery will let go of $ so that other libraries like Prototype (http://www.prototypejs.org/) are free to use that name.

Finally, we suggest that jQuery might be something like a "virtual higher-level language" built on top of JavaScript. A programmer's first reaction after viewing the JavaScript code, on seeing code using jQuery, might well be, "Is that really JavaScript? *It doesn't look like JavaScript!*" A programmer using jQuery can operate on element sets, and refine or expand, without ever typing out a JavaScript variable assignment or keyword such as `if`, `else`, or `for`, and even without cross-browser concerns, one runs into jQuery code that does the work of dozens of lines of "bare JavaScript" in a single line. But these are single lines that can be very easily read once you know the ground rules, not the cryptic one-liners of the Perl art form. This "virtual higher-level language" of jQuery is not Python and does not look like Python, but there is something "Pythonic in spirit" about how it works.

In this chapter, we will cover:

- How jQuery simplifies "Hello, world!" in Ajax
- The basic Ajax facilities jQuery offers
- How jQuery effectively offers a "virtual higher-level language"
- jQuery selectors, as they illustrate the kind of more Pythonic "virtual higher-level language facilities" that jQuery offers
- A sample "kickstart Django Ajax application," which covers every major basic feature except for server-side persistence management
- An overview of a more serious, in-depth Django application, to be covered in upcoming chapters

Let's explore the higher-level way to do things in jQuery.

jQuery and basic Ajax

Let's look at a "Hello, world!" in Ajax. A request containing one variable, `text`, is sent to the server, and the server responds with "Hello, [*contents of the variable text*]!" which is then put into the `innerHTML` of a paragraph with ID `result`:

```
if (typeof XMLHttpRequest == "undefined")
    {
    XMLHttpRequest = function()
        {
        try
            {
            return new ActiveXObject("Msxml2.XMLHTTP.6.0");
            }
        catch(exception)
            {
```

```
            try
                {
                return new ActiveXObject("Msxml2.XMLHTTP.3.0");
                }
            catch(exception)
                {
                try
                    {
                    return new ActiveXObject("Msxml2.XMLHTTP");
                    }
                catch(exception)
                    {
                    throw new Error("Could not construct
                        XMLHttpRequest");
                    }
                }
            }
        }
    }

var xhr = new XMLHttpRequest();
xhr.open("GET", "/project/server.cgi?text=world");
callback = function()
    {
    if (xhr.readyState == 4 && xhr.status >= 200 && xhr.status < 300)
        {
        document.getElementById("result").innerHTML =
          xhr.responseText;
        }
    }
xhr.onreadystatechange = callback;
xhr.send(null);
```

With the simpler, "virtual high-level language" of jQuery, you accomplish more or less the same with only:

```
$("#result").load("/project/server.cgi", "text=world");
```

$() selects a wrapped set. This can be a CSS designation, a single HTML entity referenced by ID as we do here, or some other things. jQuery works on wrapped sets. Here, as is common in jQuery, we create a wrapped set and call a function on it. $.load() loads from a server URL, and we can optionally specify a query string.

How do we do things with jQuery? To start off, we create a **wrapped set**. The syntax is based on CSS and CSS2 selectors, with some useful extensions.

Here are some examples of creating a wrapped set:

```
$("#result");
$("p");
$("p.summary");
$("a");
$("p a");
$("p > a");
$("li > p");
$("p.summary > a");
$("table.striped tr:even");
```

They select nodes from the DOM more or less as one would expect:

- `$("#result#")` selects the item with HTML ID `result`
- `$("p")` selects all paragraph elements
- `$("p.summary")` selects all paragraph elements with class `summary`
- `$("a")` selects all anchor tags
- `$("p a")` selects all anchor tags in a paragraph
- `$("p > a")` selects all anchor tags whose immediate parent is a paragraph tag
- `$("li > p")` selects all `p` tags whose immediate parent is a `li` tag
- `$("p.summary > a")` selects all anchor tags whose immediate parent is a paragraph tag with class `summary`
- `$("table.striped tr:even")` selects even-numbered rows from all tables belonging to class `striped`

The difference between `$("p a")` and `$("p > a")` is that the first selects any tag contained in a `p` tag, whether its immediate parent is the `p` tag or whether there are intervening span, em, or strong tags, and the second selects only those tags whose immediate parent is a `p` tag; the latter yields a subset of the former. This last approach lends itself to a straightforward and clean way to address the chore of tiger-striping tables:

```
$("table.striped tr:even").addClass("even");
```

The statements before this last example are not useful in themselves, but they lay a powerful foundation by creating a wrapped set. A wrapped set is an object that encapsulates both a set of DOM elements and a full complement of operations, such as `.addClass()`, which assigns a CSS class to all elements from a wrapped set, or `.load()`, which provided a one-line Ajax solution earlier.

One of the key features of a wrapped set is that these operations return the same wrapped set, unless they are one of a few exceptions, such as operations designed to change the set by adding or removing members. This means that operations can be **chained**; for a somewhat artificial example, our code to stripe items in a table could be extended to slowly hiding them, waiting for a second (specified as 1000 milliseconds), and then showing them again:

```
$("table.striped tr:even").addClass("even").hide("slow").delay(1000).
show("slow");
```

In this statement, all of the operations return the same wrapped set. Dozens of further operations could be appended after the .show() call if desired. In chaining of operations, the additional functions can function as separate "virtual statements". The previous line of code, in pseudocode, could be written:

```
Select even-numbered table rows from tables having the class
"striped".
Add the class "even" to them.
Slowly hide them.
Wait 1000 milliseconds.
Slowly show them.
```

The final appearance of the page should be as if merely $("table.striped tr:even").addClass("even"); had been called.

jQuery Ajax facilities

jQuery provides good facilities both for Ajax and other JavaScript usage. The API is excellent and can be bookmarked from http://api.jquery.com/.

We will be going through some key facilities, Ajax and otherwise, and making comments on how these facilities might best be used.

$.ajax()

The most foundational and low-level workhorse in jQuery is $.ajax(). It takes the arguments as shown in the following *Sample invocation*. Default values can be set with $.ajaxSetup(), as discussed below:

```
$.ajax({data: "surname=Smith&cartTotal=12.34", dataType: "text",
error: function(XMLHttpRequest, textStatus, errorThrown) {
        displayErrorMessage("An error has occurred: " + textStatus);
        }, success: function(data, textStatus, XMLHttpRequest) {
        try
            {
```

```
            updatePage(JSON.parse(data));
        }
        catch(error)
        {
        displayErrorMessage("There was an error updating your
            shopping cart. Please call customer service at
            800-555-1212.");
        }
    }, type: "POST", url: "/update-user"};
```

Some of the fields that can be passed are described in the following sections.

context

The context, available as the variable `this`, can be used to give access to variables in callbacks, even if they have fallen out of scope. The following code prompts for the user's name and e-mail address and provides them in a context, anonymously, so that the data are available to the callback function but are never a part of the global namespace.

```
$.ajax({success: function(data, textStatus, XMLHttpRequest)
    {
    alert(this.name + ", your email address is " +
        this.email + ".");
    processData(data, this.name, this.email);
    }, context:
    {
    name: prompt("What is your name?", ""),
    email: prompt("What is your email address?", "")
    }, …
});
```

Closures

The principle at play is the principle of **closures**. The wrong way, perhaps, to learn about closures is to look for academic-style introductions to what you need to know in order to understand them. There's a lot there, and it's a lot harder to understand than learning by jumping in. Closures represent a key concept in core JavaScript, along with other things such as functions, objects, and prototypes. Closures are part of the conceptual landscape and not only because they are the basis on how to effectively create an object with private fields. So we will jump in and give a closure that serves as a proof of concept as, effectively, an object with private fields. To give a standard, "bare JavaScript" example of using a closure to create an object with private variables, which creates an object that stores an integer value, has a getter and setter, but in Java fashion ensures that the field can only have an integer value.

We define a function, which we will be immediately evaluating; `closureExample` stores not the anonymous function but its return value. The variable field is a local variable:

```
var closure_example = function()
    {
    var field = 0;
    return {
```

The getter is an unadorned getter as in Java:

```
        get: function()
            {
            return field;
            },
```

The setter could be an unadorned setter, storing `newValue` in a field and doing nothing else. However, we provide a more discriminating behavior: we make a string of the object and then see if it can be parsed as an integer. This will be an integer if we obtain an integer and NaN (Not a Number) if it cannot be parsed as an integer. If the value is not a number, then we return false; if it gives us an integer, then we store the integer and return true:

```
        set: function(newValue)
            {
            var value = parseInt(newValue.toString());
            if (isNaN(value))
                {
                return false;
                }
            else
                {
                field = value;
                return true;
                }
            }
        }
    } ();
```

This creates and evaluates an anonymous function. Local variables (in this case, `field`) do not enter the global namespace but also remain around, lurking, accessible to the object returned and its two members: functions that can still access `field`. As long as the object stored in `closure_example` is available, its members will have access to its local variables, which are not gone and garbage collected until the object in `closure_example` itself is gone and eligible for garbage collection.

We can use it as follows:

```
closure_example.set(3);
var retrieved = closure_example.get();
closure_example.set(1.2);
var assignment_was_successful = closure_example.set(1.2)
```

Prototypes and prototypal inheritance

Prototypes and **prototypal inheritance** are a basis for object-oriented programming, with inheritance, but without classes. In Java, certain features of a class are fixed. In Python, an object inherits from a class but features that are fixed in Java cannot be overridden. In JavaScript, we go one step further and say that objects inherit from other objects. Class-based objects run in a Platonic fashion, where there is an ideal type and concrete shadows or copies of that ideal type. Prototypal inheritance is more like the evolutionary picture of single-celled organisms that can mutate, reproduce asexually by cell division, and pass on (accumulated) mutations when they divide. In JavaScript, an object's prototype is set by, for instance:

```
customer.prototype = employee;
```

Redefine members for a customer when one wants to change from the attributes of an employee. (Members that are not redefined default to the prototype's values, and if not found on the prototype, default to members on the prototype's prototype, going all the way up the chain to the object if need be.) Also note that this inheritance may or may not mean moving from more general to more specific; inheritance may better be seen as "`customer` *mutates from* `employee`" than "`customer` is a *more specific type* of `employee`."

Let us return to the parameters of `$.ajax()`.

data

This is the form data to pass, whether given as a string as it would appear in a GET URI, as follows:

```
query=pizza&page=2
```

or given as a dictionary, as follows:

```
{page: 2, query: "pizza"}
```

dataFilter

This is a reference to a function that will be passed two arguments: the raw response given by an `XMLHttpRequest`, and a type (`xml`, `json`, `script`, or `html`). This offers an important security hook: JSON can be passed to an `eval()`, but malicious JavaScript that is passed in place of JSON data can also be passed to an `eval()`.

One of the cardinal rules of security on both the client-side and server-side is to treat all input as guilty until proven innocent of being malicious. Even though it is a "double work" chore, user input should both be validated at the client-side and the server-side: client-side as a courtesy to the user to improve the user experience and *not* as trustworthy security, and on the server side as a security measure against malicious data even if it is malformed malicious data that no normal web browser would send.

We might comment that the Django principle of **Don't Repeat Yourself (DRY)**, is a major Django selling point but is *not* a reason to dodge handling both the user interface side of validation, and the security side. In practice, this means both validating from Django on the server-side and JavaScript on the client-side, for what we are doing. Needlessly repeating yourself in Django is a sign of bad code, but this is not *needless* repetition, even if it is a chore. It's *needed* repetition.

jQuery does not automatically include functionality to test whether something served up as JSON is malicious, and methods like `.getJSON()` trustingly execute what might contain malicious JavaScript. One serious alternative is the `JSON.parse()` method defined in http://www.json.org/json2.js. It will return a parsed object or throw a SyntaxError if it finds something suspicious.

dataType

This is something you should specify, and provide a default specified value via `$.ajaxSetup()`, for example:

```
$.ajaxSetup({dataType: "text"});
```

The possible values are `html`, `json`, `jsonp`, `script`, `text`, and `xml`. If you do *not* specify a value, jQuery will use an unsecure "intelligent guessing" that may trustingly execute any JavaScript or JSON it is passed without any attempt to determine if it is malicious. If you specify a `dataType` of `text`, your callback will be given the raw text which you can then test call `JSON.parse()` on. If you specify a `dataType` of `json`, you will get the parsed JSON object. So specify `text` even if you know you want JSON.

error(XMLHttpRequest, textStatus, errorThrown)

An error callback that takes up to three arguments. For example:

```
$.ajax({error: function(XMLHttpRequest, textStatus, errorThrown)
    {
    registerError(textStatus);
    }, …
});
```

success(data, textStatus, XMLHttpRequest)

A callback for success that also takes up to three arguments, but in different order. For example:

```
$.ajax({success: function(data, textStatus, XMLHttpRequest) {
    processData(data);
    }, …
});
```

If you want to do something immediately after the request has completed, the recommended best practice is to specify a callback function that will pick up after the request has completed. If you want to make certain variables available to the callback function that would not otherwise remain available, you may specify the context as discussed above.

type

The type of the request, for example GET, POST, and so on. The default is GET, but this is only appropriate in very limited cases and it may make sense to simply always use POST. The more serious the work you are doing, the more likely it is that you should *only* use POST. GET is appropriate only when it doesn't matter how many extra times a form is submitted. In other words, GET is only appropriate when there are no significant side effects, and in particular no destructive side effects. In a shopping cart application, GET may be appropriate to view the contents of a shopping cart, although POST is also appropriate and has the side effect of guaranteeing a fresh load. GET is not, however, appropriate for creating, modifying, fulfilling, or deleting an order, and you should use POST when any or all of these are involved.

url

The URL to submit to; this defaults to the current page.

$.aj0axSetup()

This takes the same arguments as `$.ajax()`. All arguments are optional, but you can use this to specify default values. In terms of DRY, if something can be appropriately offloaded to `$.ajaxSetup()`, it probably should be offloaded to `$.ajaxSetup()`.

Sample invocation

A sample invocation is as follows:

```
$.ajaxSetup({dataType: "text", type: "POST"});
```

$.get() and $.post()

These are convenience methods for `$.ajax()` that allow you to specify commonly used parameters without key-value hash syntax and are intended to simplify GET and POST operations. They both have the same signature.

The sample invocation is as follows:

```
$.get("/resources/update");
$.post("/resources/update");
$.post("/resources/update", "user=jsmith&product_id=112");
$.post("/resources/update", {user: "jsmith", product_id: 112});
$.post("/resources/update", function(data) { ("#result").html(data)
});
$.get("/resources/update", "user=jsmith&product_id=112",
   function(data, textStatus, XMLHttpRequest) {
        ("#result").html(data);
        logStatus(textStatus);
        });
$.post("/resources/update", "user=jsmith&product_id=112",
   function(data, textStatus, XMLHttpRequest) {
        ("#result").html(data);
        logStatus(textStatus);
        }, "text");
```

These are convenience methods for `$.ajax()` and make several common features from `$.ajax()` available, but notably not an error callback function. If you want a callback called in the case of an error for appropriate handling, as well as when everything goes perfectly well, register a global error handler or use `$.ajax()`.

> For the real world, this is a substantial endorsement of not using the convenience methods alone, but either specifying a global error handler or using `$.ajax()`.

Something can go wrong in front of your boss, or worse, work perfectly when you show your boss and then proceed to blow up completely when your boss shows it to your customer. Heisenbugs, (subtle and hard-to-pin-down bugs that just show up under circumstances that are difficult to repeat), network errors, and server errors will occur, and unless a noop response is appropriate and production-ready behavior when an error prevents successful completion, you will want to specify an appropriate error callback.

Or, alternatively, it may be acceptable to specify a global error handler using `$.ajaxSetup({error: myErrorHandler})` if you can write something appropriate to generically but correctly handle all Ajax error conditions where you did not directly call `$.ajax()` and specify an error handler. This includes all calls to `$.get()`, `$.load()`, and `$.post()`.

.load()

This is a very convenient convenience method. If you're looking for a simple, higher-level alternative to `$.ajax()`, you can call this method on a wrapped set to load the results of an Ajax call into it. There are some caveats, however. Let's give some sample invocations, look at why `.load()` is attractive, and then give appropriate qualifications and warnings.

Sample invocations

The sample invocation is as follows:

```
$("#messages").load("/sitewide-messages");
$("#messages").load("/user-messages", "username=jsmith");
$("#hidden").load("/user-customizations", "username=jsmith",
function(responseText, textStatus, XMLHttpRequest) {
        performUserCustomizations(responseText);
    });
```

On the surface, this looks like a good example of an alternative to doing JavaScript work that incorporates jQuery, and instead using the "virtual higher-level language" that jQuery provides. `.load()`, like many jQuery functions, is a function of a wrapped set and returns a wrapped set (as often, the wrapped set it was given). It is, therefore, *in principle* something that can be put in a chain.

Why "in principle"? It makes sense, upon some condition, to hide all of the paragraphs in a form containing a checkbox that is not checked:

```
$("form p:has(input[type=checkbox]:not(:checked))").hide("slow");
```

This says, "For all p elements in a form that have an unchecked checkbox, slowly hide them."

Furthermore, one could want to do several actions instead of one:

```
$("form p:has(input[type=checkbox]:not(:checked))").
addClass("strikethru").delay(500).hide("slow");
```

That is a more elaborate animation: "For all p elements in a form that have an unchecked checkbox, add the class `strikethru` (which can be defined in CSS to have a strikethrough line through text), then wait half a second (500 milliseconds), and then slowly hide it as was done before."

But for a wrapped set like this, it would not make much sense to insert a `.load()` after the wrapped set is generated:

```
$("form p:has(input[type=checkbox]:not(:checked))").load("/updates");
```

What that says is, "For all p elements in a form that have an unchecked box, load the contents of the relative URL `/updates` and replace whatever the selected p elements contain with what was loaded." That's *legal*, but it's not as clear *why* someone would want to do this. Ordinarily, if you are going to load something from Ajax to add to the web page, it will make sense to insert it in one place and not every element in a multi-element wrapped set. So the possibility of calling `.load()` on any wrapped set, instead of a single DOM element as can be encapsulated in a wrapped set like `$.("#results")`, is not obviously such a terribly great improvement.

Furthermore, `.load()` will return immediately, not when things are loaded, so items following it in the chain should not be assumed to have the data loaded. But they also should not be assumed *not* to have the data loaded; we have a race condition, and we should only chain other items after `.load()` when race conditions about the order of execution do not matter. So the fact that we can chain other operations after `.load()`, which is arguably the glory of jQuery, does not mean that it is always wise to do so.

Another point to be made is as above: `.load()`, like `$.get()` and `$.post()`, effectively forces a noop error handler, and therefore should be used only when it is acceptable for nothing to be done when any of a number of things that can go wrong, do go wrong. There may be some cases where a noop is the best error handler, but usually best practices in Ajax are to give some feedback that something has gone wrong.

Convenience methods exist, but we recommend using `$.ajax()` because it provides callback facilities for error situations as well as for success, or writing an appropriate generic, all-purpose error callback to give to `$.ajaxSetup()` or equivalent (there are other alternatives, including `$.ajaxError()`). The best practices are to use a convenience method in conjunction with a global error handler, which can be made more sophisticated by examining the information in its arguments to tell what went wrong.

jQuery as a virtual higher-level language

There are some other basic functions that we have seen in jQuery besides direct Ajax. One example of other kinds of functions includes selectors.

The selectors

Selectors create a wrapped set. Some examples of selectors include:

- `$("*")`: Selects all DOM elements.
- `$(":animated")`: Selects all elements that are in the process of an animation at the time the selector is called.
- `$("id|=header")`: Selects all elements with attribute `id` (in this illustration), whose content matches `header` or `header-*`, like `header-image`. In this case, this would be an element ID. This and following selectors matching text are case sensitive, meaning that an ID of "HEADER" or even "Header" would not be matched.
- `$("value*=import")`: Selects all elements with attribute `value` containing the string `import`. This would include both strings like "Then import the following class." and "This is important."
- `$("value~=import")`: Matches elements having a value that contains the string `import`, but is delimited by spaces. This would include "Then we import the following class." but exclude "This is important."
- `$("id$=wrapper")`: Matches all elements having an ID that ends with `wrapper`. This would include an ID of "comment-wrapper" as well as `wrapper`.
- `$("http-equiv=refresh")`: Matches all elements where the `http-equiv` attribute exactly equals `refresh`.
- `$("id!=result")`: Matches all elements having IDs, where the ID does not equal `result`. This will not match elements that do not have IDs.
- `$("class^=main")`: Matches all elements having a class that begins with `main`.
- `$(":button")`: Selects all buttons, whether button elements directly or inputs of type button.
- `$(":checkbox")`: Selects all inputs of type checkbox.
- `$(":checked")`: Selects all checked inputs.
- `$(":contains('important')")`: Selects all elements containing the text `important`.
- `$(":disabled")`: Selects all inputs that are disabled.

- `$(":empty")`: Select all elements that have no children, not even a text node. This would include a node from `<img src='logo.png' height='120' width='100' alt='Widgets, Inc.' />"` or `"<p></p>"`, but not `"<p>Hello.</p>"` or the outer element of `"<p><span></span></p>"`.
- `$(":enabled")`: Selects all elements that are enabled.
- `$("p").eq(0)`: This gives two examples. First, all tags of a name may be found by calling their tag name; hence `$("li")` returns all `li` elements (regardless of the case in the source HTML). The `.eq()` function performs zero-based array indexing on the set. It is conceptually like how a JavaScript `$("p")[0]`. `$("p").eq(0)` returns a wrapped set containing one item: the first `p` element.
- `$(":even")`: Selects all even-numbered elements, but zero-based. Counter-intuitively, `$("table#directory tr:even")`, which says "Take the table with ID `directory` and return all even-numbered `tr` elements from it," will return the first, third, fifth, and so on, `tr` elements from the table if the table contains at least five table rows.
- `$(":file")`: Selects all inputs of type file.
- `$(":first-child")`: Selects all elements that are the first child of their parent. For example:

```
<html>
    <head>
        <link rel="stylesheet"
            type="text/css" href="/style.css" />
        <title>Welcome to our community!</title>
        <meta http-equiv="refresh" content="900" />
    </head>
    <body>
        <p>Welcome to our community! We offer:</p>
        <ul>
            <li>Experienced leadership.</li>
            <li>Well-furnished facilities.</li>
            <li>Good neighbors.</li>
        </ul>
    </body>
</html>
```

- `$(":first-child")` will return the head element, the link element, the p element, and the first `li` element. Note that this does not noisily and legalistically include every DOM text element. The text node containing "Good neighbors." is technically the first child of its `li` parent, but `$(":first-child")` returns a more useful, and conceptually cleaner to use, version of the first child.

- `.(":gt(2)")` will return all elements with (zero-based) index greater than two in the wrapped set. `$("p").(":gt(2)")` will return the fourth and subsequent p elements, or an empty wrapped set if there are not at least four p elements.
- `$(":has(a)")`: Returns all elements containing an anchor. `$("p:has(a)")` returns all p elements containing an a element.
- `$(":header")`: Returns all h1, h2, h3, and so on, elements.
- `$(":hidden")`: Returns all elements that are hidden.
- `$(":image")`: Returns all images.
- `$(":input")`: Returns all buttons, inputs, selects, and text areas.
- `$(":last-child")`: Like `$("first-child")`, but selects the last instead of first element.
- `.(":last")`: Returns the last element in a wrapped set if that set is non-empty; the Python equivalent to `$("p").(":last")` would be `paragraphs[-1]`.
- `.(":lt")`: Like `.(":gt")`, but selects elements less than the (zero-based) index. `$("p").(":lt(2)")` would return the first two out of any p elements.
- `.(":not(p a)")`: `$("p:not(p a)")` would return a matched set of all paragraphs that do not contain an a element.
- `$(":nth-child(3n)")`: Would return every element that is the *one-based* third child of its parent. As well as `$(":nth-child(3n)")`, `$(":nth-child(4n)")`, and so on, being allowed, there is a more intuitive, one-based `$(":nth-child(even)")` and `$(":nth-child(odd)")`, which more predictably have odd nth children starting with the first child and even with the second.

  The reason for this inconsistency is historical: other elements are zero-based in following JavaScript's and other languages' wide precedent, while this option is one-based in strictly following the CSS specification.
- `$(":odd")`: A selector that is counter-intuitively zero-based. `$("p:odd")` returns the second, fourth, sixth, and so on, paragraph elements if available.
- `$(":only-child")`: Selects all elements that are the only child of their parent.
- `$(":parent")`: Selects all nodes that are parents of other nodes, including text nodes. (Would return the p element for `<p>Hello, world!</p>`.)
- `$(":password")`: Selects all inputs of type password.
- `$(":radio")`: Selects all inputs of type radio.

- `$(":reset")`: Selects all inputs of type reset.
- `$(":selected")`: Returns all elements that are selected.
- `$(":submit")`: Returns all inputs of type submit.
- `$(":text")`: Returns all inputs of type text.
- `$(":visible")`: Returns all elements that are visible.

There are several remarks to be made here.

The first is that the selectors in these examples are (usually) given alone, but this is like words being listed alone in an old-fashioned paper dictionary. In English, there are a few things you can say with a single word, like "Stop!" but usually you say things by combining them, as we have done for a few examples. These selectors are powerful by themselves, but they are more powerful when viewed as words that make up sentences like `$("div.product ul:nth-child(odd)")`, which returns the first, third, fifth, and so on, `li` elements in each unordered list contained in a `div` of class `product`, such as one would use for tiger-striping unordered lists. Many of these selectors are useful by themselves, but they are intended, like pipable Unix command-line tools, to work well together and to be assembled like Lego bricks.

One of the first remarks one might make to someone learning Perl is, "You are not really thinking Perl until you are thinking dictionaries/hashes/associative arrays." If you are solving problems like they do in a C class, from the basic data types such as int, long[], char**, and void*, then you are missing one of the most important workhorses Perl has to offer (and Python, for that matter). And in similar fashion, *you are not really thinking jQuery until you are thinking wrapped sets as created by selectors like the examples above.* It's a foundational part of idiomatic use of the "virtual higher-level language" jQuery offers.

In some other libraries, and in unadorned JavaScript, you operate on the DOM one element at a time. If you want to operate on several elements, you still operate on them one at a time, but you do this several times in sequence. However, the basic unit of work in jQuery is the wrapped set; it may be a wrapped set of one, such as one may create by calling `$("#main:first-child")` or `$("div").eq(0)`, or one may end up getting it by calling `$("h2")` when the DOM contains exactly one `h2` header. However, even then it is missing something about jQuery to think of the set as simply a wrapper for an isolated, unitary element.

The list of the selectors above is something like a paper dictionary of nouns. We haven't yet discussed the verbs, or how to put them together in speech. Let's explore one example of including jQuery in simple Django Ajax. This example does not demonstrate jQuery's power and elegance yet. That is part of the goal in subsequent chapters, as they show Django Ajax put together using jQuery.

A closure-based example to measure clock skew

Let's put some things together in making a simple Ajax example. We will load a web page that will measure how long it takes to make a request from the server, and given a request that gives the time on the server, estimate clock skew between the server and the client. The server will give its answer in JSON, and we will do some DOM manipulations: we will use jQuery rather than an inline onclick-style attribute to register with the button's click event, and we will update the DOM without ever using innerHTML. And, for good measure, we will use a closure to make one incursion into the global namespace, so that if our code or some extension of it is reused, it will not overwrite other global variables.

First, let us make the template, for the sake of discussion starting from `base.html` as defined at the end of the last chapter. We will include it in the same directory as `base.html`, **saved as** `clockskew.html`:

```
{% extends "base.html" %}
{% block title %}Measure Clock Skew{% endblock title %}
{% block body_header_title %}Measure Clock Skew{% endblock body_header_title %}
{% block head_css_page %}<style type="text/css">
<!--
.error
    {
    color: red;
    }
.success
    {
    font-weight: bold;
    }
// -->
</style>
{% endblock head_css_page %}
{% block footer_javascript_page %}<script language="JavaScript" type="text/javascript" src="/static/js/json2.js"></script>
<script language="JavaScript" type="text/javascript"
        src="/static/js/clock_skew.js"></script>
{% endblock footer_javascript_page %}
{% block body_content %}<ul id="results"></ul>
<button id="button">Measure Clock Skew</button>
{% endblock body_content %}
```

Now this page could stand to be refactored on a couple of grounds. Firstly, it includes as page-specific /static/js/json2.js, which as a library for safer parsing of JavaScript presented as JSON should probably be included sitewide, or to go one step further, it should be concatenated with /static/js/jquery.js at least for sitewide deployment, and any other sitewide includes, so that only one JavaScript HTTP request slows things down. (As far as HTTP requests go, a 2 KB download plus another 2 KB download, especially if they are 2 KB JavaScript downloads, add up to more slowness in page rendering than one 4 KB download.) Secondly, one of the major principles of Django is DRY, and the fact that this page repeats "Measure Clock Skew" three times is an invitation for refactoring. This example and what follows deliberately have room left for refinements. (*Can you spot any further improvements to make?*)

We will also define a couple of models, one to serve up this template and one to serve JSON, adapt and extend the urls.py file, and write the Ajax to add behavior to the page. Here is the JavaScript clock_skew.js file:

```
var MeasureClockSkew = function()
    {
    var that = this;
    var lastButtonPress = new Date().getTime();
    var registerError = function(XMLHttpRequest, textStatus,
      errorThrown)
        {
        $("#results").append("<li class='error'>Error: " +
          textStatus + "</li>");
        $("#button").removeAttr("disabled");
        };
    var registerSuccess = function(data, textStatus, XMLHttpRequest)
        {
        try
            {
            var remote = JSON.parse(data).time;
            var halfway = (lastButtonPress +
              new Date().getTime()) / 2;
            var skew = (remote - halfway) / 1000;
            $("#results").append("<li class='success'>Estimated clock
              skew: <span class='measurement'>" + skew + "</span>
              seconds.</li>");
            }
        catch(error)
            {
            $("#results").append("<li class='error'>Error parsing
              JSON.</li>");
            }
```

```
            $("#button").removeAttr("disabled");
            };
        var buttonPress = function()
            {
            lastButtonPress = new Date().getTime();
            $("#button").attr("disabled", "disabled");
            $.ajax({data: "", dataType: "text", error: registerError,
                success: registerSuccess, type: "POST",
                url: "/time/json"});
            };
        return {
            buttonPress: buttonPress
            }
        } ( );
    $("#button").click(MeasureClockSkew.buttonPress);
```

Before going further, we would like to make a few comments about double submission and race conditions. If our test script is deployed live on a faraway web server, with netlag we could fairly easily click the button twice before the response came back, and then it would calculate invalid data. The object, as a means of accounting for netlag, estimates that the server gave its timestamp halfway between when we submitted the click and when we received it, and if we clicked a button twice before the response came back, in addition to any inaccuracies in this estimation, it would combine the time the second click was made and when the first click's response came back, making the calculation corrupt. There are other ways this could have been dealt with; we could make a closure within a closure that would create a separate object for each click and allow overlapping trials with each end time matched to the corresponding start time. But here we have followed a much more generally applicable pattern from the e-commerce world, which is to disable the submit button so the user should not be able to generate overlapping clicks. This is another area where doing things right, even if it means doing double work, means that on the client side you prevent a second submission when that would not be in your visitor's best interests (you don't want your customers charged twice because they got impatient and pressed the button again), and on the server side you also take actions to prevent undesirable forms of double submission (remember, not all visitors have JavaScript enabled).

Furthermore, there is one other best practice worth mentioning: `this` is available only when an object is being constructed; but we can save a reference as `that`.

A Django model is a class that corresponds to a table in a database in Django's object-relational mapping. A Django model instance corresponds to a table row. The division of labor, or separation of concerns, is not exactly MVC, or model-view-controller, but MTV, model-template-view, where the model is a class of object that corresponds to a table in the database, a template is a designer-editable component that gets most HTML out of Python code, and a view is what renders a template or otherwise generates a loaded page. We will create two Django view methods to serve things up on the server side. One is like what we have seen before, and another is new but in principle self-explanatory. A view that serves up JSON is as follows:

```
#!/usr/bin/python/

import json
import time
from django.core import serializers
from django.http import HttpResponse
from django.shortcuts import render_to_response

def home(request):
    return render_to_response(u'clock_skew.html')

def timestamp(request):
    return HttpResponse(json.dumps({u'time': 1000 * time.time()}),
      mimetype=u'application/json')
```

We save both views in `clock_skew.py`, and then edit `urls.py`, so that after

```
(r'^$', 'sample.views.home'),
```

we also have:

```
(r'^time$', 'sample.clock_skew.home'),
(r'^time/json$', 'sample.clock_skew.timestamp'),
```

This is a brief nutshell example of many, but not all, of the kinds of features we will use in our more in-depth case study. The astute reader may have noticed that this brief microcosm does not have the server storing information and saving the state for the user later. However, this does provide Ajax, jQuery, JSON, and some of the most foundational features that Django offers. As we move on we will take these features, incorporate Django models and database usage, and move into a more complex and more sophisticated usage of the features that are presented in this brief example.

Case study: A more in-depth application

In the following chapters, we will build a Django Ajax web application and use jQuery. The web application will be meant to work as a company's intranet employee photo directory, and we hope to put you in a position both to use our model application and customize it to your company's specific needs. In this test application, we will demonstrate both basic features and best practices in putting together a web application using our core technologies. The chapters in our case study will include the following sections.

Chapter 3: Validating Form Input on the Server Side

In this chapter, we will send an Ajax request to the server via jQuery, and validate it on the server side based on the principle that all input is guilty until proven innocent of being malicious, malformed, incomplete, or otherwise invalid. We will look at standard server validation approaches in light of usability practices and look for improvement.

Chapter 4: Server-side Database Search with Ajax

We will compare the merits of server-side and client-side searching, and look at the limitations of JavaScript, both in terms of language limitations, and in terms of client-side performance issues associated with doing too much in the client. We will look both at the merits of handling searching and other backend functions with the full power of a backend environment, and explore why, on the client side, we should work hard to be as lazy as possible in doing network-related work.

We might clarify that "lazy" here does not *specifically* refer to the programmer's virtue of a proactive laziness that tries to solve a problem once, correctly, rather than dash off a bad solution and then spend a lot of time cleaning up after a suboptimal solution. That is worth encouraging, but it is not what we are talking about here. "Lazy" refers, for instance, to Python's xrange(), a generator which yields integers one at a time as they are requested, rather than Python's range(), that builds a complete array immediately and takes significantly more memory for large ranges.

In our case, "lazy" refers in particular to not having the client try to anticipate user needs by fetching what might or might not be needed beforehand, but requesting the minimum necessary to meet user requests, only when requested. We will be exploring several approaches; "lazy" is one approach that we should definitely know about and be able to use.

Chapter 5: Signing Up and Logging into a Website Using Ajax

This chapter will introduce Django authentication facilities and account management, and explore how we can attractively handle the client side of authentication through Ajax client-side communication with the server and corresponding Ajax client-side updates.

Chapter 6: jQuery In-place Editing Using Ajax

In this chapter, we will show a way to use jQuery to make an in-place replacement of a table that allows in-place editing, which communicates with the server in the background, adding persistence to changes.

Chapter 7: Using jQuery UI Autocomplete in Django Templates

We will discuss jQuery's basic intention as having a useful core that's designed to invite plugins to the point of it not being uncommon for programmers to write plugins their first day doing jQuery. We will use autocomplete from the jQuery UI. We will then integrate this into Django templates and our project's user interface.

Chapter 8: Django ModelForm: a CSS Makeover

Django comes with a straightforward way to easily build forms from Django models. We will explore this feature and how to use it.

Chapter 9: Database and Search Handling

In this chapter, we will be showing "lazy" best practices in developing our application.

Chapter 10: Tinkering Around: Bugfixes, Friendlier Password Input, and a Directory That Tells Local Time

If you are interested in having an employee photo directory for your intranet, we not only want to provide an application but also help you have a starting point to create a customized application around your company's needs.

Chapter 11: Usability for Hackers

If you are reading this book, you may have some surprising strengths for usability. This chapter explores them. With this chapter we take a step back from our application and take a look at usability and the bedrock competencies hackers can leverage to do usability.

Appendix: Debugging Hard JavaScript Bugs

In this appendix, we take a look at the state of mind that is needed to debug difficult bugs.

Summary

The goal of these first two chapters has been to provide both a big picture and a sense for how things fit together. Ajax is a bit interdisciplinary; it involves server-side technologies (Django for us), client-side scripting and libraries (including jQuery for us), CSS, HTML, and the DOM, and the goal is very human in character. Ajax is interesting because it opens doors in user interface, usability, and user experience, and in that regard doing well with Ajax isn't just technical; it's also a bit like the arts and humanities.

We have covered the technical side of Django Ajax with jQuery in broad strokes, including:

- A tour of "Hello, world!" in Ajax, and how jQuery makes this an easier operation than library-free, "bare metal" JavaScript
- The basic facilities jQuery offers for Ajax
- A tour of jQuery selectors as an illustration of how jQuery offers a more Pythonic "virtual higher-level language"
- A minimal Django Ajax application with jQuery, with a discussion of what is going on
- An overview of the in-depth application to be covered in the upcoming chapters

These upcoming chapters will move from broad strokes to more in-depth competencies with specific technologies integrated into a more in-depth application.

Let's begin!

3
Validating Form Input on the Server Side

This chapter will look at the topic of server-side validation, albeit from a lens that is unorthodox on a couple of counts.

First, part of the established school of thought is that server-side validation should define what is correct and be as strict as possible in enforcing the expectations. What this claim means is that server-side validation should impose assumptions as rigidly as possible. Perhaps there was a day when it was legitimate to assume that all addresses worked like United States addresses and were written in ASCII, not Unicode. In today's world, websites will see users from the whole world, and it is no longer best practice to strive to be strict in enforcing assumptions, such as can be made about United States postal addresses.

Second, in a bygone era where a hard drive was comparable in size to a large laundry appliance and had a storage capacity in the tens of megabytes, it made sense to be as thrifty with individual bytes as possible and truncate data so the databases could have limited column widths.

Now, both obsolete assumptions should be modified in favor of usability and globalization best practices.

In this chapter, we will:

- First, look at what has been the standard security perspective, a perspective still worth understanding even as we depart from it on *some* points.
- Look at what is provided "for free" in terms of security and validation in Django.
- Look at what Django provides as of version 1.2 in terms of hooks that can be used and adapted for specific validation needs.

- Discuss usability best practices as they are mostly followed in Python—but not as well in Django's default way of doing things—and how the defaults can be compensated for.
- Look at GPS coordinates as an example of a legitimate place to exercise server-side validation.
- Discuss validation as an area where less is more.
- Look at why traditional validation is "negotiating with pistols", and what can be done as an alternative—underscoring that Python and Django already take care of several important security considerations.
- Look at a better usabilility/UX alternative requiring every field be filled out before a user may move on.

The standard lecture: low-level validation

Let us look first at the mindset for low-level validation, and look at the use of regular expressions in validation for security.

Matching regular expressions

Though, strictly speaking, validation on the server-side is more than a security measure, client-side validation is not the right place for security validation. Client-side validation is a courtesy to the user that can allow more graceful handling of honest end-user mistakes. Server-side validation should be based on the premise that input is guilty until proven innocent of being malicious, and no assumption may be made that input comes from your client-side software at all. If you have a page or subsite that handles Ajax requests, it should stand up to any malicious request that could be sent to that URL from a standard or *non-standard* client.

For example, you have a JavaScript date picker that sets a form field to an ISO-8601 *yyyy-mm-dd* format, such as "2001-01-01" for when an event is to be scheduled. You want to at least perform a regular expression check or equivalent, such as:

```
is_valid = re.match(r"^\d{4}-\d{2}-\d{2}$")
```

This may be appropriate as a first layer of validation, although by itself it is incomplete. "9999-99-99" matches this regular expression but does not qualify as a valid date. Furthermore, if the date is for an event being scheduled, it should be in the future. "1327-12-25", however valid as a date, cannot be a valid date in the future. On that point there is a moral tale:

> A programmer has a problem involving validating strings.
> The programmer thinks, "I know! I'll use regular expressions."
> Now the programmer has two problems.

Regular expressions may have a place, but they bear liabilities: they are terse and cryptic. So errors will not jump out as easily as in Python-style "executable pseudocode". This is a major problem for a tool used for security, and there are some things that are either very difficult to do or impossible. A regular expression that would accurately test for valid dates would be a completely undecipherable screenful of code. A regular expression that would in addition test for a date that is today or in the future would not only be a completely undecipherable screenful of code—it would have to be a *dynamically generated* completely undecipherable screenful of code!

All this is to say that regular expressions should not be our only tool for validation, even if it is tempting to use them that way.

You cannot guarantee absolutely valid data

One further point is that though we speak of "validation", in general it is not possible to fully validate input, in the sense that we have guaranteed it is correct. If a user has selected a date from a date picker, and accidentally clicked on the option next to the intended date; there is no real way we can protect against such errors. There might be some things we can do to the user interface so such errors are more likely to be noticed by the user, but "validation" can't prove that we have the date the user intended.

Likewise, if we request a user's name, "dfsjkhlasdlhjksdfjhklds" is not appropriate input. Although, it would be a fool's errand to try to make an input validation routine that would accept any real personal name in Unicode but would avoid garbage like "dfsjkhlasdlhjksdfjhklds". The point of validation is not to guarantee that input is valid, but to guarantee that certain foreseeable types of invalid input are not given, and in particular to avoid malicious input.

Validating can detect (some) malicious input

A canonical example of malicious input is SQL injection. If, in PHP, you execute a constructed query of:

```
"INSERT INTO comments_log (comment, timestamp) VALUES (
                    '" . $_POST['comment'] . "', NOW());"
```

And `$_POST['comment']` is something like:

```
"', NOW()); DELETE FROM comments_log; --"
```

Then the executed SQL statements will effectively be:

```
INSERT INTO comments_log (comment, timestamp) VALUES ('', NOW());
DELETE FROM comments_log; --', NOW());
```

With that, the `comments_log` table is effectively wiped out.

I gave the example in PHP, not specifically to pick on PHP, but because there is no particularly straightforward way to accidentally create this vulnerability in Python (or Django). In Python and Django you can't shoot yourself in the foot like this unless you really go out of your way to do so. If you write direct SQL in Python in the preferred, standard way, Python will handle "escaping" of the SQL so that this doesn't happen. And if you do standard things in a standard way in Django, Django will use Python in such a way that this doesn't happen. To minimally correct our PHP example, if the query is constructed as follows, with a backslash added before each single quote, we have:

```
"INSERT INTO comments_log (comment, timestamp) VALUES (
    '" . str_replace("'", "\\'", $_POST['comment']) . "', NOW());"
```

That still isn't 100% correct because backslashes themselves aren't escaped. But, even without correcting that additional bug, we have addressed the vulnerability so that the code behaves in the programmer's intended way when people enter text that includes a single quote. (The genuinely correct solution in PHP is to use provided escaping functions: `pg_escape_string()`, `mysql_escape_string()`, `mssql_real_escape_string()`, and similar functions.)

The Django way of validation

In Django, many of the low-level requirements are irrelevant. This is not because they need to be done, but because the framework takes care of certain things for you. Django assumes that the input is guilty of being potentially malformed, until proven innocent.

Django gives you some things for free

In Django, much validation is already taken care of for you. Django offers a set of fields including: (`forms.`)`BooleanField`, `CharField`, `ChoiceField`, `TypedChoiceField`, `DateField`, `DateTimeField`, `DecimalField`, `EmailField`, `FileField`, `FilePathField`, `FloatField`, `ImageField`, `IntegerField`, `IPAddressField`, `MultipleChoiceField`, `NullBooleanField`, `RegexField`, `SlugField`, `TimeField`, and `URLField`.

These fields are stored in the database using the database's built-in types: an `EmailField` or a `URLField` ends up being stored by default as a `VARCHAR`. However, Django provides validation that they are correct as e-mail addresses or URLs, and (though this can be optionally turned off) Django will check that a URL exists and does not give a 404 on attempted access. The validation that comes along more or less "for free" in Django is quite a lot; malformed input like `GET /?%?%?%?%%%%&&&& HTTP/1.1` will be rejected as malformed before your validation has to deal with it. If input is passed on, it has probably passed a sanity check. `FloatField` and `IntegerField`, for instance, will be coerced to floats and integers with an exception raised if the text of the CGI input value cannot be so coerced.

There are several steps in validation; the different steps serve as hooks that can be customized, often (but not always) by overriding the appropriate method. Note that in some cases the best practice is to add specific validation to an existing field type rather than create a new field type. If we wish to confirm that a product key passes our cryptographic check for a valid product key, we could make a `CharField` of appropriate size and set its validator to throw a `ValidationError` if it did not pass our check.

The steps in Django's validation

The specific steps of validation as of Django 1.2, in rough order, are:

1. `to_python()` returns an appropriate Python datatype, such as `int` for `IntegerField`, or else throws a `ValidationError`. Here and elsewhere, any `ValidationError` should be constructed with a string explaining how the form input failed validation.

2. `validate()`, for the field, handles any validation that shouldn't be handled by validators (which are functions that can be specified in a field's construction). It takes a value in the correct datatype and raises a `ValidationError` on error. It should not alter the value.

3. `run_validators()` runs all of a field's validators, and aggregates any `ValidationErrors` (if there are more than one) into a single `ValidationError`.
   It should not usually be necessary to override the `run_validators()` method itself; validators to feed into `run_validators()` can be specified on field construction.

4. The field's `clean()` method runs `to_python()`, `validate()`, and `run_validators()`, and propagates any errors generated. The cleaned version is returned, and used to populate the form's `cleaned_data` dictionary.

5. Any form subclass's `clean_<fieldname>()` method can be overridden, will need to look up data from the form's `cleaned_data` dictionary, and will return the cleaned data (whether changed or unchanged). If we subclassed form and wanted to confirm that an included serial number was legitimate, a `clean_serialnumber()` method would be appropriate and should raise a `ValidationError` if the serial number is not legitimate.

6. Any form subclass's `clean()` method. This hook in particular is intended for requirements that do not strictly belong to individual fields. For instance, if you require that someone filling out a help request provide either phone or e-mail contact information, then neither the phone nor the e-mail field individually is required. But, a form subclass's `clean()` method is a natural place to check and raise an error if the user has not provided at least one. Alternatively, a feedback form might be explicitly intended for users who wish to leave feedback but may or may not wish to be contacted. In that case, it may make sense to have a checkbox for whether the user wishes a response, and require contact information only if the user desires a response. If a user is presented a form to specify options for an order and some combinations do not make sense, the form subclass `clean()` method can also be used to check that the user has not selected a combination of options that cannot be fulfilled.

A more sensible and cruelty-free approach to validation

To give an example of use, let us initially develop a form to collect a telephone number from end users. One basic usability concern is that while it may be entirely appropriate to store a telephone number in the database as a string of digits, it is both lazy and rude to users to impose "validation" that says "If you type any non-digit character at all, I'm going to reject it as wrong." The same principle is true with credit cards, although if we are writing code to handle credit cards in Django and we are not (for instance) the developer of a major ecommerce app, we are probably reinventing the wheel and therefore creating trouble for ourselves, when we could reuse existing debugged software. For credit cards, it is rude to demand that people type in credit cards as "4111111111111111" because you choose not to show the courtesy to write software that will overlook non-numeric characters and accept credit card numbers entered like "4111 1111 1111 1111" or "4111-1111-1111-1111".

Returning to telephone numbers, for very good reason people usually do not write, for example, U.S. telephone numbers like "8005551212". There is some variety in the wild between formats like "(800) 555-1212", "800-555-1212", and "800.555.1212"; but all of them break the numbers up because giving people 10 digits in a row is unnecessarily cruel. Furthermore, standardizing a credit card number to a string of digits desired for database storage is an introductory-level exercise:

```
from django.db import models

class CreditCardNumber(models.TextField):
    def clean(self):
        return re.sub(r'\D', '', str(self))
```

Or, if we wish to be able to store "(800) 555-1212 x123" as "8005551212x123" and perhaps vanity numbers like "(888) 4-VANITY" as "8884VANITY," then:

```
from django.db import models

class PhoneNumber(models.TextField):
    def clean(self):
        return re.sub(r'\W', '', str(self))
```

And perhaps add .lower() or .upper() to standardize case. (Alternatively, it may make sense to only allow a whitelist of letters, perhaps just 'x'. Where a digit means a number dialled and an 'x' only means "This is not for dialling; wait for the phone to be picked up and then go on dialling digits," or perhaps an algorithm could store upper-case letters for vanity values and a lowercase 'x' for extensions.)

Things get murkier

So what would this look like in Django? We would subclass form and add a validator, but there's another issue that comes up. What's the maximum length of a phone number that we need to support? Even if we restrict our attention to U.S. telephone numbers, the previous examples show a 10 character limit to be shortsighted, and sometimes a bit of a straitjacket. It is a relatively common occurrence that the number a person leaves is 10 digits, plus an extension of 3 to perhaps 5 digits. Less commonly, conference calls can have more like 7-10 digits conference PINs.

In the U.S. alone, possible phone numbers can be a bit open-ended in length, and writing code with only the U.S. in mind is breakage by design. How many digits can phone numbers be worldwide?

The zero-one-infinity rule: a cardinal rule of thumb in usability

This is a good time to make a point that the Django documentation at http://docs.djangoproject.com/en/1.2/ or http://djangobook.com/ never make clearly: there is a rule of thumb in interface design of "Don't allow _____ at all, or allow up to one of _____ but not more, or allow as many of _____ as available resources support." This principle is called the **zero-one-infinity rule**, and while zero and one both have a place, two or twenty but not more are breakage by design.

In traditional SQL, breaking the zero-one-infinity rule is almost required. Normally in declaring a column, you declare where it will break the zero-one-infinity rule. You may try to add a healthy bit of slack in *how* you do this, but you ordinarily create a column for people's names as VARCHAR(20), or VARCHAR(100), or whatever, but whatever the limit you choose, you specify an arbitrary line and guarantee that if a user enters *one* character more, let alone twenty, you will drop it on the floor.

An improvement on Django's advertised approach

Django is Pythonic in many ways, and Python observes the zero-one-infinity rule well:

- Strings can be of any length that available resources will support
- Lists and tuples may likewise be as large as can be supported
- Partly through deft handling of integer overflow, you can have correct integer calculations with integers of three digits or three thousand

However, Django follows SQL and not Python to present "breakage by design" as the normal way of handling most situations: fields such as CharField, EmailField, and the like are built on SQL's VARCHAR and presented in the documentation with the request that you specify an arbitrary length for CharField, EmailField, and the like so that if a user provides just one character more, the data will be truncated.

Fields like EmailField can be subclassed to use TEXT instead of VARCHAR, so that there is no arbitrary threshold beyond which data will be corrupted. For instance:

```
from django.db import models

class TextEmailField(models.EmailField):
    def get_internal_type(self):
        return 'TextField'
```

To return to telephone numbers, yet another solution, and perhaps a better one, would be to preserve the formatting characters so that the formatting provided by the user is still available, save it as TEXT, and declare that two phone numbers are equal if they contain the same digits:

```
from django.db import models

class TextPhoneField(models.TextField):
    def __eq__(self, other):
        try:
            return self.remove_formatting() == other.remove_formatting()
        except:
            return False
    def remove_formatting(self):
        return re.sub(ur'\D', u'', str(self))
```

This overloads ==, and respects Python's duck typing by avoiding `isinstance`: if someone else creates a class that does the work of a `TextPhoneField` but is not descended from it, we don't want to declare all of its instances unequal to any `TextPhoneField`, because it is not an instance or a subclass. The way we remove formatting has been offloaded to its own method, both to make it available and to allow changes (for instance, if we decide to change what characters we do and do not remove, perhaps by replacing the regular expression `ur'\D'` with `ur'\W'`).

Let us look at one more detail of Django validation before building a validated form for our case study. Django fields can be created with the argument `required = True` or `required = False`, defaulting to `required = True`. For instance, a `CharField` or `TextField` created the default way will register a validation failure on an empty value. There are at least two different cases where you will want to set `required = False`: if you ever might want to allow an empty value (it is usually not a user interface best practice to make people fill out all fields, all the time); or if you want to have a useful `BooleanField`, normally rendered as a checkbox (the `BooleanField`, like other fields, defaults to being required that you fill it in, meaning that it defaults to being rejected as invalid if you do not click a checkbox — the meaning of the checkbox is not "Do you mean 'Yes' or 'No'?" but "Say 'Yes', and give your rubber stamp here.").

A validation example: GPS coordinates

Let's take a slightly more involved example of input validation: a field for GPS coordinates. This is complicated in part because "GPS coordinate" does not *exactly* mean a single system, but one of a few different systems. For this specific system, which is something of an exception, we *could* use the VARCHAR based CharField. This is because like the information stored in a Date or DateTime, there actually is an upper limit to how long a useful value will be. A measurement to the nearest thousandth of a second is specific to within a distance you could measure with a handheld ruler. We will allow some added space, but the goal is not specifically to create a GPS coordinate field that allows subatomic precision.

Among the ways an address could be specified are the following:

```
36° 09' 55.8"N, 86° 46' 58.8"W
36.16586 -86.78425
37° 25.330'N, 122° 5.039'W

N36 09 55.781
W86 46 58.287
```

We may find it helpful to use regular expressions at some point. While it should, in principle, be recommended to make a single regular expression call to handle all these cases, much better would be to break it down into a series of manageable tests, in this case returning success if input matches a test as valid, and then raising a ValidationError if none of the tests could interpret it as valid. We will specify a maximum length, but for now leave it unspecified, something to be determined after we know how long the longest validating entry will be.

Our code is as follows:

```python
from django.db import models
from django.core.exceptions import ValidationError
import re

def gps_validator(value):
    # Create a normalized working copy of the value.
    working_copy = value
    working_copy = working_copy.replace(u'\n', u',')
    working_copy = working_copy.replace(u'\r', u',')
    working_copy = re.sub(ur',*$', '', working_copy)
    working_copy = re.sub(ur',+', u',', working_copy)
    if not u',' in working_copy and not \
        re.match(ur'.* .* .*', working_copy):
            working_copy = working_copy.replace(u' ', u',')
```

```
        working_copy = re.sub(u'[\00B0\2018\2019\201C\201D\'"]', ' ',
                        working_copy)
        working_copy = working_copy.replace(u',', u' ')
        working_copy = re.sub(ur'\s+', u' ', working_copy)
        working_copy = working_copy.strip()
        working_copy = working_copy.upper()
        # Test the normalized working copy against regular
        # expressions for different kinds of GPS format.
        if re.match(ur'[-NS]? ?\d{1,3} [0-5]\d [0-5]\d(\.\d+)[NS]?,
                 [-EW]? ?\d{1,3} [0-5]\d [0-5]\d(\.\d+)[EW]?',
                 working_copy):
            return working_copy
        elif re.match(ur'[-NS]? ?\d{1,3} [0-5]\d(\.\d+)[NS]?,
                   [-EW]? ?\d{1,3} [0-5]\d(\.\d+)[EW]?',
                   working_copy):
            return working_copy
        elif re.match(ur'[-NS]? ?\d{1,3}(\.\d+)[NS]?,
                   [-EW]? ?\d{1,3}(\.\d+)[EW]?',
                   working_copy):
            return working_copy
        else:
            raise ValidationError(u'We could not recognize this as a valid
GPS coordinate.')

class GPSField(models.TextField):
    default_error_messages = {
        u'invalid': u'We could not recognize this as a valid GPS
coordinate.',
    }
    default_validators = [gps_validator]
```

The regular expressions are cryptic and ugly, but, in a nutshell, what is done is to coerce the data to a normalized form, and then test for whether the normalized form of the input looks like "N36 09 55.781, W86 46 258.287" or other comparable forms.

Avoiding error messages that point fingers and say, "You're wrong!"

We might also briefly stop to note a principle of user experience and user interface. The computer must at times bear bad news, but there is a difference in how the software comes across between saying, "We could not recognize this as valid input" and "You messed up."

Your software will be better liked and better received if it handles validation failures by saying "**We** could not recognize this as valid input", "**We** need additional information before we can continue", and so on than if it says, "**You** entered data that was invalid", or "**You** failed to provide required information". If nothing else, there is much less egg on the programmer's face if the senior vice-president is an avid geocaching hobbyist who knows GPS inside and out, and enters GPS data in a perfectly valid format that we didn't know about. It is much better to tell a hobbyist vice-president who knows GPS better than we do, "We couldn't recognize this as a valid format." than, effectively, *You idiot, we know better than you that you don't know how to write a valid GPS location.*

Now, after the fact, if we allow for specification of up to a thousandth of a second, a "maximally long believable cleaned input" might be:

```
N100 10 10.111, S100 10 10.111
```

That creates a Unicode string of length 30. We might suggest that a good programmer might be slightly nervous about fixing a length of 30, probably because if someone adds extra whitespace, or in light of unforeseen future developments, it makes sense to use GPS coordinates to sub-millimeter precision and so people start to enter data like:

```
N 100°, 10', 10.11111",
S 100°, 10', 10.11111"
```

Our regular expressions may be slightly more future-proof because they are written flexibly. But even here, there is reason to be a bit nervous about choosing VARCHAR over TEXT.

Validation as demanding that assumptions be met

To validate is to demand that user data conform to your expectations, meaning *assumptions*, about what constitutes valid data. It's hard to make assumptions that are valid the world around.

Old-school: conform to our U.S.-based assumptions!

Let's take a somewhat standard, old-school approach to validation of what goes in the database. This approach says that you don't want junk data in your database and you define strict rules and take every possible step to prevent junk data entering. The initial, U.S.-centric form has:

- Street address, line 1 (*required*)
- Street address, line 2 (*optional*)
- City (*required*)
- State (*required, and specified by a dropdown menu*)
- Zip code (*required*)

This is U.S.-centric but not entirely fair to U.S. residents themselves. For starters, some forms like this out in the wild reject valid input. There is a five-digit and a nine-digit version of a ZIP code. Although the diligent nine-digit zip code is preferred and is intended to allow mail to reach its destination faster, enter a nine-digit zip code on many forms like this and you will get a response amounting to "This is unacceptable; please try again and give a real zip code this time."

But even if that problem is not present, there is another problem as far as the state goes. If we just let people type in a two-letter state code, we are inviting typos, even if many of them could be caught by straightforward server-side checks. But if we require a drop-down menu so they *can't* type an invalid state, something really funny happens even if every single record has a real state. Valued customers who may not have spent long hours on Pac-Man (let alone growing up on smartphones and SecondLife) try their best to handle the long dropdown menu but still leave addresses like:

Ashley Jones

1745 Broadway

New York, **NC** 10019

Whereas we could tell there was a problem if this person accidentally made a typo corresponding to an invalid state, here the error is that a different valid state has been (mis-)registered as the customer's state. And what is worse, we get many more of these invalid records than if we just let customers type in their own states. Not only is the long dropdown menu cruel to users, it makes a good many users have more trouble entering the data they intended. As a result, the dropdown menu delivers more than a painful user experience. It delivers significantly and substantially more corrupt data in the database than if we had just been "lazy" and let them type a two-letter state code. And it delivers corrupt data that is harder to identify than typos like "NU" which are usually not valid state codes and are therefore often more straightforward to identify as corrupt data.

What do we do if we want to take a form like this and make it more international? One solution that perhaps all of us have seen is:

- Address, line 1 (*required*)
- Address, line 2 (*optional*)
- City (*required*)
- State, province, district, region, or territory (*required*)
- Zip or postal code, if applicable (*optional*)
- Country (*required*)

And we can particularly offend Canadians, who wince at (real or imagined) evidence that the U.S. lumps them in as the 51st state, by making a "state/province/..." menu that intermingles U.S. states and Canadian provinces and then leaves the rest of the world's regions as "Other (please specify below:)". This solution is probably meant as a gesture of warmth from the U.S. to Canada, but it is a gesture of warmth that quite probably did not include consulting a Canadian about Canadian sensibilities.

There is at least one U.S.-specific concession that actually makes a lot of sense. For the New Yorker who didn't grow up on video games, putting all of the countries in alphabetical order may end up with a problematic number of street addresses like:

> Ashley Jones
>
> 1745 Broadway
>
> New York, NC 10019
>
> United Arab Emirates

If we wanted to trust the user's judgment a little more, we could let people fill out their country as text. That could result in less-uniform data, as "USA", "US", "U.S.A.", and "U.S." would probably all appear in any number of U.S. residents. But it would both be merciful to the end user and refrain from the cruelty of making people pick a needle out of the haystack of a long dropdown menu, *and* result in better and more correct information in our database.

Adding the wrong kind of band-aid

The solution that is taken, in many cases, is to make "United States of America" the first option of the menu so as to avoid giving U.S. residents the needle-in-a-haystack cruelty of finding their country buried under the "U" section of an alphabetical list of every country in the world. And it is needlessly cruel to residents of the United States of America... or the United Kingdom... or United Arab Emirates... or...

This leaves out the internationalization issue that not all addresses are constructed like U.S. addresses. If you take the original structure of:

- Street address, line 1 (*required*)
- Street address, line 2 (*optional*)
- City (*required*)
- State (*required, and specified by a dropdown menu*)
- Zip code (*required*)

Appending country and making the "State" and "Zip" slots generic does not make the structure flexible enough to accommodate internationalized address handling. Some countries have more lines in their street addresses, while some have fewer. Part of this is absorbed by the optional second street address line, but there are still addresses worldwide that are mangled if you demand that they fit this format. Even if you will allow letters in a postal code and freeform text for the state-like field.

Then what can be done? It should be almost theoretically possible to just present a dropdown menu first, specifying country, and then have Ajax adjust the form so that there is an appropriate form for the country. On the backend, an equally Rube Goldberg system of rules could enforce this mentality for every locality worldwide, and on the backend at least, people wouldn't get frustrated waiting for the enormous Ajax application to load and possibly crash their browsers. But at least, in principle, this mentality can be internationalized to put its heavy hand on every international address in fully localized form.

But there is an alternative—*A single textarea.*

Perhaps some programmers might feel like they're not doing their jobs if they "just" give a textarea for address without further doing diligent work, like making people suffer through long dropdown menus, to convince themselves they're preventing people from getting bad data into the system. Even if it means that for every one case where they prevent an address like "...New York, NU..." from entering the system, ten addresses like "...New York, NC..." get through validation. But really, honestly, it's better to let go of the control freak mentality, stop making people jump between fields on your particular form, and just type an address they know well in an ordinary, clearly legible, and attractively styled textarea. *Really, less is more.*

And one additional point to underscore that less is more: Even in the U.S., I've run aground with "more is more" computers that negotiated with pistols. One "negotiated with pistols" demand is that if you have a valid address, you include a street address with a house number. And my address was:

> Jonathan Hayward
>
> Department of Theology
>
> Fordham University
>
> Bronx, NY 10458-9993

And this was treated as not an acceptable address, **period**. Never mind that the ZIP+9 alone told which department in the university to send correspondence to. I did not have the expected street address beginning with a number, and therefore, by definition it seemed, I could not have entered a valid address and I could not be allowed to move forward. And this occasional loss of U.S. customers is a way to drive away customers the world around. People in other parts of the world may wish to pat me on the head and say, "Poor baby! You had a taste, once, of what happens to us all the time!"

Making assumptions and demanding that users conform

Let's look at one other type of basic information: a person's name. For this discussion, we will ignore Unicode issues completely and look at problems that come up even if we stick to ASCII. LinkedIn and Facebook alike request a first and last name, but this isn't quite right.

At least names are simple, right?

On the surface, one obvious validation, if we do not coerce case, is that a person will have a first and last name, each of which is an uppercase letter followed by one or more lowercase letters. That's easy enough to test for, but it doesn't allow for a lot more than a first initial, optionally followed by a period. And strictly speaking, it doesn't allow even most American full legal names at birth. Though "Firstname Lastname" is often treated as a person's full name, most full legal names are "Firstname Middlename Lastname." And most people will treat the common exception of the CamelCased last name, such as the Scottish "MacDonald" or the Irish "McDonald".

But here we have the Monty Python sketch where the Cardinals announce "Our two chief weapons are fear and surprise," because there's at least one more common exception. The French "de Balzac"/"de BALZAC", the German "von Friar", or the Dutch "van Driel" or "van den Driel", which in European convention are alphabetized under the capitalized name because "de"/"von"/"van…" is not strictly part of the name. So our two chief exceptions are Celtic CamelCase, and European words translating to "of" (namely "de"/"von"/"van…") that are added before the proper part of the name. And also the case where Americans of Dutch ancestry have CamelCased or otherwise altered the European convention, making a name of VanDriel or Vandriel.

Even in ASCII, things keep getting murkier

So now our three chief exceptions to our general-purpose validation rule are as above, and also that it is becoming more common practice for women to list both their maiden and married names as last names.

Our four chief exceptions to the general-purpose validation rule include Celtic CamelCasing, variations on European "de"/"von"/"van…", women listing two last names, and Orthodox monks and nuns. An Orthodox woman named Sarah Smith who becomes a nun will take a new first name such as Xenia and give up her last name, will be properly addressed as "Mo. Xenia" (that is "Mother Xenia"), and not be referred to with her last name at all. When it is necessary from context to perhaps specify which Mo. Xenia is being referred to, parentheses are expected around her last name. So she would then for clarification be referred to by name as "Xenia (Smith)". So our validation, if it allows for this, will need to allow for no last name, or a last name that begins and ends with parentheses, or both. Orthodox bishops are monks and thus have only one name, but it is written in ALL CAPS, for example "His Grace BASIL".

Our simple validation rule is imposing certain assumptions, and the list of exceptions seems to get longer each time we list it.

Furthermore, the pattern of a first and last name, where the first is a personal name and the last is a family name, is far from universal. In Chinese culture, people have a first and last name, but the first name is the family name and the last is a personal name.

We would propose the following, which almost assuredly imposes some cultural assumptions that do not hold in all cultures:

- An optional Unicode slot for any honorific(s)
- A Unicode slot for a person's name

- An optional Unicode slot for what in Western culture are letters after a person's name, including not only academic degrees but religious order membership, titles, and an open-ended list of other things that should not exclude being a LinkedIn Open Networker

In U.S. culture, there is an informal society where it is considered unpretentious to simply be addressed by your first name and no honorific. This is not a pattern worldwide and giving people a place to indicate what honorifics are proper to address them by is appropriate. Or, as an alternative which may be pursued for the greater good of the UI, we may have a single slot that holds honorifics, name, and post-nominals.

Now there is nothing wrong with creating heuristics that will try to extract a first and last name, and Django server-side heuristics could be made that would be quite accurate in handling U.S.-style names.

Better validation may be less validation

As far as server-side validation goes, *really, less is more*. Perhaps we as programmers are always looking for ways we can be more diligent, and we look for ways we can work harder that will deliver a better solution. But there's something we need to understand about validation.

Each requirement in validation is a demand that data meet an assumption. Each assumption is a way to make a solution more culture-specific and harder to internationalize, and also less future-proof.

Validation that requires a real five-digit U.S. zip code creates an unpleasant surprise to the customer who diligently gave a perfectly valid nine-digit form in the hope that a product might arrive one day sooner. Old U.S. validation requirements, from when a database really would only hold U.S. information, are almost invariably a legacy obstacle to gracefully handling internationalized and localized information in today's world. There may as well not be a single database validation measure for data like addresses that originally only took U.S. data into consideration that does not create obstacles to handling internationalized data gracefully. Almost by definition, they demand that data meet assumptions that things behave the way they do in the U.S. What if our GPS validator is used in French localization? In English, a period is used to specify a decimal; π to two decimal places would be written, "3.14". In French numbers, the comma does this job, as in "3,14". Our GPS validation routine above, in English localization, would validate "36.16586 -86.78425" but reject a French-style "36,16586 -86,78425".

Caveat: English is something of a lingua franca

Surely our GPS validator could be adjusted to tolerate either locale's decimal marker, but this is the road to Rube Goldberg nightmare code. It might make sense to ask people entering GPS data to use English localization as *lingua franca* for that part of the code. And not only because a GPS field is something we might want to parse and have the computer understand, and it would be a Rube Goldberg code nightmare to write a parser for every possible localized form of GPS coordinates. To native English speakers concerned about cultural chauvinism, we might suggest that it makes a lot more sense, internationally, than we might suspect.

When I was studying in Paris, I remember seeing a keyboard synthesizer, looking to see what was selected, and being utterly shocked to see "HONKY-TONK PIANO," *in English*. I had assumed that in the U.S. synthesizers were labeled in English, and in France synthesizers would just as naturally be labeled in French. But the markings, instrument names, and so on were pure English and I was the only one to find this strange. English is *lingua franca*, or close to it, for technology, and speakers of some other languages find it normal to have an online forum with the user interface in English (and forum threads in their native language).

Latin remained the language of scholarship and international discourse in Europe whether or not there were any native Latin speakers at all. When Europe moved to writing scholarship in people's native languages, book titles remained in Latin for much longer. The 20th century German Ludwig Wittgenstein's seminal *Tractatus Logico-Philosophicus* is written in German, but the title *is in Latin*. And when the work is dealt with in English, the contents are translated to English. But the title, which could be translated in English like "Logical-Philosophical Treatment", is abbreviated to *Tractatus* but seems to *only* be given in Latin even among English speakers who have never studied Latin.

English now is a bit like Latin: it is something of a standard language, especially in matters of technology. And many non-native speakers make it their first choice in discussing technology. Furthermore, it might be pointed out that Google has made extraordinary efforts at localization, with meticulous attention to detail for giving directions in Japan for instance. Google Maps at the time of this writing accepts "36.16586 -86.78425" and pulls it up immediately, but for a location of "36,16586 -86,78425", answers, "We could not understand the location 36,16586 -86,78425".

[We might point out that the error message, "We could not understand..." is well done and minimizes any message of "You don't know what you're doing."]

Django comes with validated, *and worldwide*, `EmailField` and `URLField` fields. And it was designed by journalist professionals who would know perfectly well that it is desirable to be able to store phone numbers and postal addresses. However, there is no `PhoneField` or `StreetAddressField` because making worldwide validation for these is a tarpit. There are tools to make a U.S.-centric address field, complete with long, cruel dropdown menus to specify a valid state, but no `WorldStreetAddressField` because that would be a Rube Goldberg tarpit.

Then is there any validation to be done, or do we simply drop it? We might propose one alternative.

We don't have to negotiate with pistols

The standard rule of practice is for validation to negotiate with pistols. So if data doesn't meet your assumptions, you say "I will not let you move forward until you change this data to what I assume it should be." As far as Django server-side validation goes, if you specify that an input fails validation, you guarantee that the input as submitted could never be entered into the database. But there is another client-side option.

For the client side, possibly the most common error is not specifying a complete address including country. And it would be both possible and sensible to run a client-side test to see if you can recognize the provided address as including a country. If you cater to a mainly U.S. clientele, it is also entirely permissible to have the system infer a U.S. address if the address ends in something like "New York, NY 10019-4343".

But you don't have to negotiate with pistols. Instead of refusing to continue unless the user enters an address that meets our assumptions, we could give a dialog that says, "We could not identify what country this address belongs to" with buttons of **Go back and specify a country** and **This address is correct**. This provides a way to identify foreseeable data errors, and asks the user to correct them. But at the same time, it avoids creating an absolute roadblock to the user who specifies an entirely appropriate address that our validation routines didn't foresee.

For a U.S. company keeping a directory of telephone numbers, with, say, four-digit phone extensions. A phone number might be tested, client-side, by stripping out non-word characters, and accepting a phone number of at least ten digits as valid; or a phone number of ten digits, an 'x', and at least one more digit as valid; or exactly four digits optionally preceded by an 'x' as valid; or warn for any other number. That offers significantly better flexibility for people coming from outside the U.S., even if it does not undertake the (again) Rube Goldberg task of checking for country codes and numbers that correspond to the given country code. But if the validation warns, instead of demanding that its assumptions be met, someone who tries to make an entry of "466453" (for texting queries to Google) will be allowed, after a warning, to enter a number not foreseen in the validator's assumptions.

Doing our best to solve the wrong problem: a story

Perhaps the most inappropriate textbook example of why we need precise requirements tells of a professor who assigned as homework that students should program a four-function calculator. One student turned in a flawless four-function calculator using *Roman numerals*, complete with a full user's manual in Latin. The obvious point that was presented in the example is that the professor would have been better to be more precise in the homework specification, but this is naïve and stupid. The student was giving a crystal-clear signal, "I'm in the wrong class!" It is stupidity worthy of Dilbert's boss to try to solve this problem with more specific requirements. Had the professor been more specific, stating that Arabic numerals were acceptable and Roman numerals were not, this would have accomplished two things:

- First, it would have made the assignment more confusing for most of this student's classmates
- Second, it would have thrown down the gauntlet to any student who was in the wrong class

The student, perhaps, would have produced a fully functional four-function calculator, implementing the specification to the legalistic letter, and the professor, perhaps, would have been surprised to type:

```
>  7*8
56
```

And then find, ostensibly to provide enhanced accessibility, that the program played a sound clip of a painfully loud note on an out-of-tune piano fifty-six times before moving on. And the student had taken thought to set a Unix terminal mode that included disabling the usual ways to send a suspend or interrupt from the keyboard.

The problem when a student hands in a four-function calculator—with Roman numerals and a full Latin user's manual—is that the student is bored silly in the wrong class. The correct solution is to bump the student up some classes until the student's ability and the class's challenge level are in sync. Kneejerk reactions to move towards more legalistic requirements do not help. Part of the Agile experience is that handling requirements more legalistically does not help in the real world, either, not as much as one might think. (The documents and communication of Agile delivering its best solutions probably never have the legalistic precision of a heavyweight waterfall requirements document solving a badly identified problem as precisely as possible.) Communicating clearly, of course, is always an asset, but trying to manage risk and change by trying to be legalistic and pin things down that way is an attempt to solve the wrong problem, which rarely does a good job of addressing the correct real-world problem.

It really does apply to validation

And the same insight holds for the "Big Design Up Front," heavyweight design process mentality for validation. If we deal only with U.S. contacts, we can use a form with:

- Address, line 1 (*required*)
- Address, line 2 (*optional*)
- City (*required*)
- State (*required*)
- Zip (*required*, any valid zip code accepted)

If we are afraid that people will give junk values, with a city like "afdjkfdkj", we may be able to use USPS web services or the website to test whether an actual street address is given. But then what if people use an address across the country? Conceivably, we could locate their IP's geographical location in relation to the address. But this is being silly, not to mention that customers might find it a tad creepy. People who really want to provide junk data, perhaps to preserve the anonymity of their addresses when it is inappropriately demanded, will do so. We can try to do things that will catch common data entry errors; but trying to legalistically keep invalid data out of our databases will accomplish little more than a more legalistic wording for the four-function calculator assignment.

But don't we need to assume data is guilty until proven innocent of being malicious and possibly malformed? Not personally if we are using Django, because Django is intended to take care of those basics for us. If we can find a way to straightforwardly build a model with Django-provided fields, with Django managing the SQL, and still succeed in executing arbitrary SQL by an injection attack, we should contact security@djangoproject.com about how we managed to straightforwardly use Django models and fields and create such a vulnerability.

For that matter, if you manage to find a strange and convoluted setup that exposes any vulnerability that you didn't deliberately create, please notify security@djangoproject.com. They would like to know even if it turns out, on later inspection, to be spurious. They have tried very hard to make "naïve" use of their models and fields as safe as possible. And while no programmer worth trusting would say "We know that our program is free from vulnerabilities," they have tried very hard, and undergone intense public scrutiny, so that Django can take care of being paranoid about attacks like malformed input and SQL injection for us. At least as far as security basics are concerned, Django is designed to take care of assuming that data is guilty until proven innocent of being malicious and possibly malformed.

Facebook and LinkedIn know something better

We would last make an observation from social networks. Social networks, like Facebook and LinkedIn, thrive on full profiles but demand surprisingly little information to be let in, at least to start off with. The initially required information asks little beyond the core essentials without which the network cannot handle the user. But then they use another dynamic: while demanding lots of information up front is off-putting and would kill them, people like to have complete profiles. And both social networks provide feedback that a particular account is 25% filled in, or 80% filled in, and suggest a concrete and manageable step to take to improve on that percentage.

We will be developing as our model application, an intranet employee photo directory. While not intended to compete with social networks, we will take a cue and require to start with a minimal amount of information and then let people move towards a 100% complete profile, one step at a time.

Summary

We've looked at server-side validation with an emphasis on usability and internationalization concerns, and raised the idea that a validation requirement, especially on the server side, is a demand that user input conform to your assumptions. That is exactly how U.S.-centric assumptions in data validation can leave non-U.S. visitors with no way to move forward giving their address in a form that will pass validation.

Django does a lot for us, including a lot of work to gracefully handle Unicode. We might be advised to use `TextField` instead of `CharField`, and `TEXT` in preference to `VARCHAR` due to a basic usability concern, but Django already does a lot for us, including quite a lot of holding data innocent until proven guilty of being malicious and possibly malformed.

In this chapter we have covered the insights traditionally considered essential to optimal server-side validation. Then we moved on to how Django addresses certain basic security concerns and provides a framework for validation. We introduced one usability principle and best practice—the "zero-one-infinity rule"—and discussed how Django can be adapted to observe it. We also provided an example of how to make a validated field for GPS coordinates, discussed when and where "less is more" with validation, and how this relates to usability and internationalization. We then discussed usability best practices to encourage profile completion while not demanding that users fill in every field before being allowed to continue; this we will see in the next chapter.

Next, let's look at searching on the server side with Django, for which it provides excellent tools.

4
Server-side Database Search with Ajax

In this chapter we will cover some of Django's database and persistence basics, create a model, and create an Ajax-oriented search for that model. We will build on the observation that context switching between Python and SQL, especially if it is frequent, bears a "cognitive tax" and makes for buggier code. The way the Django developers have tried to offer an improvement is to create features so that most of the work addressed by writing SQL can now be managed without disrupting a programmer from "Python mode." We will both take an overview of the basics and then see a simple case of these basics in action.

More specifically, we will:

- Compare client and server roles and discuss reasons for a server-side home to search functionality
- Introduce Django models, and build an in-depth sample Django model
- Begin work on our intranet employee photo directory
- Discuss what kind of functionality is desirable in a search tool
- Create a Django view to serve as the JSON backend part of the search tool
- Tour the Django database search functionality, and discuss how it is similar to things we have already seen in jQuery selectors

Let's take a look at searching on the client or server side.

Searching on the client side and server side

There exist powerful options for an in-memory client-side JavaScript database. This much means that the difference between server-side and client-side options is not a choice between excellent and terrible. However, two features are worth considering.

Persistence: Much of the attraction and reason for using a server-side database is that it offers persistence. Having a database that does not support persistence defeats the point, like a car without any room for passengers or the driver. This is not to say that a client-side JavaScript database cannot have persistence. With Ajax, it is possible to create a persistence solution. However, it *is* to say that creating a server-side database is a solution to the persistence problem, and a client-side in-memory database is *not*.

Scaling: For the application we are using, and for personal and test use of that application, delivering everything in the database we might possibly need except the files themselves is not that terribly big a download. For some production purposes, "everything in the database we might possibly need" is still not that big a deal in terms of download speed or memory footprint. *However,* for many production purposes the database becomes large enough to make delivering an in-memory database problematic. In many cases the recommended best practice is to work hard to be as lazy as you can. In other words, the best practice is not to have the client download what might sometime be needed, but download what actually *is* needed on a "just-in-time" basis. A production database is designed so that if anticipated or unanticipated reasons cause the dataset to grow ten times bigger, performance will not necessarily take too much of a hit. But if it does, there are things that can be done to compensate. If you define your solution to deliver an in-memory database, the problems with a tenfold increase in the dataset are not so easily resolved.

Let us explore the server side first.

Handling databases through Django models

The power of Ajax is derived partly from storage of information on the server-side, quite often in a database. Django provides an excellent platform for handling the database side.

Django attempts to offer certain facilities and then let you go your own way if you want. It is not as opinionated a framework as **Ruby on Rails**. You can choose, if you want, to use other packages like **psycopg2** and **sqlite3** and bypass Django's persistence facilities as much as you want, and you can also handle raw SQL while using Django's persistence facilities. However, Django database handling is very carefully thought out, and it is well worth taking the effort to understand.

One Pythonic observation feeding into Django's approach is that frequent context switching bears a "cognitive tax," even if the templating is done by a developer who handles the models, rather than the web designers Django's templating is designed for. The Django approach is meant to spare the developer the cognitive strain of repeatedly switching between Python and HTML on a single screen of code. With SQL the cognitive tax is even more important. Repeated switching between Python and SQL introduces a strain that makes it easier to introduce bugs and then easier for the bugs to pass unnoticed. Django's approach is meant to remove this strain and allow for persistence to be handled without switching out of "Python mode."

Let us look at this more concretely.

Models for an intranet employee photo directory

Let us look at the models for an employee intranet photo directory. For our directory we will attempt to cover routine information for employees, such as office, extension, tagged skills, and so on. In general, solving a problem correctly in Django means taking advantage of existing working parts, those that come standard with Django and those that are available. For the purposes of an intranet employee photo directory, it might make good sense to use a Pinax social network as a basis. Our reasons for not using Pinax are not mainly due to its deficiencies, but because we need a sample application that will let us tour Django and Ajax. Pinax may solve enough of the problem for us that we would not have as informative a tour. This is not a criticism of Pinax; it's just a statement about what makes a good sample application that will get the reader's hands dirty with the power of Django and Ajax.

The `OFFICE_CHOICES` list is only illustrative; we expect that it would be replaced for production code. This one uses a two-character code. If you were making a choice like this, you could use one, or three, or ten. The short form is stored in the database and the long form is displayed in the example dropdown menu:

The code defining this choice, and the beginning of our models.py source file, is:

```python
#!/usr/bin/python

from django.db import models
import datetime

OFFICE_CHOICES = (
    (u'CN', u'Chicago North Office, Illinois, USA'),
    (u'CS', u'Chicago South Office, Illinois, USA'),
    (u'WH', u'Wheaton Office, Illinois, USA'),
    (u'SY', u'Sydney Office, New South Wales, Australia'),
    )
```

The `ExtensionField` in this case is implemented as a `TextField`, but this may be one case where a `VARCHAR`-based `CharField` makes sense to store, for example, a four or five digit extension field can be safely assumed, and is possibly deeply entrenched. The existing `ExtensionField` is:

```python
class ExtensionField(models.TextField):
    pass
```

If you wanted to specify an extension of up to five digits, you could declare a field like the following:

```python
import django.forms
import re

EXTENSION_LENGTH = 5

def is_extension(number):
    if len(str(number)) > EXTENSION_LENGTH:
        raise forms.ValidationError(u'This extension is too long.')
    #elif len(str(number)) < EXTENSION_LENGTH:
        #raise forms.ValidationError(u'This extension is too short.')
    else:
        return text

class ExtensionField(PositiveIntegerField):
    default_error_messages = {
      u'invalid': u'Enter a valid extension.',
      }
    default_validators = [is_extension]
```

(The commented-out lines, if uncommented, enforce that the extension is exactly `EXTENSION_LENGTH` digits long, instead of being at most that length.)

Returning to the code, we have a `Location` model, which has several fields. Note the `required = False`: Django's default behavior is to treat all fields as required, and in this case we want to support several kinds of information without requiring the user to fill them in before continuing. The `notes` field is for any particular notes on a location. The `office` field is a `CharField` populated from a choice, meaning that if it is filled in, it will be one of the remaining values in the choice above. If you want a choice for a U.S. state, you don't need to reinvent the wheel, just import and use `django.contrib.localflavor.us.forms.USStateField`. And if that sort of thing wasn't covered, it would make sense to make a `CharField` of length 2 populated by a straightforward choice letting people pick full state names and guaranteeing that any value stored in the database was one of the two that were entered. Besides that issue, companies around the world have a use for specifying a department, product line, or other item where there is a fixed list. It may be less of a real strength that one can save a few bytes by using an abbreviation for database storage and other internal use. However, a choice like this is a useful and powerful tool for our toolbox, and it's nice that Django allows us to decouple what is displayed from how it is represented internally.

Again, the `Location` object is designed to allow and encourage information to be filled, instead of requiring everything be given up front:

```
class Location(models.Model):
    notes = models.TextField(required = False)
    office = models.CharField(max_length = 2,
                              choices = OFFICE_CHOICES,
                              required = False)
    postal_address = models.TextField(required = False)
    room = models.TextField(required = False)
    coordinates = GPSCoordinate(required = False)

class TextEmailField(models.EmailField):
    entity = models.ForeignKey(Entity)
    def get_internal_type(self):
        return u'TextField'

class TextPhoneField(models.TextField):
    number = TextField()
    description = TextField()
    def __eq__(self, other):
        try:
            return self.remove_formatting() == \
                other.remove_formatting()
        except:
            return False
```

```
        def remove_formatting(self):
            return re.sub(ur'\D', u'', str(self))

    class TextURLField(models.URLField):
        def get_internal_type(self):
            return u'TextField'
```

We have text-based fields that work similarly to Django's `EmailField` and `URLField`, but in the database are represented by `TEXT` fields instead of `VARCHAR`, which breaks the zero-one-infinity rule.

One specific design decision that needs to be explained is why the following class is not called the `Person` or `Employee` class, but the `Entity` class. Scope creep is one of the facts of life in the programming world: if something is working, people want it to do more. The same insight lies behind the saying, "A successful tool is one that is used to do something its original creator never imagined." The baseline of success for this project is whether it works as an intranet employee photo directory, and if it doesn't, it fails, period. If it succeeds, people are going to want to put information besides specific employee details into the database, *guaranteed*. While no amount of foresight will get us a product that is officially certified to be future-proof, if we design for flexibility from the beginning, we will less certainly have painted ourselves into a corner.

Calling the class `Entity` by itself sounds like a move Dilbert's boss would encourage. But the class is designed for flexibility, and the name `Entity` is a carefully chosen reminder that the directory may include not only employees, but potentially departments, customers, events, or other things we cannot foresee. Perhaps some of these are more likely to happen than others. It may be unlikely that a company with any kind of serious CRM solution would want to be duplicating that kind of information in their employee directory.

If the people using our software—who will *rarely* do what we expect, and almost *never* do what we intend them to do—decide to store customer contact information in our directory, we want our solution to behave as gracefully as we can manage. Calling the class `Entity` is a reminder that we are trying to make a flexible solution: a solution that behaves gracefully when users do things that go against our assumptions. And while we cannot guarantee something future proof, at least we can minimize imposing the kind of assumptions that make for gratuitous failure to be future proof. (We will give our users enough pain even if we try not to.)

```
    # This class is basically the "Person" class; however, it is called
    # "Entity" to emphasize that it is intended to accommodate people,
    # offices, organizational units, and possibly other areas.
```

```
class Entity(models.Model):
    active = models.BooleanField(required = False)
    department = models.ForeignKey(Entity, required = False)
```

Note that at this point we are trying to make, and internally "dog food," one entity class that should be flexible enough to serve as a department. What this last line says, in slightly opaque form, is that the department, *if one is specified*, is another entity:

```
    description = models.TextField(required = False)
    email = TextEmailField(required = False)
    extension = ExtensionField(required = False)
    homepage = TextURLField(required = False)
```

One remark here about not being control freaks and the last line: many corporations, at least the larger ones, have enough intranets with varying degrees of official support that "How many intranet sites do we have?" is the sort of question that no one likely knows the answer to. If you are in charge of a project on an officially sponsored intranet site, wonderful. But do not think in terms of the *real* intranet and then the unimportant, unofficial fluff.

If it makes sense in terms of your company to use a `homepage` field for personal homepages, Twitter feeds, and the like, that is one valid use of a `homepage` field. But even if personal links are discouraged, it makes excellent sense for the "official" intranet to have at least a little bit of a roadmap to connect people to "spontaneous intranet" sites. Perhaps a `homepage` field is not enough, and such functionality may or may not belong in a directory. Although, there would seem to be real added value in an official directory that had data on departments, organizations, and groups, *including* a link to the unofficial intranet sites that not only are not going away, but probably should not go away.

We will cover ways to associate more than one of X with a model. There could be a `Website` class created, with a URL and a displayed name, and then entities could list zero, one, ten, or more than twenty URLs. That would not be a bad idea; it is just something not included in this implementation but left as room for the reader to expand and tinker with the starting point provided here:

```
    image = models.FileField(required = False)
```

Server-side Database Search with Ajax

Since we are working on an employee intranet *photo* directory, this is an important field, and one comment is apropos here: we have chosen to allow at most *one* image. This is not the only option; it is a defensible choice to design to allow for a gallery with arbitrarily many photos, and one selected to be displayed first. In our case, it makes a page like:

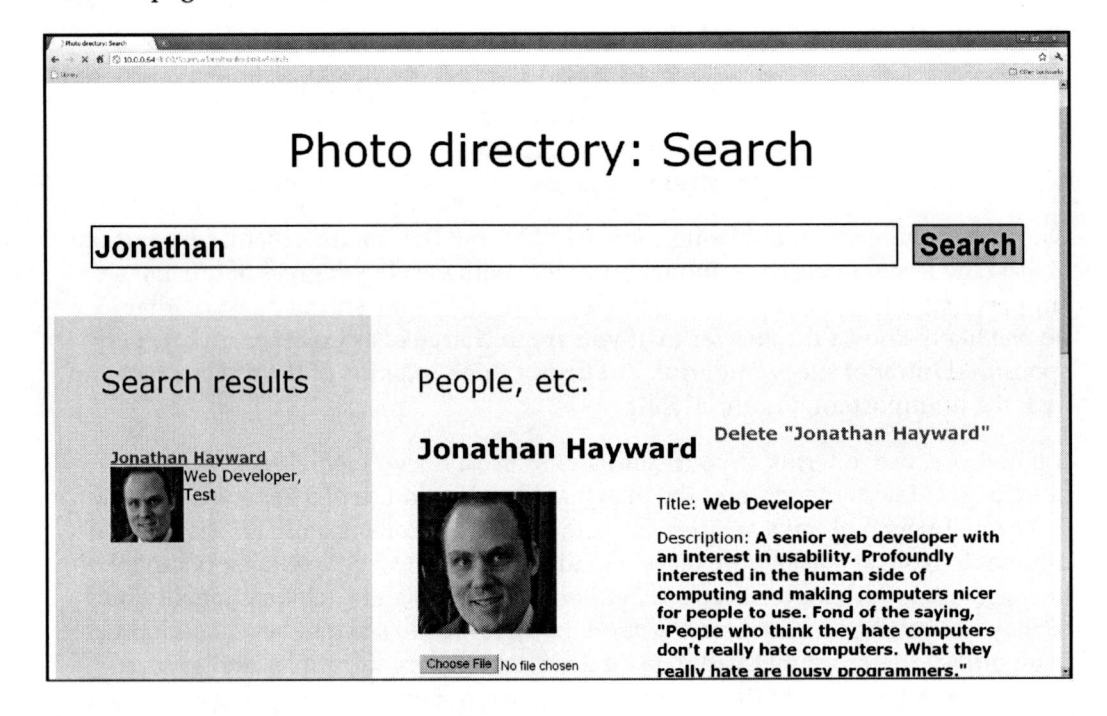

The point underscored here is not that there is anything wrong with photo galleries (even if it may not be obvious that a mere photo directory needs to give Facebook's multiple galleries a run for their money). But in terms of the zero-one-infinity rule, both "at most one" and "as many as you want" are sensible design choices. The iPhone and iPad interface, with one app at a time, and the Droid interface allowing multiple apps, are *both* sound design decisions and are *both* part of a carefully designed interface, partly because they *both* respect the zero-one-infinity rule. We will not try to resolve the question of which is better, but we would pointedly suggest that *both* make sense.

If you want to make a version of the directory that allows arbitrarily many photographs, and more power to you, then this book is intended to put you in a position to hack and tinker. If your first action is to explore how you can change this design decision, that's excellent. We'll be glad that we helped get you tinkering.

```
location = LocationField(required = False)
honorifics = models.TextField(required = False)
name = models.TextField(required = False)
post_nominals = models.TextField(required = False)
```

In these fields we incorporate a name and how a person should be addressed, as discussed earlier. The `name` is a `TextField`, and there is an optional field for any honorifics, and an optional field for any letters after a person's name, whether for academic degrees or any other reason. (In this case `name` is also optional, as we are trying to let people create an empty initial entry and fill it in later, but of all the fields on the form, this may have the strongest case to be required.)

```
publish_externally = models.BooleanField(required = False)
```

This is a field that is placed as room to grow. At present, the conceived use of the directory is one that will live behind a firewall and allow anyone on the trusted network area to read information, and appropriately authorized users to write. If it is additionally used to present information externally, this is used for an entity to "opt-in" to external placement. Note that in that case it may make sense for whitelisted fields only to be displayed.

In terms of the Agile "You ain't gonna need it," it would be entirely defensible to delete this field if you do not need it now. If you find you need it later, it can be added when it is needed, and omitting such features now does not paint any Pythonist into a corner if they turn out to be needed later on.

```
reports_to = models.ForeignKey(Entity, required = False)
start_date = models.DateField(required = False)

# Tagging is intended at least initially to locate areas of expertise
# tagging.register(Entity)
```

In Django-tagging, the way you make a model subject to tagging is not to add a field, but by calling `tagging.register()` on the model.

```
class TextStatus(models.Model):
    datetime = models.DateTimeField(default=datetime.now)
    entity = models.ForeignKey(Entity)
    text = models.TextField()
```

An Entity may have many `TextStatus` tags; the intent in this field is to allow status within the company to be published. While not all corporate cultures would really have a use for such things, and certain corporate cultures could squelch any really useful functionality, having a Twitter-like status for current projects and the like could render very valuable internal communication services.

That could look like the following:

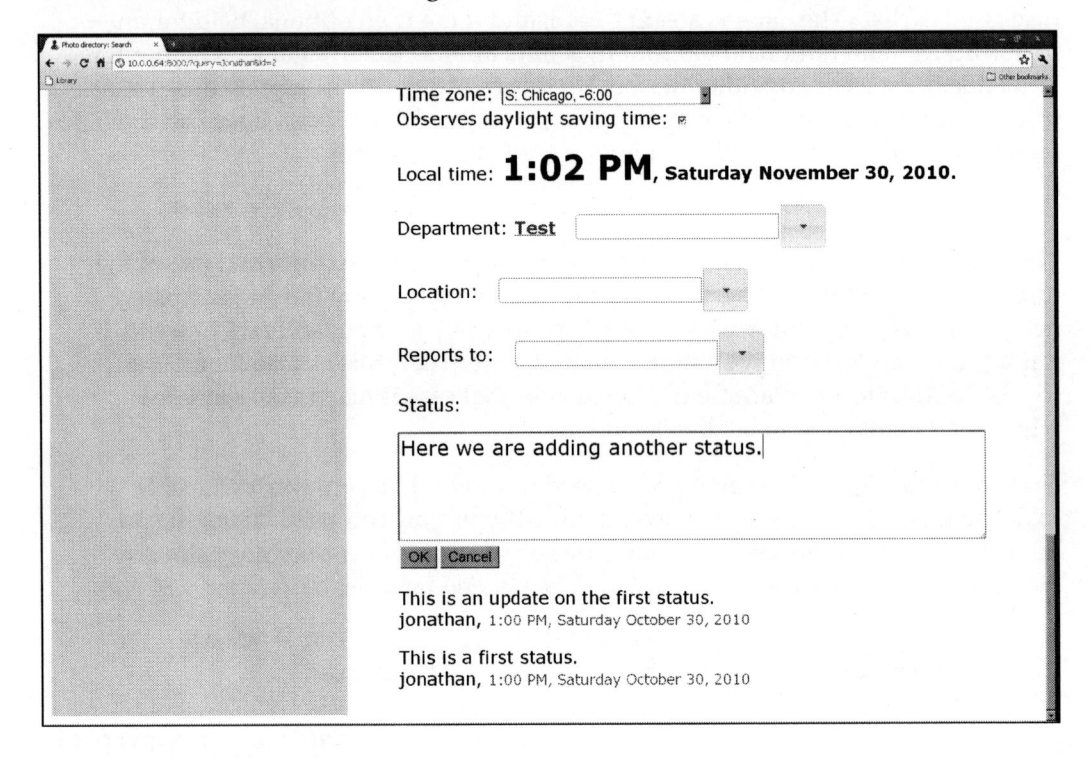

Note that no specific character limit is given, and it may make sense to post updates that are copies of the previous ones, updated where a change is warranted.

You are welcome to disable or delete this feature if it does not make enough sense in your organization.

Other many-to-one fields could be given. A many-to-one phone field is:

```
class EntityPhoneField(TextPhoneField):
    entity = models.ForeignKey(Entity)
```

If you want to support multiple images, the database backend could be handled by a model containing a `models.FileField()` and a foreign key as shown. You would presumably want to delete the single image field. Or, alternatively, the existing could be kept as a main image field. In addition, there could be galleries supporting as many images as desired.

We might comment that making this change correctly would involve appropriately adapting the user interface. The bulk of the work in doing it right would be user interface work rather than making a couple of changes on the backend.

Searching our database

We will be making a deliberately limited basic search field, but one that is carefully chosen.

One basic user interface principle is that if there is a standard user interface, it is almost always the right decision to go with the standard interface rather than make something completely different, however clever. In terms of office software, that means the correct solution will be one that "feels like" Microsoft Office, and it is not an accident that at least before the ribbon, OpenOffice looked a lot like Microsoft Office. If some feature of the standard interface is patented, that throws in a monkey wrench, but it doesn't change the basic principle that the optimal interface is the one people expect.

In terms of searching, Bing has made inroads but Google is still the standard, and that rather cleanly answers the question of what we should be aiming for: one text input that people enter search terms into, no **Advanced search** to fight with, a **Submit** button you press to search, and then you get results, beginning with the ones that are probably most relevant. (Even if Bing's interface departs from Google's at points, they still have one query input field front and center, one button to press, and serve up a result page with the most relevant results first. Even if you're competing with Google, you will probably want to imitate Google on the all-important basics.) Compare Google with Bing:

And the Bing search page:

We will be aiming to achieve Google-like basics with Ajax. What this means is that while we will be implementing our search with partial page refreshes and Ajax internals, we will still aim for that familiar feel. Of course we might not be quite as good as Google in our implementation, but we have a very clear reference about what to aim for. If we shoot for a Google quality interface and miss, we might still land among the stars.

In terms of backend functionality we will take a deliberately restrained search and only search in one text field, the entity's name. A full-text search might be highly desirable but would be very easy to get wrong. For instance, a search for "Alice" could bury all employees named Alice under a mountain of employees who have ever registered a status of, for example, "Worked with Alice to investigate bug 1234. Marked RESOLVED INVALID." An appropriately done full-text search might include entities with a status containing the string "Alice", but it should presumably prioritize entities named "Alice" and place them earlier in the results.

If the tagging is used to denote employee areas of expertise, it would be very desirable to be able to search by tags, and we note as an area for improvement that our implementation does not address that desirable feature. Another desirable feature might be to make searches tolerant of spelling errors. The `py-editdist` package (http://www.mindrot.org/projects/py-editdist) is one package used to calculate the Levenstein edit distance between two strings, which can be used to guess a near-miss spelling match. Completing some of these features may involve doing work in Python beyond what is done through the Django database functionality, and in fact we will do this in our implementation. There are functions to match by regular expressions, but backend functionality varies from database to database, and an implementation that used the Django database regular expression functionality may work reasonably well with some database backends and break completely for non-ASCII Unicode names with others. We will be taking advantage of the features provided, before providing a discussion of other facilities Django offers, but we will also be writing our own code to provide a consistent and correct behavior across database backends.

What we want to do first is break the search string into words. This will be done by a Unicode-sensitive regular expression split into non-word characters, although this is not globalization-wise a perfect solution. Some languages have more or less one character per word, instead of one character per sound, and so separating words by non-word characters is not a universally assumed pattern. We will mark this as a known issue and move forward with this solution for lack of knowing a better obvious *and straightforward* solution.

We define a view:

```
#!/usr/bin/python

from django.core import serializers

RESULTS_PER_PAGE = 10

def search(request):
    query = request.POST[u'query']
    split_query = re.split(ur'(?u)\W', query)
    while u'' in split_query:
        split_query.remove(u'')
```

The `(?u)` passes a flag to be Unicode sensitive. With it, any letter/word character in any language is recognized as a word character. Without it, only some ASCII characters would be recognized, so the split query would fail to preserve non-ASCII letters.

Server-side Database Search with Ajax

Having found the query, we will do an OR search by searching for all the query words. However, this is one point where we will depart from standard use of the database. We will be doing a case-insensitive search for exact words, so that people with short names or parts of names don't spuriously match. We do not want a search for "ed"/"Ed" to register as an exact match for "Ted", "Edna", "Edward", and similar names. And Django's database facilities allow a case-insensitive search for a substring, but matching word boundaries correctly in Unicode appears to be inconsistently supported by database backends. We will be using Django's database facilities to pull results containing query terms (so "ed" will pull "Ed", "Ted", "Edna" and "Edward", among other possibilities), but we will enter Python territory by doing the equivalent of the above code. Out of *all* the database hits, *some* are ones we will want.

```
results = []
for word in split_query:
    for entity in Entity.objects.filter(name__icontains = word):
        if re.match(ur'(?ui)\b' + word + ur'\b'):
            entry = {u'id': entity.id, u'name': entity.name,
                     u'description': entity.description}
        if not entry in results:
            results.append(entry)
```

This is creating a list containing select fields, and this much (namely `Entity.objects.filter()`) is working with Django's persistence facilities normally. The next few lines of code are working with Python objects in memory, not Django persistence facilities, for reasons partly discussed, and also partly discussed in the following.

Later in this chapter, we will provide a more direct look at Django persistence facilities.

```
for entry in result:
    score = 0
    for word in split_query:
        if re.match(ur'(?ui)\b' + word + ur'\b'):
            score += 1
    entry[u'score'] = score
def compare(a, b):
    if cmp(a[u'score'], b[u'score']) == 0:
        return cmp(a[u'name'], b[u'name'])
    else:
        return -cmp(a[u'score'], b[u'score'])
results.sort(compare)
```

Two remarks before we continue with the function. What we have done has neutralized one of the major benefits of working with a database, a benefit that Django preserves: laziness, meaning that data are loaded on an as-needed basis. In the days of ancient computers where a 64 megabyte memory was an unimaginably vast dream, it meant a major strength: you could deal with information too big to fit in memory. We have lost that benefit here, but if your company is large enough that loading the information stored above is taking too much memory on the server, then your company should be able to afford a dedicated server with maxed-out memory.

Second, the scoring, which we have handled by an inner function, ranks first by number of query terms that are matched (the `-cmp` is to ensure highest scores first, not lowest), and then as a tiebreaker sorts by alphabetical order. This is a basic scoring system that should be adequate, but it is one of many parts intended to allow the reader to tinker and see if it can be improved. The goal is to put the most interesting results here, and the specific criterion is intended as a sort of "adequate placeholder" that can be used as is but also invites tinkering and customization to your company's needs.

```
try:
    start = int(request.POST[u'start'])
except:
    start = 0
try:
    results_per_page = int(request.POST[u'results_per_page'])
except:
    results_per_page = RESULTS_PER_PAGE
returned_results = results[start:start + results_per_page]
json_serializer = serializers.get_serialized(u'json')()
response = HttpResponse()
response[u'Content-type'] = u'text/json'
json_serializer.serialize([returned_results, len(results)],
            ensure_ascii = False, stream = response)
return response
```

In the last few lines, we look at some CGI variables, create an object with one page's worth of results plus the total count of results found, and put it in a JSON response. Once parsed on the client end, the client will have one page's worth of results, including the names of the entities, their descriptions, and their Django-assigned ID numbers, which can be used as a basis to link them to this person's page. Here again there is room to tinker and expand. For instance, since we are working on a photo directory, we might search for a thumbnail creator (`sorl-thumbnail` turns up quickly as a Django image thumbnailer) and work on a way to deliver a client-side page that includes thumbnail images.

Let us look at another point, beginning with an earlier remark about Django philosophy as contrasted to Ruby on Rails—Rails is an unapologetically opinionated framework: "You're using my framework, you do it my way." Django is intended to offer certain facilities, and then stay out of your way if you choose to do things differently. Here we have used Django persistence facilities, but not played to their usual strengths. We realized a problem existed while thinking somewhat outside the box, and chose a basic implementation that Django's documentation doesn't really suggest. This does not showcase the natural strengths of Django persistence facilities, but it does showcase how Django avoids demanding, "It's my way or the highway." With that stated, let's look a little more at Django persistence facilities and how they would be used in a solution that plays better to Django's natural strengths.

A tour of Django persistence facilities

It has been said that **Object-relational Management (ORM)** is the Vietnam War of computer science. People keep throwing money, resources, and work at the problem, and it remains unsolved. If the problem is conceived in a general way, namely to take whatever objects Python programmers may create, and straightforwardly have an automatic system that will retroactively figure out how to serialize/deserialize (pickle/unpickle) them in a relational database, that problem, in general, is a hard problem and one that may never have a good solution. However, Django handles ORM in such a way that it is not only solvable, but solved neatly.

Django models and related classes are designed from the ground up to be mappable to databases. And that is a different matter from designing out of object-oriented concerns without consideration for relational databases, and then trying to retrofit storage in relational databases. A model class corresponds to a table, an instance of a model corresponds to an individual row, and fields of the model correspond to columns in the table/row. While Django is meant to let you stay in "Python mode" and avoid frequent Python/SQL context switching, it asks you to correctly solve problems like foreign keys and many-to-one relationships (as we have used) or many-to-many relationships. This means that the programmer is asked to solve the problem so that the ORM is straightforward, and keeps Django's ORM code from the tarpit of correctly implementing "Do what I mean!" functionality of mapping any object(s) to a relational database correctly, and do what the programmer would have meant to do. Django's approach to ORM is to provide carefully designed, Pythonic facilities and asks us as developers, "Say what you mean!"

For search and lookups, you can, on the model class, call something like:

```
Entity.objects.get(name__icontains = u'ed')
```

For `name__icontains`, on the left of the double underscore separator is a field name, and to the right is an operator, such as:

- `contains`: the string you supply is contained in the field value, case-sensitive. One compatibility note: `description__contains = u'book'` is translated into SQL of `...description LIKE '%book%'....` On some database backends, `LIKE` preserves case sensitivity; on other backends, the interpretation of this SQL command forces case insensitivity. Django seems not, in general, to smooth over differences between database backends to provide uniform behavior; this means that switching the database backend could cause a change in how identical Django searches behave. In one case, `description__contains = u'book'` will match a description of `u'Books for sale!'`, and in another case it won't.
- `day`: for date/datetime fields, exact one-based day match.
- `endswith`: ends with, case-sensitive.
- `exact`: a case-sensitive, exact match.
- `gt`: greater than.
- `gte`: greater than or equal to.
- `icontains`: the string you supply is contained in the field value, case-insensitive.
- `iexact`: a case-insensitive exact string match.
- `in`: the field value is in a list you provide.
- `iendswith`: ends with, case-insensitive.
- `iregex`: case-insensitive regular expression search.
- `isnull`: if this is equal to true, specifies that a field is null; if it is false, specifies that the field is not.
- `istartswith`: starts with, case-insensitive.
- `lt`: less than.
- `lte`: less than or equal to.
- `month`: for date/datetime fields, exact one-based month match.
- `regex`: case-sensitive regular expression search.
- `startswith`: starts with, case-sensitive.
- `week_day`: Day of week, from 1 (Sunday) to 7 (Saturday).
- `year`: for date/datetime fields, exact four-digit year match.

There is some similarity between the combinations of field names and the list above, and jQuery selectors like $(".emphasized") that served as a "virtual higher-level language" from JavaScript. There are several parallels, and we could say in similar fashion that just as jQuery offers a "virtual higher-level language" on top of bare JavaScript, Django offers a "virtual higher-level language" over a mixture of bare Python and bare SQL. And the similarity goes further. Just as jQuery is intended to allow chaining, Django allows chained operations. Let's suppose that we want to search for entities with descriptions containing the string "book", take out all entries containing the string "bookworm", be case insensitive in both instances, and sort them in alphabetical order by name and then description. In Django this looks remarkably similar to jQuery chaining:

```
queryset = Entity.objects.filter(description__icontains = u'book').
exclude(description__icontains = u'bookworm').order_by(u'name',
u'description')
```

We've made a few different adjustments as we've refined our requirements in the code above. Now how many database hits has this cost us? Trick question: the answer is, "None." Django's database handling is lazy, and doesn't fetch results until it knows what results are really needed, when they are needed. If we make an initial request and then make adjustments, all it does is keep its notes up to date. If and when we want results, we can get them, with database hits as needed, by something like the following:

```
for entity in queryset.all():
    # Do something with each entity
```

And in classic relational database tradition, this means that you can have a much bigger dataset without increasing the memory taken. If you want to, you can create a computer with a more than a terabyte hard drive and only 64 megabytes of RAM, and do database searches through genomic data without running out of memory.

> This example was for illustration purposes. If you are a researcher working with genomic data, don't reinvent the internal combustion engine. Use BioPerl. It's a far more Pythonic solution than building in Python from scratch.

The objects we have been dealing with are queries and QuerySet and further Django documentation is online.

Summary

We have taken an overview of Django's persistence facilities, its way of building models so that ORM is not a tarpit but is solved cleanly, and we have looked at how a solution might work using these building blocks. Specific points covered include why the server is a natural home to address persistence issues though a database or otherwise, as well as what a Django model that demonstrates several key features could look like, to make a view that performs a basic search on this model and returns JSON, which could be useful to client-side Ajax parts of an application, finally, what some of the other Django search functionality is, and how it resembles one of jQuery's selling points.

Let us continue. Our next chapter, *Signing Up and Logging into a Website Using Ajax* covers both front end and back end tools to have a Django Ajax login. This will get our hands dirty, and we will be working to build a graceful Web 2.0-style login process.

5
Signing Up and Logging into a Website Using Ajax

Authentication and logins using Django Ajax can be accomplished using the following:

- On the server-side, an `@ajax_login_required` decorator for views that is used similarly to Django's `@login_required`, and also server-side Ajax authentication handling.
- On the client-side, a function that will, if an Ajax call returns a specific message saying authentication is needed, will provide an appropriate client-side `div` requesting login credentials and other details, and allow the request to be resubmitted after authentication has been cleared.

A **decorator** is a function that encapsulates another function and provides some added or modified functionality compared to the bare original. It is one of the patterns defined in the "gang of four" patterns book, *"Patterns: Elements of Reusable Object-Oriented Software"* by *Erich Gamma, Richard Helm, Ralph Johnson,* and *John Vlissides; Addison-Wesley Professional.*

Signing Up and Logging into a Website Using Ajax

In this specific decorator, an inner function wrap is defined, which calls the original function if the user is authenticated and returns a JSON message that the user is not authenticated otherwise.

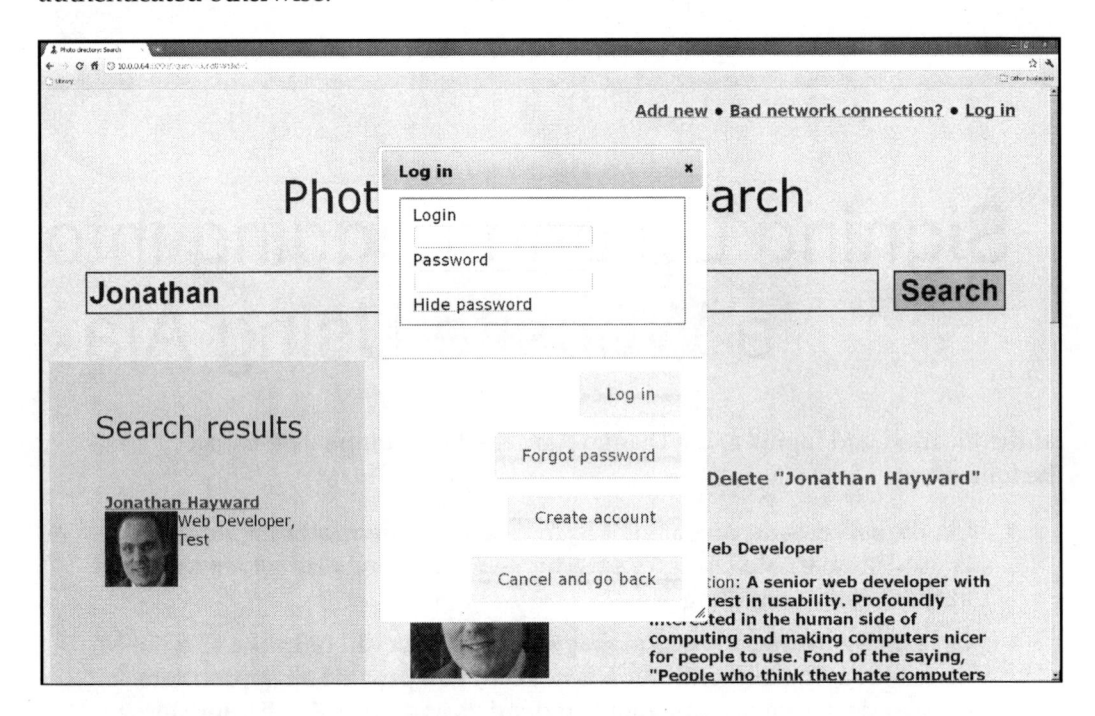

We will go over both server-side and client-side details to do this. The initial search page will present a regular search interface whether or not a user is logged in. If a user is not logged in, the screen should be dimmed and the user should see an Ajax modal dialog allowing the user to log in, as in the screenshot.

In this chapter we will look at both server-side and client-side code, covering:

- `admin.py`, used to have functionality called once and only once on the server-side.
- `functions.py`, with different utility functions, such as the `@ajax_login_required` decorator.
- `views.py`, which has functions that render web pages and the server's responses to Ajax requests. One view shows how we can slowly build a view by hand, and another shows an excellent Django shortcut.
- `style.css`, which has basic styling for utilitarian needs and usability.

- `search.html`, which has basic client-side Ajax for our search. Normally Ajax is factored out into its own files; this could be done to some degree but we have chosen an implementation that means that settings changes are centralized to the top of `settings.py`. Part of our solution entails JavaScript files that are populated as Django templates rather than being completely static, separate files.
- The Django admin interface, which we can use to create test data.

Let's begin!

admin.py: administrative functions called once

In `admin.py`, we have certain things that we wish to have called once and only once. This sets up the admin interface to be able to handle Entities:

```
import django.contrib.admin
import directory.models

django.contrib.admin.autodiscover()
django.contrib.admin.site.register(directory.models.Entity)
django.contrib.admin.site.register(directory.models.Location)
```

functions.py: project-specific functions, including our @ajax_login_required decorator

This is our `functions.py` file, which incorporates a `StackOverflow` solution. Traditionally in Django the `@login_required` decorator is placed before a view to have Django check to see if a user is authenticated and request authentication the old-fashioned way if a user is not logged in. This `@ajax_login_required` decorator works along the same lines: it is intended for Ajax-oriented views that return JSON, should pass along the view's output if the user is authenticated, and should otherwise output JSON with `not_authenticated` as `TRUE`.

On the client side, the appropriate behavior is to take a returned JSON value, and see if it has `not_authenticated` defined as TRUE. If so, the client should behave in an appropriate fashion to the user not being authenticated. In our case, we will present a modal dialog form via jQuery UI, which will allow a user to log in and eventually register for an account. Note that we should allow an escape hatch, as sometimes the user would rather not register. However important the website may be to us, it may not be so important to all users, and we want to gracefully handle the case where the user isn't interested enough to log in or register.

```
from django.http import HttpResponse

import json

def ajax_login_required(view_function):
    def wrap(request, *arguments, **keywords):
        if request.user.is_authenticated():
            return view_function(request, *arguments, **keywords)
        output = json.dumps({ 'not_authenticated': True })
        return HttpResponse(output, mimetype = 'application/json')
    wrap.__doc__ = view_function.__doc__
    wrap.__dict__ = view_function.__dict__
    return wrap
```

This is a good working example of creating a decorator. Its docstring (`__doc__`) and dictionary (`__dict__`) are assigned to be those of the inner function, and the inner function is returned. We see this decorator used in the first function in `views.py`, as will be shown in the following section.

views.py: functions that render web pages

The pattern that has been perhaps the most popular, the most used, and the most misused is the MVC pattern. Here there is a separation of concerns between the Model, the View, and the Controller. Theoretically, the concerns are separated.

In Django, the most common pattern is the MTV pattern, where the three letters mean Model, Template, and View. We have edited models before, and we will be using a simple template later on in this chapter. Here we will be looking at two views. At least in their classical definitions, a Django MTV view is not quite the same thing as an MVC view. While MVC and MTV models may be doing basically the same thing, a Django MTV view has a job description that includes some responsibilities of an MVC controller. There are many similarities between MVC and MTV, and both make a careful separation of concerns, but the division of labor is different and the Django view has some of the responsibilities of both the view and controller under MVC.

```
#!/usr/bin/python

from django.contrib.auth import authenticate, login
from django.core import serializers
from django.http import HttpResponse
from django.shortcuts import render_to_response
from directory.functions import ajax_login_required

import directory.models
import json
import re

RESULTS_PER_PAGE = 10

def ajax_login_request(request):
    try:
        request.POST[u'login']
        dictionary = request.POST
    except:
        dictionary = request.GET
```

The preceding code is important for debugging purposes: it checks for a basic key first in `request.POST`, defaulting to `request.GET` if this is not found.

The benefit of this is not relevant to production, and more pointedly it should not be used in production, where credentials should be submitted via POST over SSL. In production Ajax calls to this function should always use POST rather than GET, but for debugging purposes it can be highly desirable to fall back to GET. The reason is to provide one way of dealing with an uncaught exception. If there is an uncaught exception and Django has DEBUG set to True, it will serve up a detailed and informative error page. Unfortunately, if jQuery is expecting JSON and gets a detailed HTML error page, it will offer a singularly uninformative account of the error, which is not useful for debugging.

As a workaround for this phenomenon, you can manually make GET requests for at least some queries. If, for example, the base URL is `http://127.0.0.1:8000/ajax/login` for this view, you can add GET data at the end and manually visit a URL like `http://127.0.0.1:8000/ajax/login?login=mylogin&password=mypassword`.

Signing Up and Logging into a Website Using Ajax

If your system isn't working correctly, and your (POST) Ajax query is throwing an error, manually querying by GET in a browser window can be a good way to access a detailed error page designed to help pinpoint what exact exception is being thrown, and where.

```
user = authenticate(username = dictionary[u'login'],
                    password = dictionary[u'password'])
if user and user.is_active:
    login(request, user)
    result = True
else:
    result = False
response = HttpResponse(json.dumps(result),
                        mimetype = u'application/json')
return response
```

The `authenticate()` and `login()` functions do different jobs. For Django's normal (non-Ajax) login procedures, inactive accounts cannot log in. But here we need to check for ourselves that `authenticate()` returns a valid user, and furthermore that the valid user `is_active` (that is, has not been marked inactive). This function both logs the user in (if appropriate) and then returns a Boolean value telling whether the login has been successful. It is recommended procedure not to delete user accounts, but set them to inactive. This best practice avoids creating holes in the database where something refers to a user who is no longer available.

The following function is protected by the `@ajax_login_required` decorator. It is relatively long; let us walk through it:

```
@ajax_login_required
def search(request):
    try:
        query = request.POST[u'query']
        dictionary = request.POST
    except:
        query = request.GET[u'query']
        dictionary = request.GET
```

Here we repeat what we have discussed before: besides the decorator, we look for POST but default to GET to make debugging easier. Note that the debugging information is exposed only if `settings.py` has DEBUG set to TRUE. In general, it is bad security practice to give information about internals in error messages. And if Django's `settings.py` has DEBUG set to FALSE, it will shut off detailed error messages and give generic messages intended to avoid exposing your program's internal structure. However, when we are developing with DEBUG set to TRUE, this gives us a chance to load an equivalent to a query that triggered an error by typing the equivalent `GET` query in our browser. This could be made a `DEBUG` only feature, but it may not be clear what the advantage or added security would be to that.

```
split_query = re.split(ur'(?u)\W', query)
```

Here are a couple of notes on syntax for this regular expression operation. We have been using strings like `u'test'` to indicate a Unicode string. Here we want to give a raw string, as is usual for regular expressions. This means that (in this case) the backslash will not be interpreted, as `u'(?u)\W'` will be interpreted simply as the backslash escaping the W, which doesn't do anything particularly interesting, giving a string that will effectively be treated as `u'(?u)W'`. We could achieve the intended effect by giving `u'(?u)\\W'`, but manually keeping track of extra backslashes is a consolation prize as a solution compared to simply asking Python to interpret the string as raw. This is done by changing the u to ur; note that the u comes first: we want `ur'(?u)\W'`, not `ru'(?u)\W'`; the latter will cause a syntax error. It is generally recommended to make a practice and habit of using raw strings when dealing with regular expressions.

In the regular expression, we pass the Unicode flag with `(?u)` at the beginning of the string. This will cause the `\W`, the regular expression sequence for a non-word character, to recognize Unicode word versus non-word characters, rather than (for instance) recognizing only ASCII word characters and treating other alphabets, ideograms, and so on as non-word characters.

The possibility of consistently doing this in Python is why we are doing, in Python, the kind of work that Django developers often offload to the databases. The database backends offer inconsistent support for Unicode-sensitive word breaks.

```
while u'' in split_query:
    split_query.remove(u'')
```

We are interested in blocks of word characters; the regular expression call may leave both the blocks of word characters we want, and empty strings. We remove the empty strings to get the sequences of word characters included in the search string.

This solution may not separate words for languages where one character represents one word rather than a sound or part of a word. If a workaround is needed, users can put a space between each word. (But if this is a significant concern, it would be better to adapt the solution so that people can give search terms in the way that is natural to them, and the computer seems to auto-magically do the right thing.)

```
results = []
for word in split_query:
    for entity in directory.models.Entity.objects.filter(name__icontains = word):
```

```
            if re.match(ur'(?ui)\b' + word + ur'\b', entity.name):
                entry = {u'id': entity.id, u'name': entity.name,
                    u'description': entity.description}
            if not entry in results:
                results.append(entry)
```

For each word in the split query, we search for objects containing the word, and then if the word matches, we add it to our list of results if it is not already there.

The `directory.models.Entity.objects.filter(name__icontains = word)` is a brief example of the kind of workhorse one uses in Django's ORM; the usual correct solution would be based on that. Here we do a case-insensitive search for objects containing the word. So if the word is "ed", this will turn up results containing the names "Ed", "Ted", "Edna", and other similar names. For the purposes of this discussion, we only want exact matches, so we perform a regular expression check: `(ui)` requests both "Unicode aware" and "case-insensitive," and \b specifies a word boundary, so "Ed" will match "ed" while "Ted" and "Edna" will not.

```
    for entry in results:
        score = 0
        for word in split_query:
            if re.match(ur'(?ui)\b' + word + ur'\b', entry[u'name']):
                score += 1
        entry[u'score'] = score
```

This is a bare-bones scoring algorithm, and one of many places where you should be able to play around with the provided starting point and make it better.

```
    def compare(a, b):
        if cmp(a[u'score'], b[u'score']) == 0:
            return cmp(a[u'name'], b[u'name'])
        else:
            return -cmp(a[u'score'], b[u'score'])
    results.sort(compare)
```

This defines a function that sorts first by score, and then by name in alphabetical order.

```
    try:
        start = int(dictionary[u'start'])
    except:
        start = 0
    try:
        results_per_page = int(dictionary[u'results_per_page'])
    except:
        results_per_page = RESULTS_PER_PAGE
```

```
        returned_results = results[start:start + results_per_page]
        response = HttpResponse(json.dumps([returned_results,
            len(results)]),
            mimetype = u'application/json')
        return response
```

Here we take a slice of the result set, and send a response with a JSON encoding of the appropriate slice of a result set (so the client can obtain page 2 at 10 results per page, or page 3 of 50 results per page, and so on and so forth), and the total number of results. Both of these are hooks meant to support pagination. The default behavior if the client does not specify our POST/GET fields for pagination is to return the first 10 results (or all results if there are less than 10) and the number of results total.

```
    def homepage(request):
        return render_to_response(u'search.html')
```

This two-line view is a Django shortcut in action, and an example of how Django can save us time.

style.css: basic styling for usability

The CSS we use is straightforward. There is little ornament, but there is styling to make text easier to read, such as requesting a font that was very carefully designed for readability on screen: one of the best fonts optimized for usability. Some of the styling is utilitarian: the form to log in via Ajax is not shown by default. There is a notifications div, which has certain styles, and the text input for the search query is prominent and large:

```
body
    {
    font-family: Verdana, Arial, sans;
    }

#login_form
    {
    display: none;
    }

#notifications
    {
    background-color: #ff8080;
    border: 3px solid #800000;
    display: none;
    padding: 20px;
    }
```

```
#search_form
    {
    margin-left: 40px;
    }

#submit
    {
    border: 2px solid black;
    font-size: 2em;
    margin-left: 10px;
    }
```

search.html: a template for client-side Ajax

Next we will go through the template that defines the search page. We note in advance that while this template gets a lot done, it is not a showcase of Django templating features. The Django templating engine is intended for designers and allows designers to access variables, perform looping and conditionals, and other major features while not being given the power to execute arbitrary code. But even without harnessing most of the templating engine's features, we can still get quite a lot done.

```
{% extends "base.html" %}
{% block head_title %}Photo Directory: Search{% endblock head_title %}
```

The first line states which template it extends, and the second gives it a title. The code that follows contains HTML, and in many cases hooks for Ajax, to serve as a base for client-side work.

```
{% block body_main %}
<div id="notifications"></div>
```

The `notifications div` is meant to serve as a hook that will be available for Ajax manipulations as a message area. With a bit of Ajax shown later on, notifications will fade in, stay there for five seconds, and fade out. When a notification is fully faded in it can look like the following:

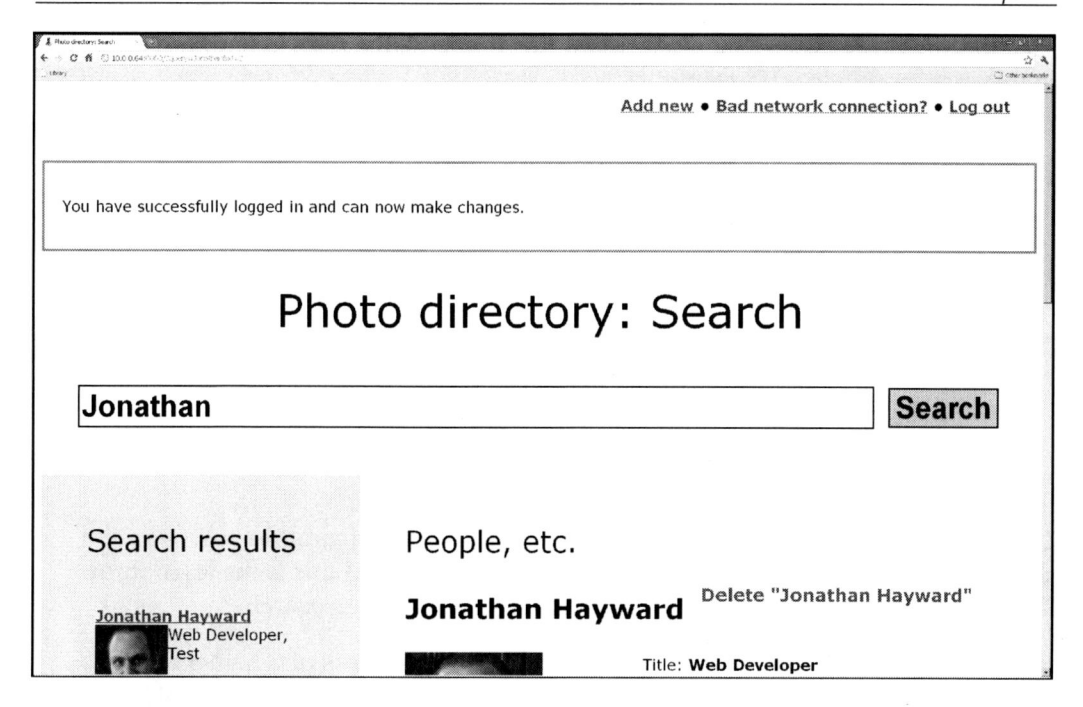

[Screenshot of Photo directory: Search page showing a search for "Jonathan" with results for Jonathan Hayward, Web Developer.]

The HTML is:

```
<form name="search_form" id="search_form" action="/">
  <input type="text" name="query" id="query" /><br />
  <input type="submit" name="submit" id="submit" value="Search" />
</form>
```

This is the search form. In keeping with semantic markup, we define the form semantically, and then use jQuery to submit searches and do partial page updates with the results. Note that every HTML element has an ID. This is not required for semantic markup as such, but it helps for styling elements via CSS when desired, for customizing behavior via jQuery or other Ajax tools, and for graceful degradation.

Although we have not implemented server-side support for this, the form as it stands could work perfectly well for a graceful degradation strategy to let people search the old-fashioned way with JavaScript turned off. (Such support will be added later.)

```
<div id="results"></div>
```

Signing Up and Logging into a Website Using Ajax

Like the `notifications` div seen earlier, this is a hook for Ajax to manipulate and, in this case, populate with results.

```
<div id="login_form" title="Log in">
    <form>
        <fieldset>
            <label for="login">Login</label>
            <input type="text" name="login" id="login"
                class="text ui-widget-content ui-corner-all" /><br />
            <label for="password">Password</label>
            <input type="password" name="password" id="password"
                class="text ui-widget-content ui-corner-all" /><br />
        </fieldset>
    </form>
</div>
```

This `div`, initially hidden, is used for Ajax login. For demonstration purposes, the directory is only searchable to users who are logged in, and this is the login form that is displayed when someone who is not logged in tries to search.

If you wish the search functionality to be available regardless of whether a user is logged in, simply comment or remove the `@ajax_login_required` decorator before `search()` in `views.py`.

In the next two lines, we indicate that we are done with content for the `body_main` hook, and are moving on to the page-specific JavaScript hook, `footer_javascript_page`.

```
{% endblock body_main %}
{% block footer_javascript_page %}
```

We include a JavaScript file, and then write functionality for this page. The main jQuery script has already been included in the `base.html` Django template; we don't need to do anything more for that here.

The following is a helper function. Right now, on both the server-side and client-side we have not discussed the several reasons a user might not be treated as logged in:

- No attempt has been made to log in
- The user has attempted to log in with an invalid account
- The user has attempted to log in to a valid account but got the password wrong
- The user has correctly authenticated to an account that does not have `is_valid` set

In terms of room for expansion, it might be helpful to distinguish which of these several options has occurred. Particularly in the Palaeolithic era, when programmers sat down on stone benches and logged in to monochrome terminals, it made sense to answer either an invalid login or password with "login incorrect" and avoid divulging whether the login or password is wrong. Now refusing to give any hint of an answer to "Did I get my login or password wrong?" is needless and usually doesn't do much to improve websites' security. One way this program could be improved is for the server and client to distinguish between possible reasons an attempted login did not succeed.

```
<script language="JavaScript" type="text/javascript"
        src="/static/js/jquery.effects.fade.js"></script>
<script language="JavaScript" type="text/javascript">
<!--
function check_authentication(parsed_json)
    {
    if (parsed_json.not_authenticated)
        {
        return false;
        }
    else
        {
        return true;
        }
    }
```

The following function is a less generic helper function. It mostly draws on functionality that is defined elsewhere:

```
function offer_login()
    {
    $("#login_form").dialog("open");
    }
```

The following function kicks off a notification appearing and disappearing—with animation—in the notifications area. setTimeout() is called so that send_notification() will return control to its caller quickly, instead of slowing down any caller by five seconds plus the duration of two animations:

```
function send_notification(message)
    {
    $("#notifications").html("<p>" + message + "</p>");
    setTimeout(function()
        {
        $('#notifications').show('slow').delay(5000).hide('slow');
        }, 0);
    }
```

Signing Up and Logging into a Website Using Ajax

The following function encapsulates the search submission. Its `success` function does not assume that the user is logged in, because a successful `XMLHttpRequest` call could happen whether or not the user is logged in, and could be search results, but could only be a message saying that the user is not authenticated.

If the user is not authenticated, it offers the *option* of logging in. That part is indirectly recursive in that a successful login from the `offer_login()` call will resubmit the search and should pull the results. Whether or not the implementation details could be done differently, this is the correct user interface behavior if login is required to do a search:

1. The search form is presented.
2. If the user is not authenticated, the user is given the option of logging in, but is also free to decide that this isn't worth logging in.
3. If the user authenticates successfully, the flow of activity continues from where it was left off. The user doesn't have to hit **Search** again, retype the query, or otherwise start over on the request. Instead, on successful authentication, the flow of activity continues without disruption as if the user had already been authenticated.

The function encapsulates a call to jQuery's low-level `$.ajax()`. This is an option worth considering in this case, but in many cases higher-level functions will be called, with a signature like `$("#messages").load("/messages/current")`.

```
function submit_search()
    {
    $.ajax(
        {
        data:
            {
            query: document.search_form.query.value
            },
        datatype: 'json',
        success: function(data, textStatus, XMLHttpRequest)
            {
            if (data)
                {
                if (check_authentication(data))
                    {
```

If `data` is "real" data, instead of a "not authenticated" message, we use jQuery to display the results. The system is designed with an eye to allowing pagination, but for now we simply display all results. The following code illustrates how one may manipulate the DOM using Ajax. Another approach would be to build the HTML constructed here on the server, perhaps make the HTML as a string stored in `data.html`, and simply call something like `$("#results").html(data.html);`. Both approaches can work, although we will focus on Ajax DOM manipulation:

```
                $("#results").html("");
                var results = data[0];
                var length = data[1];
                for (var index = 0; index < results.length;
                    ++index)
                    {
                    var result = results[index];
                    $("#results").append("<p><a href='/entities/"
                        + result["id"] + "'>" + result["name"] +
                        "</a><br />" + result["description"] +
                        "</p>");
                    }
                }
            else
                {
                offer_login();
                }
            }
        },
        type: 'POST',
        url: '/ajax/search',
        });
    }
```

The `$(function(){...});` in the following code specifies functionality to be executed when the DOM is ready. Note that this is not identical to the `onload` event because the DOM can be ready before images are loaded, and this will be executed sooner. An arbitrary number of functions can be requested this way; we have wrapped the function calls we want in one anonymous outer function, but it would have been equivalent to use two `$(function(){...});` calls, one per wrapped call. However, doing things this way and specifying a `body onload` do not work together; we should do things this way when we want something executed when the DOM is available and ready.

Signing Up and Logging into a Website Using Ajax

The following `function()` call is a bare bones example of **hijaxing**: replacing an element's default behavior on a given event with an Ajax effect. In this case, the **submit** button, which will perform a Web 1.0-style form submission and whole page replacement on a click, is hijaxed with a function that, in our case, calls a function, and then returns `false`, which prevents the default event handling from taking place. Unlike other facets of JavaScript, we cannot return `0`, `''`, or other non-true values besides `false` and achieve the same effect; we specifically need to return `false`.

```
$(function()
    {
    $("#submit").click(function()
        {
        submit_search();
        return false;
        });
```

The text input field is shrunk to make room for the **submit** button.

This is an example of using jQuery to get pixel-perfect CSS-style effects. The intended effect is that the query field and the **submit** button make up one line, and that one line is centered. This may degrade if the user has selected a larger or smaller font, but the basic effect of two items, with the query text input sized so that together with the **search** button it is centered, is an example of presentation that is more easily achieved with jQuery than CSS.

```
$("#query").width($(window).width() - 240);
```

The following call is based on jQuery UI rather than jQuery core alone, and uses the `login_form` div as the basis for a modal dialog. It adds a **Log in** button, which will attempt to log in and submit the search on being clicked, and presently unimplemented **Forgot password** and **Create account** buttons, which should be created for production purposes and should be doable by the same principles as the server-side and client-side code enabling Ajax login.

```
$("#login_form").dialog({
    autoOpen: false,
    height: 150,
    width: 350,
    modal: true,
    buttons:
        {
        'Log in': function()
            {
            $.ajax({
                data:
                    {
```

```
                        login: $("#login").val(),
                        password: $("#password").val(),
                        },
                datatype: 'text',
                success: function(data, textStatus,
                                XMLHttpRequest)
                    {
                    if (data)
                        {
                        send_notification(
                            "You have successfully logged in.");
                        $(this).dialog('close');
                        submit_search();
                        }
                    else
                        {
                        send_notification(
                            "Your login was not successful.");
                        }
                    },
                type: 'POST',
                url: '/ajax/login',
                });
            $("#password").val("");
            },
        'Forgot password': function()
            {
            send_notification(
                "This feature has not been implemented.");
            },
        'Create account': function()
            {
            send_notification(
                "This feature has not been implemented.");
            },
        },
    });
});
```

The following call registers a global error handler that will be called by default by all Ajax operations. At present this is an error handler for developers rather than end users. `textStatus` and `errorThrown` are the sort of innards that can be helpful for a developer but are not appropriate to inflict on innocent users. Depending on the browser, the `textStatus` and `errorThrown` may not even be the sort of thing that would help a developer. In my case they were, respectively, "error" and "undefined" in every case, although much more useful debugging information was presumably available from digging through the `XMLHttpRequest` argument's data.

In terms of a production-ready message, neither "error"/"undefined" nor digging up the response received by the `XMLHttpRequest` are appropriate. It would be better to send a notification of **There was an error handling your request. We apologize for the inconvenience**, or if you want to make a more sophisticated error handler, see what information can be obtained from the `XMLHttpRequest`, and then give a more customized user-friendly error like **We're sorry, but we had an error trying to save your information. The development team has been alerted and will try to address the root problem. If you need help, please contact [email/phone/contact link]**.

```
        $.ajaxSetup(
            {
            error: function(XMLHttpRequest, textStatus, errorThrown)
                {
                send_notification(textStatus + "</p><p>" +
                                  errorThrown);
                },
            });
        });
// -->
</script>
{% endblock footer_javascript_page %}
```

The Django admin interface

The Django admin interface is a full Create, Read, Update, and Delete (**CRUD**) capable interface. The basic philosophy behind the interface is that some forms of Create, Read, Update, and Delete operations need to be done in project-specific ways, which are often interesting challenges, and the Django admin interface is not intended for that purpose. What the admin interface is intended for is to address certain routine boilerplate Create, Read, Update, and Delete functionality, so that the more chore-like features are taken care of for you well.

The steps to make the admin site in Django 1.2.x available are:

1. Go to your `settings.py` and ensure that `INSTALLED_APPS` contains `django.contrib.admin`, `django.contrib.auth`, and `django.contrib.contenttypes`.

2. Put a line like the following in your `admin.py` file for every model that you want to be available via the admin interface:

   `django.contrib.admin.site.register(directory.models.Entity)`

3. Include in your `urls.py` the following lines, firstly at the top:

   `import admin`

   And in your `urlpatterns` include the following line or anything of its equivalent:

   `(r'^admin/', include(admin.site.urls))`

4. Restart the server.

After that, we should see a screen like the following once we have logged in with the user we've created:

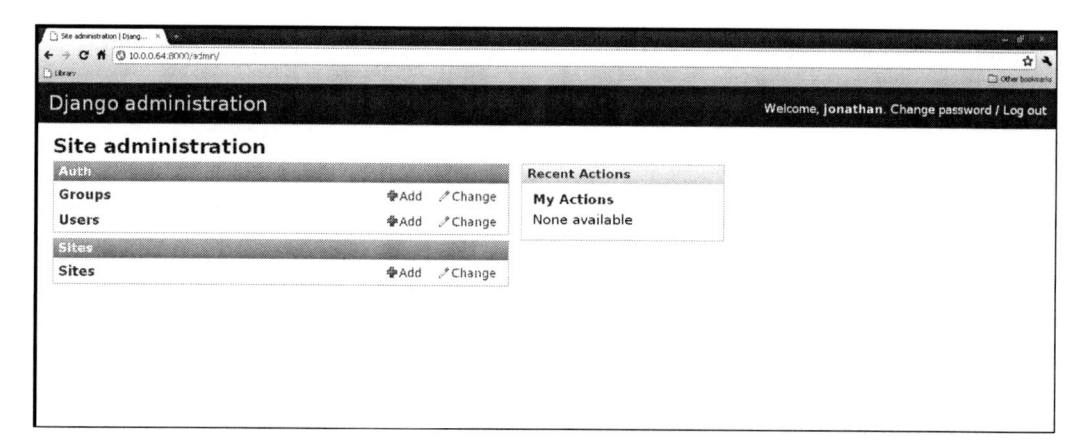

We can then click on **Entity** (or **Locations**), and add an entity. We have set things up so all fields are optional.

We will be working later on to make a more responsive, Ajax-based interface with in-place editing. It has been said, "Where there is output, let there be input." Ideally, if someone wants to change information that is displayed, and that person has privileges to do so, it should be possible to click on that information and update it there, rather than scout out what other part of the site is responsible for giving input. However, the Django admin interface is decent, and we can use it for test data in particular.

Summary

With all the pieces put together, you should be able to use the Django admin interface to create test data, and then search and see a basic results page. There is room to expand and improve in almost all of what we have done, and we invite you to tinker around and make something better. But this is a substantial working system, and we have dealt with real and serious code.

We have covered `admin.py`, for functions that we want called exactly once when the server starts. We have also covered `functions.py`, a file we have created for utility functions and in particular an `@ajax_login_required` decorator that requires users to authenticate before seeing a view, but unlike the standard `@login_required` workhorse is optimized to respond appropriately to Ajax clients expecting JSON rather than web browsers rendering whole HTML pages. We have covered `views.py`, which defines two views. Again, these are views under Django's MTV Model-Template-View division of labor and separation of concerns, and not the classic MVC Model-View-Controller separation of concerns. We have covered `search.html`, a template that renders the desired web page without even needing to use many Django templating engine features. We have also covered the Django admin interface, which lets us handle routine Create, Read, Update, and Delete operations almost for free. We can (and in this case will) work on another interface, but for now we have a powerful and friendly way to create test data and one that would serve us well for production purposes if we wanted.

jQuery is a library designed to allow an ecosystem of plugins. In our next chapter, we will look at a snazzier interface that heeds the words, "Where there is output, let there be input." We will use a jQuery plugin to allow in-place Ajax editing, giving a Web 2.0 shine. Furthermore, we will log changes: in terms of successful intranets, companies that turn on anonymity tend to turn it off very quickly. Making the directory more like a wiki can result in better and more up-to-date information. This isn't the only option, but it is the one we will explore next.

On to in-place editing!

6
jQuery In-place Editing Using Ajax

jQuery as a library is intended to have a good, solid, lightweight core that invites an ecosystem of plugins. Ordinary JavaScript programmers have been known to learn jQuery and start writing new plugins on their first day. In this chapter, we will take advantage of the **Jeditable – Edit In Place Plugin For jQuery**, with homepage at http://www.appelsiini.net/projects/jeditable. Jeditable is not the only plugin out there, nor the only good one; it is one of a number of interesting and useful plugins that are available in the jQuery plugin ecosystem. If you would like to find or explore jQuery plugins, http://plugins.jquery.com/ is a good place to start.

In this chapter, we will cover:

- How to include a plugin on a page
- How to use jQuery with the Jeditable plugin to add "edit-in-place" functionality
- How to use Django to keep track of the server-side responsibilities
- How to make a detailed profile page that supports in-place editing, as well as adding the same functionality to the search results page

In our next chapter, we will complete the profile pages, building on autocomplete features to allow an employee's supervisor to be specified without a long dropdown menu, as well as exploring autocomplete for search.

This will allow us to create a results page as shown:

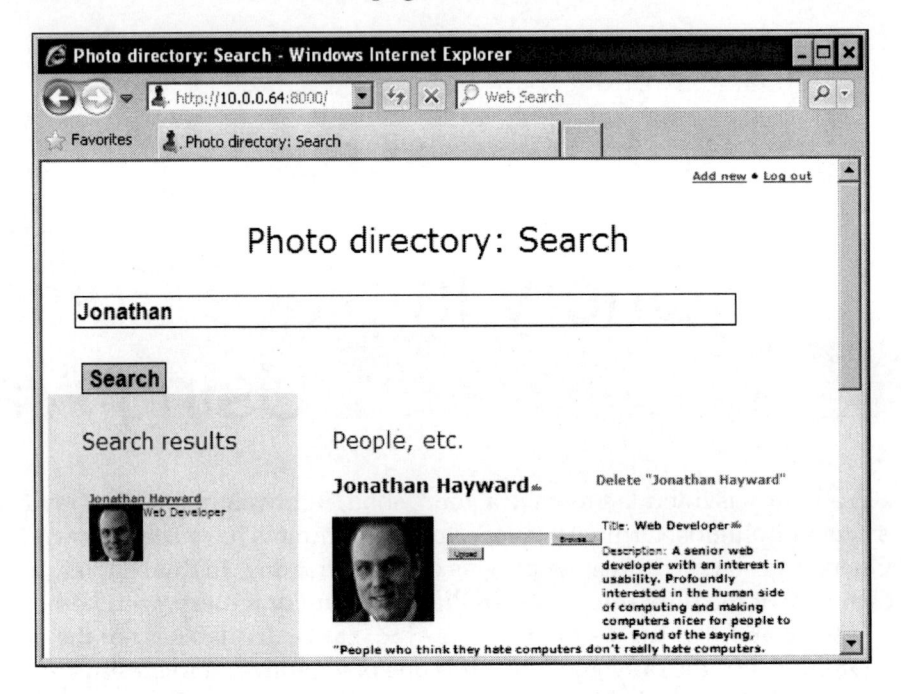

If someone clicks on the name, for instance, it becomes:

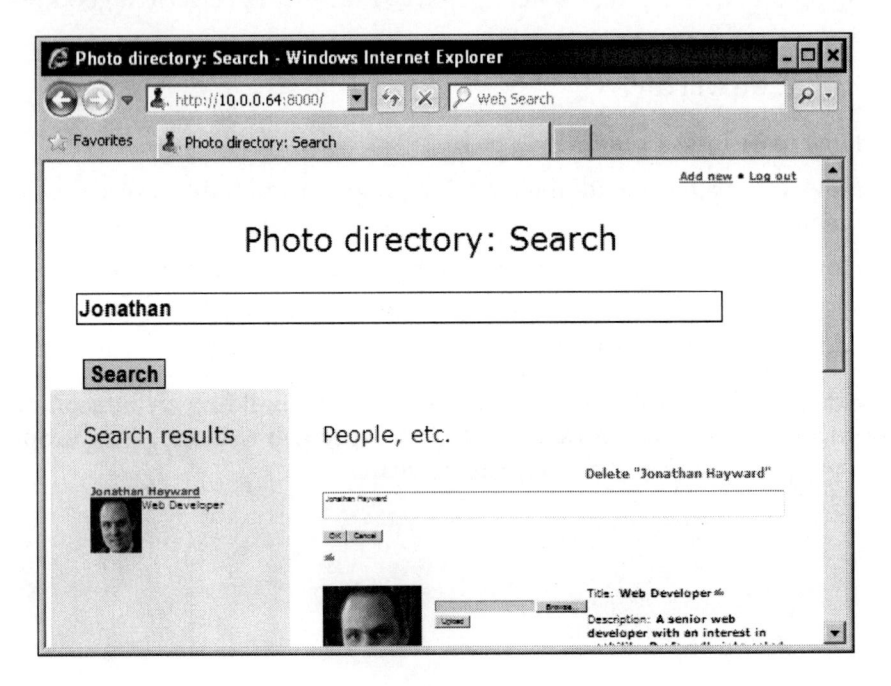

When someone clicks **OK**, the data is saved on the server, and also shown on the page.

Let's get started on how this works.

Including a plugin

We include a jQuery plugin on a page by including jQuery, then including the plugin (or plugins, if we have more than one). In our `base.html`, we update:

```
{% block footer_javascript_site %}
  <script language="JavaScript" type="text/javascript"
          src="/static/js/jquery.js"></script>
  <script language="JavaScript" type="text/javascript"
          src="/static/js/jquery-ui.js"></script>
  <script language="JavaScript" type="text/javascript"
          src="/static/js/jquery.jeditable.js"></script>
{% endblock footer_javascript_site %}
```

This is followed by the `footer_javascript_section` and `footer_javascript_page` blocks. This means that if we don't want the plugin, which is the last inclusion, to be downloaded for each page, we could put it in overridden section and page blocks. This would render as including the plugin after jQuery.

How to make pages more responsive

We would also note that the setup, with three JavaScript downloads, is appropriate for development purposes but not for deployment. In terms of YSlow client-side performance optimization, the recommended best practice is to have one HTML/XHTML hit, one CSS hit at the top, and one JavaScript hit at the bottom. One of the basic principles of client-side optimization, discussed by Steve Souders (see http://developer.yahoo.com/yslow/) is, since HTTP requests slow the page down, the recommended best practice is to have one (preferably minified) CSS inclusion at the top of the page, and then one (preferably minified) JavaScript inclusion at the bottom of each page. Each HTTP request beyond this makes things slower, so combining CSS and/or JavaScript requests into a single concatenated file is low-hanging fruit to improve how quick and responsive your web pages appear to users.

For deployment, we should minify and combine the JavaScript. As we are developing, we also have JavaScript included in templates and rendered into the delivered XHTML; this may be appropriate for development purposes. For deployment though, as much shared functionality as possible should be factored out into an included JavaScript file. For content that can be delivered statically, such as CSS, JavaScript, and even non-dynamic images, setting far-future Expires/Cache-Control headers is desirable. (One practice is to never change the content of a published URL for the kind of content that has a far-future expiration set, and then if it needs updating, instead of changing the content at the same location, leave the content where it is, publish at a new location possibly including a version number, and reference the new location.)

A template handling the client-side requirements

Here's the template. Its view will render it with an entity and other information. At present it extends the base directly; it is desirable in many cases to have the templates that are rendered extend section templates, which in turn extend the base. In our simple application, we have two templates which are directly rendered to web pages. One is the page that handles both search and search results—dealt with earlier—and the other, the page that handles a profile, from the following template:

```
{% extends "base.html" %}
```

Following earlier discussion, we include honorifics before the name, and post-nominals after. At this point we do not do anything to make it editable.

```
{% block head_title %}
{{ entity.honorifics }} {{ entity.name }} {{ entity.post_nominals }}
{% endblock head_title %}
{% block body_main %}
```

There is one important point about Django and the title block. The Django developers do not find it acceptable to write a templating engine that produces errors in production if someone attempts to access an undefined value (by typos, for instance). As a result of this design decision, if you attempt to access an undefined value, the templating engine will silently insert an empty string and move on. This means that it is safe to include a value that may or may not exist, although there are ways to test if a value exists and is nonempty, and display another default value in that case. We will see how to do this soon. Let's move on to the main block, defined by the last line of code.

Once we are in the main block, we have an `h1` which is almost identical to the title block, but this time it is marked up to support editing in place. Let us look at the `honorifics` span; the `name` and `post_nominals` spans work the same way:

```
<h1>
    <span id="Entity_honorifics_{{ entity.id }}" class="edit">
        {% if entity.honorifics %}
            {{ entity.honorifics }}
        {% else %}
            Click to edit.
        {% endif %}
    </span>
```

The class `edit` is used to give all `$(".edit")` items some basic special treatment with Jeditable; there is nothing magical about the class name, which could have been replaced by `user-may-change-this` or something else. `edit` merely happens to be a good name choice, like almost any good variable/function/object name.

We create a naming convention in the span's HTML ID which will enable the server side to know which—of a long and possibly open-ended number of things we could intend to change—is the one we want. In a nutshell, the convention is *modelname_fieldname_instanceID*. The first token is the model name, and is everything up to the first underscore. (Even if we were only interested in one model now, it is more future proof to design so that we can accommodate changes that introduce more models.)

The last token is the instance ID, an integer. The middle token, which may contain underscores (for example `post_nominals` in the following code), is the field name. There is no specific requirement to follow a naming convention, but it allows us to specify an HTML ID that the server-side view can parse for information about which field on which instance of which model is being edited.

We also provide a default value, in this case `Click to edit`, intended not only to serve as a placeholder, but to give users a sense on how this information can be updated.

We might also observe that here and in the following code, we do not presently have checks against race conditions in place. So nothing here or in the following code will stop users from overwriting each others' changes. This may be taken as a challenge to refine and extend the solution to either prevent race conditions or mitigate their damage.

```
<span id="Entity_name_{{ entity.id }}" class="edit">
    {% if entity.name %}
        {{ entity.name }}
```

```
            {% else %}
                Click to edit.
            {% endif %}
        </span>
        <span id="Entity_post_nominals_{{ entity.id }}" class="edit">
            {% if entity.post_nominals %}
                {{ entity.post_nominals }}
            {% else %}
                Click to edit.
            {% endif %}
        </span>
    </h1>
```

This approach is an excellent first approach but in practice is an `h1` with three slots that say `Click to edit` on a profile, creating needless confusion. We move to a simplified:

```
<h1 class="edit" id="Entity_name_{{ entity.id }}">
    {{ entity.name }}
</h1>
```

Taken together, the three statements form the heading in this screenshot:

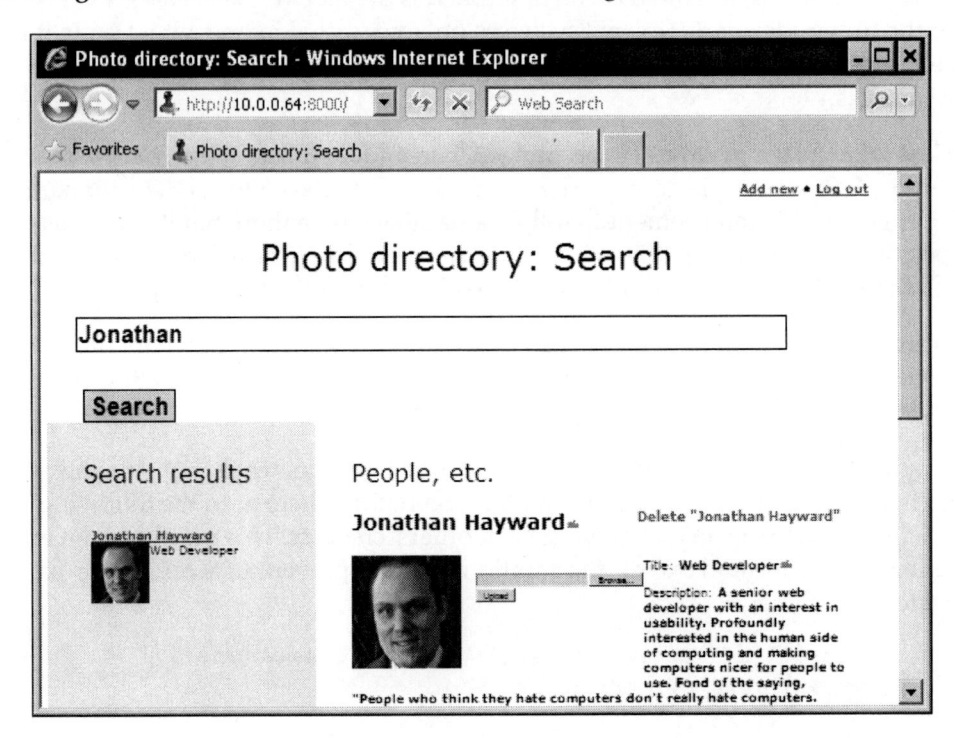

If we click on the name (for instance) it becomes:

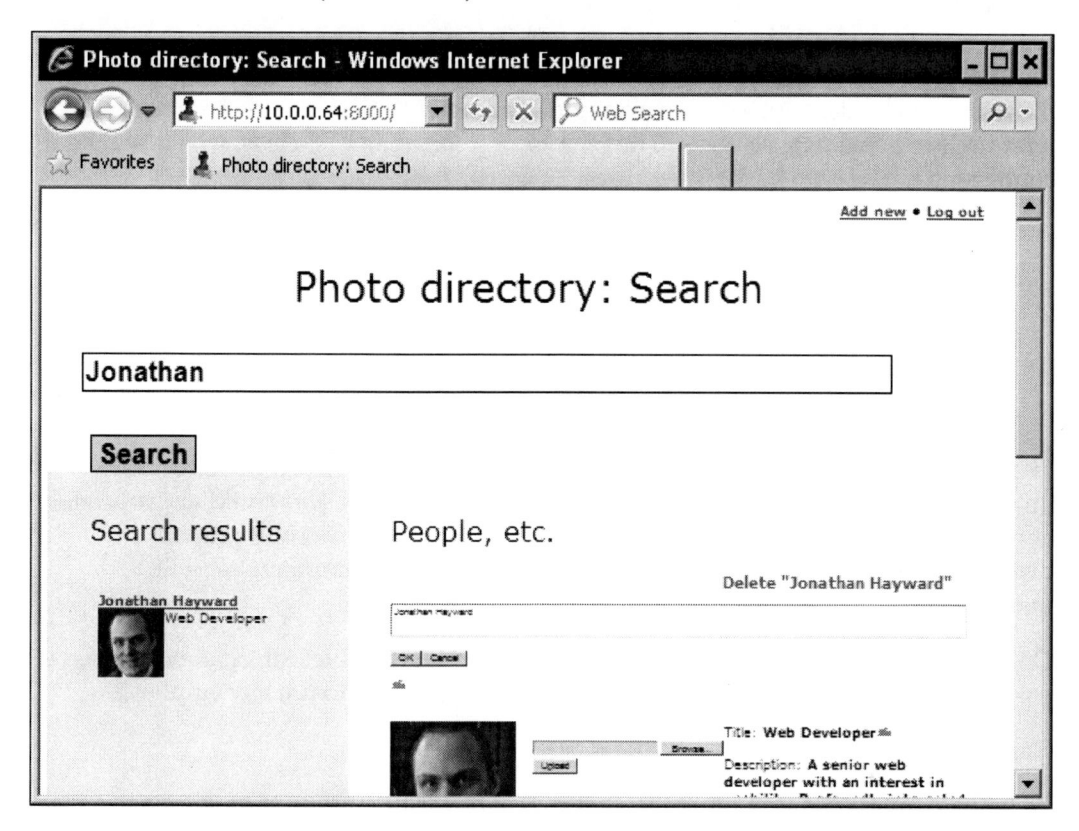

The image is presently a placeholder; this should be expanded to allow an image to be uploaded if the user clicks on the picture (implementing consistent-feeling behavior whether or not we do so via the same plugin). We also need the `view` and `urlpattern` on the backend:

```
{% if entity.image %}
<img src="/images/{{ entity.id }}" alt="{{ entity.name }}">
{% endif %}
```

The bulk of the profile

For small bits of text, we use the `edit` CSS class, which will be transformed to an input of type text on click (or double-click or mouseover, if we were using Jeditable differently). The description is an example of something that would more naturally lend itself to a textarea, so we will use the `edit_textarea` CSS class, which will be configured to use a textarea.

```
<p>
     Description
  <strong id="Entity_description_{{ entity.id }}"
        class="edit_textarea">
     {{ entity.description }}
  </strong>
</p>
```

The **Department**, as well as **Reports to** field, are not arbitrary text in our implementation; they are another entity (if one is specified). This could appropriately enough be implemented as a dropdown menu, but even a carefully pruned dropdown menu could be long and unwieldy for a large company. We will, in our next chapter, use an autocomplete plugin for this job.

One additional note on usability: When displaying "label: value" information on pages, particularly heavily used pages, the most basic option is not to use any emphasis:

Name: J. Smith

To help people's eyes find what they want, one obvious solution is to emphasize the label, as in:

Name: J. Smith

This works well the first time. However, if people are looking at the same set of fields, in the same order, on a web page they visit repeatedly, it is no longer best to emphasize the labels. Regular visitors already know what the labels are, and the motive for even looking at the labels is to see the value. Therefore, for our directory, we will be using bold for the value rather than the label:

Name: **J. Smith**

```
<p>Department:
    <strong>
        {{ entity.department.name }}
    </strong>

<p>Homepage:
    {% if entity.homepage %}
```

```
                <a href="{{ entity.homepage }}">
            {% endif %}
            <strong class="edit_rightclick"
                    id="Entity_homepage_{{ entity.id }}">
                {% if entity.homepage %}
                    {{ entity.homepage }}
                {% else %}
                    Right click to change.
                {% endif %}
            </strong>
            {% if entity.homepage %}
                </a>
            {% endif %}
</p>
```

If a homepage is defined, we give the URL, wrapped in a link and a `strong` that makes the link editable by right clicking. If the link were just editable by a regular click, Jeditable would short-circuit the usual and expected behavior of clicking on a link taking you to the corresponding page or opening the corresponding e-mail. To allow editing while also allowing normal use of links on a profile page, we assign the right click rather than click event to be the way to allow editing. From a UI consistency perspective, it might be desirable to additionally always allow a right click to trigger any (possible) editing. However, we will leave that on our wishlist for now. We will define JavaScript later on in this chapter that will add desired behavior.

Whitespace and delivery

The formatting used above is preferable for development; for actual delivery, we may wish to strip out all whitespace that can be stripped out, for this page:

```
{% if entity.homepage %}<a href="{{ entity.homepage }}">{% endif %}<strong class="edit_rightclick" id="entity_homepage_{{ entity.id }}">{% if entity.homepage %}{{ entity.homepage }}{% else %}Right click to change.{% endif %}</strong>{% if entity.homepage %}</a>{% endif %}<br />
```

Some browsers now are better about this, but it has happened in the past that if you have whitespace such as a line break between the intended text of a link and the `</a>` tag, you could get unwanted trailing whitespace with a visible underline on the rendered link. In addition, pages load faster if minified. For development purposes, though, we will add whitespace for clarity. In the next code, we will have a spurious space before rendered commas because we are not stripping out unnecessary whitespace:

```
<p>Email:
    <strong>
        {% for email in emails %}
```

```html
                <a id="EntityEmail_email_{{ email.id }}"
                   class="edit_rightclick"
                   href="mailto:{{ email.email }}">
                    {{ email.email }}
                </a>
                {% if not forloop.last %}
                    ,
                {% endif %}
            {% endfor %}
            <span class="edit" id="EntityEmail_new_{{ entity.id }}">
                Click to add email.
            </span>
        </strong>
    </p>
```

This allows e-mails to be added, like so:

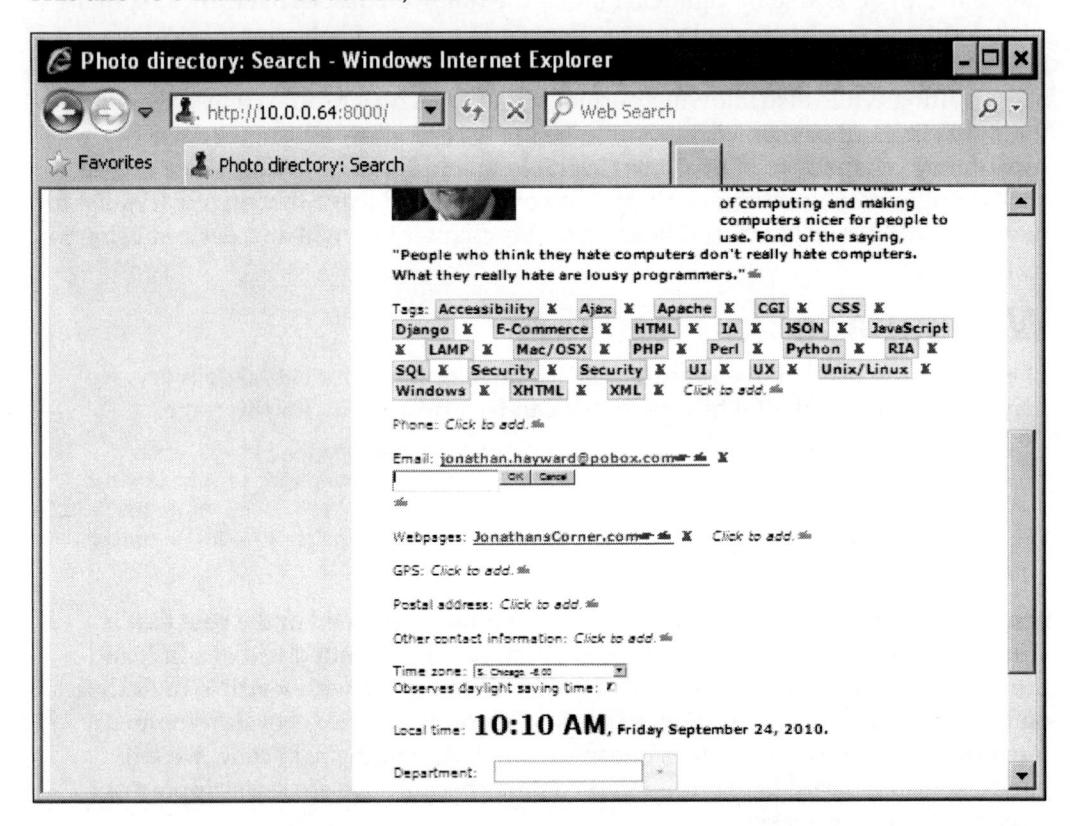

For the **Location** field, we are deferring an intelligent way to let people choose an existing location, or create a new one, until the next chapter. For now we simply display a location's identifier, which is meant as a human-readable identifier rather than a machine-readable primary key or other identifier:

```
<p>Location:
    <strong>
        {{ entity.location.identifier }}
    </strong>
</p>
```

This entails a change to the `Location` model, to allow:

```
class Location(models.Model):
    identifier = models.TextField(blank = True)
    description = models.TextField(blank = True)
    office = models.CharField(max_length = 2,
                              choices = OFFICE_CHOICES,
                              blank = True)
    postal_address = models.TextField(blank = True)
    room = models.TextField(blank = True)
    coordinates = GPSField(blank = True)
```

The **Phone** field is the last one that is user editable.

```
<p>Phone:
    <strong class="edit" id="Entity_phone_{{ entity.id }}">
        {% if entity.phone %}
            {{ entity.phone }}
        {% else %}
            Click to edit.
        {% endif %}
    </strong>
</p>
```

The following fields are presently only displayed. The **Reports to** field should be autocomplete based. The **Start date** field might well enough be left alone as a field that should not need to be updated, or for demonstration purposes it could be set to a jQuery UI datepicker, which would presumably need to have Ajax saving functionality added.

```
<p>Reports to:
    <strong>
        {{ entity.reports_to.name }}
    </strong>
</p>
```

```
<p>Start date:
    <strong>
        {{ entity.start_date }}
    </strong>
</p>
{% endblock body_main %}
```

Page-specific JavaScript

The page-specific JavaScript follows. The first few lines enable the `edit`, `edit_rightclick`, and `edit_textarea` CSS classes to have in-place editing:

```
{% block footer_javascript_page %}
<script language="JavaScript" type="text/javascript">
<!--
function register_editables()
    {
    $(".edit").editable("/ajax/save",
        {
        cancel: "Cancel",
        submit: "OK",
        tooltip: "Click to edit.",
        });
    $(".edit_rightclick").editable("/ajax/save",
        {
        cancel: "Cancel",
        submit: "OK",
        tooltip: "Right click to edit.",
        event: "contextmenu",
        });
    $(".edit_textarea").editable("/ajax/save",
        {
        cancel: "Cancel",
        submit: "OK",
        tooltip: "Click to edit.",
        type: "textarea",
        });
    }

$(function()
    {
    register_editables();
    });
// -->
</script>
{% endblock footer_javascript_page %}
```

Support on the server side

This function provides a rather unadorned logging of changes. This could be expanded to logging in a form intended for machine parsing, display in views, and so on in `functions.py`:

```python
def log_message(message):
    log_file = os.path.join(os.path.dirname(__file__),
                            directory.settings.LOGFILE)
    open(log_file, u'a').write(u"%s: %s\n" % (time.asctime(),
                               message)
```

In `settings.py`, after the `DATABASE_PORT` is set:

```python
# Relative pathname for user changes logfile for directory
LOGFILE = u'log'
```

In the `urlpattern` in `urls.py`:

```python
(ur'^ajax/save', views.save),
(ur'^profile/(\d+)$', views.profile),
```

In `views.py`, our import section has grown to the following:

```python
from django.contrib.auth import authenticate, login
from django.contrib.auth.decorators import login_required
from django.core import serializers
from django.db.models import get_model
from django.http import HttpResponse
from django.shortcuts import render_to_response
from django.template import Context, Template
from django.template.defaultfilters import escape
from django.template.loader import get_template
from directory.functions import ajax_login_required

import directory.models
import json
import re
```

In `views.py` proper, we define a profile view, with the regular `@login_required` decorator. (We use `@ajax_login_required` for views that return JSON or other data for Ajax requests, and `@login_required` for views that return a full web page.)

```python
@login_required
def profile(request, id):
    entity = directory.models.Entity.objects.get(pk = id)
    emails = directory.models.EntityEmail.objects.filter(
             entity__exact = id).all()
    return HttpResponse(get_template(u'profile.html').render(Context(
      {u'entity': entity, u'emails': emails})))
```

The following view saves changes made via in-place edits:

```
@ajax_login_required
def save(request):
    try:
        html_id = request.POST[u'id']
        value = request.POST[u'value']
    except:
        html_id = request.GET[u'id']
        value = request.GET[u'value']
    if not re.match(ur'^\w+$', html_id):
        raise Exception(u'Invalid HTML id.')
```

First we test, specifically, for whether a new e-mail is being added. The last parsed token in that case will be the ID of the Entity the e-mail address is for.

```
match = re.match(ur'EntityEmail_new_(\d+)', html_id)
if match:
    model = int(match.group(1))
```

We create and save the new `EntityEmail` instance:

```
        email = directory.models.EntityEmail(email = value,
            entity = directory.models.Entity.objects.get(
                pk = model))
        email.save()
```

We log what we have done, and for a view servicing Jeditable Ajax requests, return the HTML that is to be displayed. In this case we return a new link, and re-run the script that applies in-place edit functionality to all appropriate classes, as dynamically added content will not have this happen automatically. Our motive is that people will sometimes hit **Save** and then realize they made a mistake they want to correct, and we need to handle this as gracefully as the case where the in-place edit is perfect on the first try. We escape for display:

```
        directory.functions.log_message(u'EntityEmail for Entity ' +
          str(model) + u') added by: ' + request.user.username +
          u', value: ' + value + u'\n')
        return HttpResponse(
          u'<a class="edit_rightclick"
              id="EntityEmail_email_' + str(email.id) + u'"
              href="mailto:' + value + u'">' + value + u'</a>' +
          u'''<span class="edit" id="EntityEmail_new_%s">
              Click to add email.</span>''' % str(email.id))
```

The `else` clause is the normal case. First it parses the `model`, `field`, and `id`:

```
else:
    match = re.match(ur'^(.*?)_(.*)_(\d+)$', html_id)
    model = match.group(1)
    field = match.group(2).lower()
    id = int(match.group(3))
```

Then it looks up the selected model (under the `directory` module, rather than anywhere), finds the instance having this ID, sets the instance's `field` value, and saves the instance. The solution is generic, and does the usual job that would be done by code like `entity.name = new_name`.

```
selected_model = get_model(u'directory', model)
instance = selected_model.objects.get(pk = id)
setattr(instance, field, value)
instance.save()
```

Finally, we log the change and return the HTML to display, in this case simply the value. As with previous examples, we escape the output against injection attacks:

```
directory.functions.log_message(model + u'.' + field + u'('
    + str(id) + u') changed by: ' + request.user.username
    + u' to: ' + value + u'\n')
return HttpResponse(escape(value))
```

Summary

We have now gone from a basic foundation to continuing practical application. We have seen how to divide the labor between the client side and server side. We used this to make a profile page in an employee directory where clicking on text that can be edited enables in-place editing, and we have started to look at usability concerns.

More specifically, we have covered how to use a jQuery plugin, in our case Jeditable, in a solution for Ajax in-place editing. We saw how to use Jeditable in slightly different ways to more appropriately accommodate editable plain text and editable e-mail/URL links. We discussed the server-side responsibilities, including both a generic solution for when a naming convention is required. We looked at an example of customizing behavior when we want something more closely tailored to specific cases (which often is part of solving usability problems well), and also how a detailed profile page can be put together.

In the next chapter, we will address part of the profile page not solved here, namely, how to use autocomplete-style functionality to provide a well-scaling alternative to let people choose Entities for the `department` and `reports_to` field. Let's look at that more closely.

7
Using jQuery UI Autocomplete in Django Templates

In this chapter, we will cover ground in two different dimensions. First of all, we will use jQuery UI's autocomplete, with Django templates and views, covering both the server-side and client-side aspects and explore Django Ajax a little more deeply. Second, we will use something more like a real-world process of discovery while we are doing this. That is to say, instead of starting immediately with a finished solution, we will show what it is like to meet roadblocks along the way and still deliver a working project.

In this chapter we will cover:

- jQuery UI's autocomplete and themeroller
- A "progressive enhancement" combobox
- What needs to be done on the server-side and client-side to do the following:
    - Using Django templating to dynamically create elements
    - Client-side event handling to send autocomplete-based selections to the server
    - DOM Level 0 and iframe-based alternatives on the client-side
    - Extending server-side Django Ajax views to handle updates from the client
    - Refining the working solution
- An example of practical problem solving when issues arise

In previous chapters, we have explored how to get a solution working under optimal conditions. Here we'll look at what we can do when tools don't always work.

Adding autocomplete: first attempt

For further development, we will be using a jQuery theme. What specific theme can be used is customizable, but autocomplete and other plugins require *some* theme such as jQuery UI Themeroller provides. jQuery UI Themeroller, which lets you customize and tweak a theme (or just download a default), is available at:

http://jqueryui.com/themeroller/

When you have made any customizations and downloaded a theme, you can unpack it under your static content directory. In our `base.html` template, after our site-specific stylesheet, we have added an include to the jQuery custom stylesheet (note that you may download a different version number than we have used here).

```
{% block head_css_site %}<link rel="stylesheet" type="text/css"
href="/static/css/style.css" />
<link rel="stylesheet" type="text/css"
href="/static/css/smoothness/jquery-ui-1.8.2.custom.css" />
{% endblock head_css_site %}
```

We will be using the jQuery UI combobox, which offers a "progressive enhancement" strategy by building a page that will still work with JavaScript off and will be more accessible than building a solution with nothing but Ajax.

Progressive enhancement, a best practice

"Progressive enhancement," in a nutshell, means that as much as possible you build a system that works without JavaScript or CSS, with semantic markup and similar practices, then add appearance with CSS, and then customize behavior with JavaScript. A textbook example of customizing behavior is to make a sortable table which is originally sortable, in Web 1.0 fashion, by clicking on a link in a table header which will load a version of the table sorted by that link. Then the links are "hijaxed" by using JavaScript to sort the table purely by JavaScript manipulations of the page, so that if a user does not have JavaScript on, clicking on the links loads a fresh page with the table sorted by that column, and if the user does have JavaScript, the same end result is achieved without waiting on a network hit. In this case, we mark up and populate a dropdown menu of available entities, which the JavaScript will hide and replace with an autocomplete box. The `option` tags follow a naming convention of *fieldname.id*; all the autocomplete fields are for fields of an entity, and the naming convention is not directly for the benefit of server-side code, but so that an event listener knows which field it has been given a value for.

Here we follow the same basic formula for `department`, `location`, and `reports_to`. We produce a list of all available options. The first entry is for no selected `department`/`location`/`reports_to`; as a courtesy to the user we add `selected="selected"` to the presently selected value so that the form is smart enough to remember the last selected value, rather than defaulting to a (presumably unwanted) choice each time the user visits it.

This much of the code is run once and creates the beginning of the containing paragraph, sets a `strong` tag, and creates the entry for no `department` selected (and selects it if appropriate):

```
<p>Department:
    <strong>
        <select name="department" id="department"
                class="autocomplete">
            <option
            {% if not entity.department.id %}
                selected="selected"
            {% endif %}
            value="department.-1">&mdash; Select &mdash;</option>
```

Then we loop through the list of departments, creating an `option` that has a value of `"department."` followed by the id of the entity provided as a department. Remember that earlier we simply used a list of all entities for departments. If you are interested in tinkering, you could add a checkbox to indicate whether an entity should be considered a `department` or a `reports_to` candidate. (Locations are a different data type, so no paring should be obviously helpful for them.)

```
            {% for department in departments %}
            <option
            {% if department.id == entity.department.id %}
                selected="selected"
            {% endif %}
            value="department.{{ department.id }}">
                            {{ department.name}}
            </option>
        {% endfor %}
```

We then close the `select` and `strong`, and move on to the next line.

```
        </select>
    </strong>
</p>
```

The `location` and `reports_to` are handled similarly:

```
Location:
    <select name="location" id="location" class="autocomplete">
```

We add the default, unselected option:

```
        <option
        {% if not entity.location.id %}
            selected="selected"
        {% endif %}
        value="location.-1">&mdash; Select &mdash;</option>
```

Then we loop through available locations and build their options.

```
        {% for location in locations %}
            <option
            {% if locationi.id == entity.locationi.id %}
                selected="selected"
            {% endif %}
            value="location.{{ location.id }}">
                        {{ location.identifier }}</option>
        {% endfor %}
        </select>
    </p>
```

And likewise in `Reports to`:

```
<p>
Reports to:
    <select name="reports_to" id="reports_to" class="autocomplete">
        <option
        {% if not entity.reports_to.id %}
            selected="selected"
        {% endif %}
        value="reports_to_-1">&mdash; Select &mdash;</option>
        {% for reports_to in reports_to_candidates %}
            <option
            {% if reports_to.id == entity.reports_to.id %}
                selected="selected"
            {% endif %}
            value="reports_to_{{ reports_to.id }}">
                        {{ reports_to.name }}</option>
        {% endfor %}
    </select>
</p>
```

Our profile page is modified to provide more variables to the template. Later on, we might identify which entities can be an entity's departments and which entities can be reported to, thus improving the available options by paring away irrelevant entities, but for now we simply provide all entities.

```
@login_required
def profile(request, id):
    entity = directory.models.Entity.objects.get(pk = id)
    emails = directory.models.EntityEmail.objects.filter(
            entity__exact = id).all()
    all_entities = directory.models.Entity.objects.all()
    all_locations = directory.models.Location.objects.all()
    return HttpResponse(get_template(u'profile.html').render(Context(
      {
      u'entity': entity,
      u'emails': emails,
      u'departments': all_entities,
      u'reports_to_candidates': all_entities,
      u'locations': all_locations,
      })))
```

This provides nice-looking autocomplete functionality like:

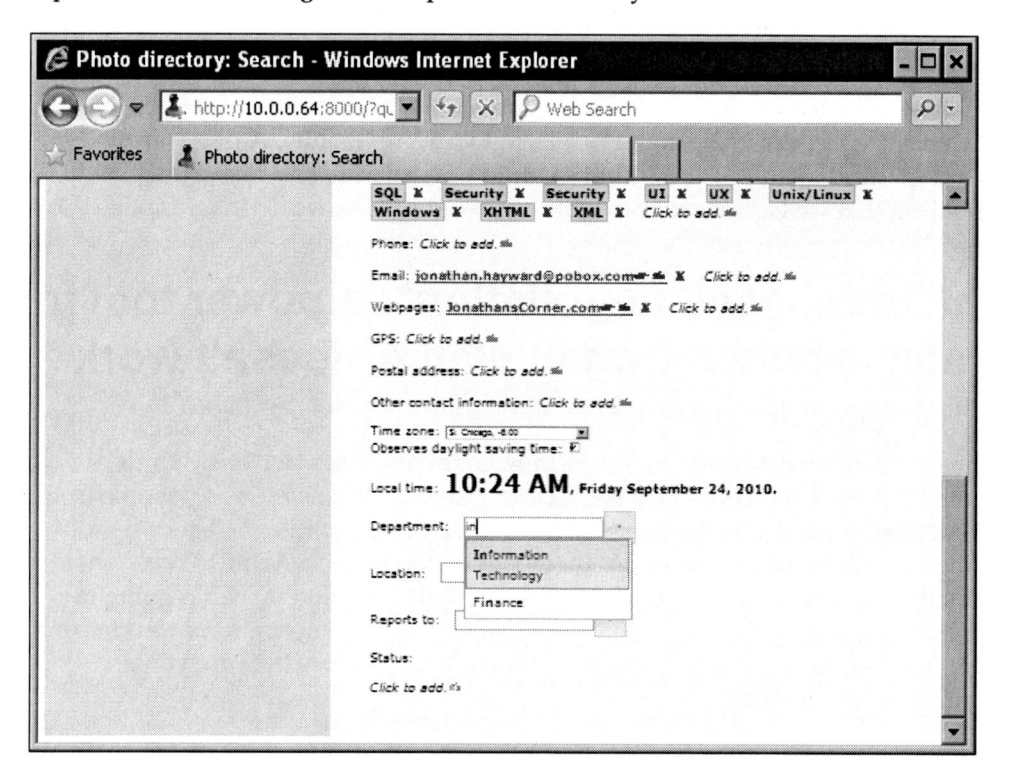

However, there's a bit of a quirk. When we use the code as implemented earlier, it does not seem to save our changes; they are not persistent across page views.

A real-world workaround

In the course of writing this book, a difficulty was encountered. We will take advantage of that opportunity to look at finding alternatives when things do not work. For those interested in jQuery UI complete specifically, the StackOverflow question at `http://stackoverflow.com/questions/188442/whats-a-good-ajax-autocomplete-plugin-for-jquery` is recommended, and a response with nine upvotes as of this writing said autocomplete doesn't work as of roughly jQuery UI 1.6. `http://pastie.org/362706` is reported as a working version. However, let's look at a workaround when things don't work—because even a recommended plugin for a good library may not work, or may not work for us. However, we will succeed later on working with the provided plugin.

The difficulty in question is as follows. jQuery UI includes autocomplete functionality. As downloaded in our case, the autocomplete functionality appeared to work from the user interface perspective, but did not appear to be saving data on the server. A callback function had been created and (attemptedly) registered, but it was not being called. Inserting `alert()` in the beginning of the function did not trigger any alert boxes, and no error appeared in the browser console. Consulting forums at `http://forum.jquery.com/` and `http://stackoverflow.com/`, which are excellent resources, did not seem to turn up results. A bug was filed at `http://dev.jqueryui.com/`, but that did not generate any response quickly. Supposing that we have deadlines looming, what should we do in a case like this?

"Interest-based negotiation": a power tool for problem solving when plan A doesn't work

At this point we might discuss a tangent from *interest-based negotiation*.

Fisher and Ury's negotiation classic *Getting to Yes* discusses two basic kinds of negotiation: hard and soft. Hard negotiation tries to bend as little as possible from its stated position; soft negotiation, such as often occurs in informal and friendly settings, is much more flexible. But they both suffer from an Achilles heel: when both sides start by defining a position, and the only question is who is going to give how much from their initial positions, the result is almost guaranteed to be suboptimal. If you play that game in the first place, you lose because you are playing the wrong game.

The alternative, interest-based negotiation, which involves finding what interests exist on both sides and doing creative problem solving based on those interests, is much more likely to produce a winner for all involved. *Getting to Yes* discusses interest-based negotiation as a power tool for hostile negotiations where the other side has the upper hand, and perhaps it may be. But some of the best mileage you can get out of interest-based negotiations is in friendly negotiations.

One such situation that keeps coming up at work is when someone has basically figured out what they consider a solution to a problem, and then asks for you to attend to the implementation. For example, a manager might have come to a system administrator in the days when pagers were the hot new thing and said, "Our disk filled up last night! In order to prevent this from happening again, is there any way you can set up an automatic process to send the output of a `df` to a pager every five minutes?" And almost the worst response in that situation is, "Yes, I'll get right on it." In cases like these, if the solution was envisioned, architected, and designed by someone nontechnical, and the technical person is asked only to handle implementation details, the solution is almost guaranteed to be wrong.

The correct solution is not to negotiate on a level of positions, but of interests. This particular solution uses a program whose output is designed for a full terminal window, which would be quite painful to scroll through on an early pager even once. It is a "boy who cried wolf" solution that means to the system administrator, "Here's some spam you have to scroll through every five minutes to find out if there is interesting data." Not, necessarily, that it is wrong to send something to a pager. It might well be an appropriate solution to periodically check and send a brief message to the system administrators if the disk is fuller than some threshold percentage, or if the disk is being filled up beyond some threshold percentage per unit of time. But in many cases the correct response is to politely receive the stated position and then get on to identifying the interests involved and trying as best you can to craft a position.

In this case, we are applying the principle of interest-based negotiation to negotiation with the computer. Our initial position, "Follow the jQuery UI instructions" has not produced the desired results, at least not yet. So the next thing we can do is identify our interests. Our interest here, without degrading anything else, is to provide autocomplete functionality to the user interface. This allows at least four potential ways to get past the obstacle:

- Resolve the problem and complete the intended solution
- Work around the bug using the same framework
- Find another jQuery plugin to handle autocomplete
- Use a standalone solution, or another library

We don't need to stay stuck; in fact, we have several options. The first option cannot be ruled out, but right now we have not succeeded. Let's say that's not an option in our case. The third and fourth possibilities almost certainly have multiple options, and multiple live options, but in this case we can bend the rules a little bit, comment out our event-handling code, and give a little nudge to let our jQuery UI-based solution work with all of the niceties of using jQuery UI. We will go with this workaround, but we are not just a workaround away from being blocked by a brick wall. There are presumably several live options, and the more we think in terms of interests rather than positions, and identify interests to feed into problem solving, the more a brick wall fades into a cornucopia of possibilities.

A first workaround

The workaround, like many workarounds, is itself an example of interest-based negotiation with the computer. What we want to happen, that isn't happening yet, is for the data to be saved. The obvious way for us to save the data is by an `XMLHttpRequest` based call but it is not strictly an interest to say that we go through `XMLHttpRequest` or jQuery for the submission. It would also work to have a form that submitted the same data to an `iframe`. This is not a first choice solution, but we should be much more cautious about ruling out positions altogether than identifying our interests. Now we don't want a spurious `iframe` on the page, but we can set it to `display: none;`, and treat it as a bit bucket, or a Unix `/dev/null`. And the graceful degradation solution provided by jQuery UI uses a `select`, so we can specify an `onchange` for the `select` that will submit the form whenever the `select` is changed, that is whenever an autocomplete value is selected. jQuery UI allows us to display the select, and we will do this, both to allow a person to see available options, and to provide a choice about means of input.

Our revised code is as follows in `static/style.css`:

```
bitbucket, #bitbucket
    {
    display: none;
    }
```

In the top of the `body_main` block in `templates/profile.html` we add:

```
<iframe class="bitbucket" id="bitbucket" name="bitbucket"
        src="about:blank"></iframe>
```

One design consideration from our implementation is that it wraps each of the `select` tags (that populate an autocomplete) in its own form element. This means that semantically we cannot have all of them in different `br` separated lines of the same `p`, but this gives an opportunity to make the design better. If we put each field in its own paragraph, it will make a more readable use of whitespace. So we give each field its own paragraph, wrap the paragraphs with `select` tags in `form` elements which submit via `POST` to our Ajax-geared URL and have a target of `bitbucket`, add a hidden form element which will receive special treatment on the server side as will be discussed later, and specify an `onchange` form submission for `select`. This workaround uses what is informally called "DOM Level 0," and is not a first choice. It does, however, allow us to keep a "close to jQuery" solution, with a workaround that is readily replaced by a more preferable solution if a bug is fixed.

The previous code is largely the same, but is wrapped in a `form` tag, and preceded by a hidden `input` designed to ensure that the view has all the information it needs.

```
<form action="/ajax/save" method="POST" name="department_form"
    id="department_form" target="bitbucket">
  <input type="hidden" name="id"
        value="Entity_department_{{ entity.id }}" />
  <p>Department:
```

The `select` has an `onchange` set to submit the form wrapping it. This kind of approach, informally referred to as DOM Level 0 scripting, is not a first choice solution; it is not exactly semantic markup. But it has been said, "In theory, theory and practice are the same. In practice, theory and practice are different." Especially if you have a deadline, given a choice between purist semantic markup that doesn't work, and a less pure solution that works, choose the solution that works. (But, of course, if you have a choice between a purist solution that works and a less pure solution that works, choose the purist solution that works, even if it involves more learning or more work up front.)

```
<select name="department" id="department" class="autocomplete"
    onchange="this.form.submit();">
  <option
    {% if not entity.department.id %}
        selected="selected"
    {% endif %}
```

We changed an option value of — Select —, such as is a common practice for `select` used for their own sake, to `None`. The reason has to do with why we are building this `select`: we wish to populate an autocomplete, and for autocomplete purposes, if someone wants to set a `value` to `None`, it is unlikely that they will start typing "Select".

But these are changes of relatively small details. The select is still essentially like it was before. And that is a benefit: if we are able to get things working in pure semantic markup using best practices, it helps to have a page that's still basically like a "best practices" implementation.

```
            value="department.-1">None</option>
        {% for department in departments %}
            <option
                {% if department.id == entity.department.id %}
                    selected="selected"
                {% endif %}
                value="department.{{ department.id }}">
                    {{ department.name }}</option>
        {% endfor %}
        </select>
    </p>
</form>
```

The other fields are changed, if slightly. They are in their own paragraphs, which is semantically at least as good as having them one per line in a large paragraph, and lends itself to display with better use of whitespace—a major benefit if people will be using our directory a lot!

We define a link for the homepage:

```
<p>
    Homepage:
    {% if entity.homepage %}
        <a href="{{ entity.homepage }}">
    {% endif %}
```

Within the link we define `strong`, which is marked up for (right-click) editing, and display the URL inside the link:

```
<strong class="edit_rightclick"
    id="entity_homepage_{{ entity.id }}">{{ entity.homepage }}
</strong>
```

Then we close the link and paragraph:

```
    {% if entity.homepage %}
        </a>
    {% endif %}
</p>
```

We define similar, but not identical, handling for the e-mail:

```
<p>
    Email:
    <strong>
        {% for email in emails %}
            <a id="EntityEmail_email_{{ email.id }}"
                class="edit_rightclick"
                href="mailto:{{ email.email }}">
```

We eliminate some whitespace so that there will not be a space between the link and the separating comma:

```
                {{ email.email }}</a>{% if not forloop.last %},
            {% endif %}
        {% endfor %}
        <span class="edit" id="EntityEmail_new_{{ entity.id }}">
            Click to add email.
        </span>
    </strong>
</p>
```

The `location` fields, as the `reports_to` field in the following snippet, follow the same pattern as the `department` previously seen.

We define a `form`:

```
<form action="/ajax/save" method="POST" name="location_form"
        id="location_form" target="bitbucket">
```

We define a hidden `input` so the server-side code has a parsable identifier:

```
<input type="hidden" name="id"
        value="Entity_location_{{ entity.id }}" />
<p>
    Location:
```

We define a `select` with a DOM Level 0 submit:

```
<select name="location" id="location" class="autocomplete"
    onchange="this.form.submit();">
```

We build the first option for when nothing has been selected:

```
<option
{% if not entity.location.id %}
    selected="selected"
{% endif %}
value="location.-1">None</option>
```

We populate the rest of the list:

```
{% for location in locations %}
    <option
    {% if locationi.id == entity.locationi.id %}
        selected="selected"
    {% endif %}
    value="location.{{ location.id }}">
        {{ location.identifier }}</option>
{% endfor %}
```

And we close tags that need to be closed:

```
        </select>
    </p>
</form>
```

The `Phone` field is an in-place edit field. It works as a regular in-place edit field, not an autocomplete:

```
<p>
    Phone:
    <strong class="edit" id="entity_phone_{{ entity.id }}">
        {% if entity.phone %}
            {{ entity.phone }}
        {% else %}
            Click to change.
        {% endif %}
    </strong>
</p>
```

And finally, we have our third and last autocomplete, which works like the first two:

```
<form action="/ajax/save" method="POST" name="reports_to_form"
    id="reports_to_form" target="bitbucket">
    <input type="hidden" name="id"
        value="Entity_reports_to_{{ entity.id }}" />
    <p>
        Reports to:
        <select name="reports_to" id="reports_to" class="autocomplete"
            onchange="this.form.submit();">
        <option
        {% if not entity.reports_to.id %}
            selected="selected"
        {% endif %}
            value="reports_to_-1">None</option>
```

```
            {% for reports_to in reports_to_candidates %}
                <option
                {% if reports_to.id == entity.reports_to.id %}
                    selected="selected"
                {% endif %}
                value="reports_to_{{ reports_to.id }}">
                    {{ reports_to.name }}</option>
            {% endfor %}
            </select>
    </p>
</form>
<p>
    Start date:
    <strong>
        {{ entity.start_date }}
    </strong>
</p>
```

The handler follows the signature for event handlers registered, as we wish to register them. While we do not use the `event` object, we keep it in the signature. `context.item` should be the `option` that was selected. Its value will look like `department.1` and is meant to carry all the information needed for this function. The data submitted follows the same `id-value` structure as we have already used for in-place editing in the previous chapter, and submits it to the same view. We will in fact have different server-side code handling these selections. The code that stores text in a field will not take an ID and look up the right instance of the intended field, at least not without significant refactoring. However, we are developing with an analogous interface in mind: submitted data in the `id-value` format, with the ID following the *ModelName_fieldname_instanceID* naming convention.

```
function update_autocomplete(event, context)
    {
    var split_value = context.item.value.split(".");
    if (split_value.length == 2 && !isNaN(split_value[1]))
        {
        var field = split_value[0];
        var id = split_value[1];
        $.ajax({
            data:
                {
                id: "Entity_" + field + "_" + {{ entity.id }},
                value: id,
                },
```

```
                url: "/ajax/save",
            });
        };
    }
```

Boilerplate code from jQuery UI documentation

It is commonplace when using software to include adding boilerplate code. Here is an example. We insert boilerplate code from the documentation pages for jQuery UI at http://jqueryui.com/demos/autocomplete/#combobox:

```
    (function($) {
        $.widget("ui.combobox", {
            _create: function() {
                var self = this;
                var select = this.element.hide();
                var input = $("<input>")
                    .insertAfter(select)
                    .autocomplete({
                        source: function(request, response) {
                            var matcher = new RegExp(request.term,
                                                    "i");
response(select.children("option").map(function() {
                                var text = $(this).text();
                                if (this.value && (!request.term ||
                                    matcher.test(text)))
                                    return {
                                        id: this.value,
                                        label: text.replace(new
RegExp("(?![^&;]+;)(?!<[^<>]*)(" +
$.ui.autocomplete.escapeRegex(request.term) +
")(?![^<>]*>)(?![^&;]+;)", "gi"), "<strong>$1</strong>"),
                                        value: text
                                    };
                            }));
                        },
                        delay: 0,
                        change: function(event, ui) {
                            if (!ui.item) {
                                // remove invalid value,
                                // as it didn't match anything
                                $(this).val("");
                                return false;
```

```
                }
                select.val(ui.item.id);
                self._trigger("selected", event, {
                    item: select.find("[value='" +
                                        ui.item.id + "']")
                });
            },
            minLength: 0
        })
        .addClass(
            "ui-widget ui-widget-content ui-corner-left");
    $("<button> </button>")
    .attr("tabIndex", -1)
    .attr("title", "Show All Items")
    .insertAfter(input)
    .button({
        icons: {
            primary: "ui-icon-triangle-1-s"
        },
        text: false
    }).removeClass("ui-corner-all")
    .addClass("ui-corner-right ui-button-icon")
    .click(function() {
        // close if already visible
        if (input.autocomplete("widget").is(":visible")) {
            input.autocomplete("close");
            return;
        }
        // pass empty string as value to search for,
        // displaying all results
        input.autocomplete("search", "");
        input.focus();
    });
        }
    });

})(jQuery);
```

Turning on Ajax behavior (or trying to)

We make autocompletes out of the relevant selects, and also display the selects, which the `combobox()` call hides by default. The user now has a choice between the select and an autocomplete box.

```
$(function()
    {
    $(".autocomplete").combobox();
    $(".autocomplete").toggle();
```

Here we have code which, from the documentation, might be expected to call the `update_autocomplete()` event handler when a selection or change is made. However, at this point we encounter a bend in the road.

The bend in the road is this: the following commented code, when uncommented, doesn't seem to be able to trigger the handler being called. When it was uncommented, and an `alert()` placed at the beginning of `update_autocomplete()`, the `alert()` was not triggered even once. And the usual suspects in terms of forums and even filing a bug did not succeed in getting the handler to be called. The `alert()` was still not called.

After this code, let's look at our updated code on the server side, and then see how this bend in the road can be addressed.

```
    /*
    $(".autocomplete").autocomplete({select: update_autocomplete});
    $(".autocomplete").bind({"autocompleteselect": update_
autocomplete});
    $(".autocomplete").bind({"autocompletechange": update_
autocomplete});
    */
    });
```

Now let us turn our attention to the server side.

Code on the server side

Here we have the updated `save()` view which has been expanded to address its broader scope. We accept either `GET` or `POST` requests, although requests that alter data should only be made by `POST` for production purposes, and save the dictionary for exploration.

```
    @ajax_login_required
    def save(request):
        try:
            html_id = request.POST[u'id']
```

```
        dictionary = request.POST
except:
    html_id = request.GET[u'id']
    dictionary = request.GET
```

If we have one of the autocomplete values, we have a hidden field named `id` which guarantees that any submission will have that field in its dictionary, either `request.POST` or `request.GET`. However, the `department`, `location`, and `reports_to` fields are not all named `value`, and we manually check for them and use `value` as a default:

```
if html_id.startswith(u'Entity_department_'):
    value = dictionary[u'department']
elif html_id.startswith(u'Entity_location_'):
    value = dictionary[u'location']
elif html_id.startswith(u'Entity_reports_to_'):
    value = dictionary[u'reports_to']
else:
    value = dictionary[u'value']
```

We perform some basic validation. Our code's HTML ID should only consist of word characters:

```
if not re.match(ur'^\w+$', html_id):
    raise Exception("Invalid HTML id.")
```

Then we handle several special cases before the general-purpose code that handles most `/ajax/save` requests. If there is a new `EntityEmail`, we create it and save it:

```
match = re.match(ur'EntityEmail_new_(\d+)', html_id)
if match:
    model = int(match.group(1))
    email = directory.models.EntityEmail(email = value, entity =
      directory.models.Entity.objects.get(pk = model))
    email.save()
    directory.functions.log_message(u'EntityEmail for Entity ' +
      str(model) + u' added by: ' + request.user.username + u',
      value: ' + value + u'\n')
    return HttpResponse(
      u'<a class="edit_rightclick"
          id="EntityEmail_email_' + str(email.id)
      + u'" href="mailto:' + value + u'">' + value + u'</a>' +
      u'''<span class="edit" id="EntityEmail_new_%s">
          Click to add email.</span>''' % str(email.id))
```

We have the added code to look up the entity, look up the appropriate `department` (if any), assign the updated `department`, and save the entity. This technique is repeated, with slight variation, for the `location` and `reports_to` fields. We still need to return an `HttpResponse`, even if the value is ignored. On the client-side, the following code we develop will report a Django error page for development purposes but even then will discard the reported value if the update runs without error.

Here we have the special case of an Entity's `department` being set. While we create the illusion on the client-side that this is just the same sort of submission as (say) an Entity's description, we need to handle a few things on the server side to give the client-side a simple appearance of "Mark it up right and save it, and it will be saved."

```
elif html_id.startswith(u'Entity_department_'):
    entity_id = int(html_id[len(u'Entity_department_'):])
    department_id = int(value[len(u'department.'):])
    entity = directory.models.Entity.objects.get(pk = entity_id)
    if department_id == -1:
        entity.department = None
    else:
        entity.department = directory.models.Entity.objects.get(
                                pk = department_id)
    entity.save()
    return HttpResponse(value)
```

The `location` code works the same way as `reports_to` and `department`:

```
elif html_id.startswith(u'Entity_location_'):
    entity_id = int(html_id[len(u'Entity_location_'):])
    location_id = int(value[len(u'location.'):])
    if location_id == -1:
        entity.location = None
    else:
        entity.location = directory.models.Location.objects.get(
                                pk == location_id)
    entity.save()
    return HttpResponse(value)
elif html_id.startswith(u'Entity_reports_to_'):
    entity_id = int(html_id[len(u'Entity_reports_to'):])
    reports_to_id = int(value[len(u'reports_to.'):])
    entity = directory.models.Entity.object.get(pk = entity_id)
    if reports_to_id == -1:
        entity.reports_to = None
    else:
```

```
                  entity.reports_to = directory.models.Entity.objects.get(
                                  pk == reports_to_id)
       entity.save()
       return HttpResponse(value)
```

Although it is last, this is the mainstream and most generic handler, handling the usual cases of text fields supporting in-place editing:

```
       else:
           match = re.match(ur'^(.*?)_(.*)_(\d+)$', html_id)
           model = match.group(1)
           field = match.group(2)
           id = int(match.group(3))
           selected_model = get_model(u'directory', model)
           instance = selected_model.objects.get(pk = id)
           setattr(instance, field, value)
           instance.save()
           directory.functions.log_message(model + u'.' + field +
               u'(' + str(id) + u') changed by: ' +
               request.user.username + u' to: ' + value + u'\n')
           return HttpResponse(escape(value))
```

Refining our solution further

This approach works, but there is room to further clean it up. First of all, we can set things up in the base template so that, for development, Django's informative error pages are displayed; we also set form submissions to POST by default. We make a target `div` for the notifications:

```
              {% block body_site_announcements %}
              {% endblock body_site_announcements %}
              {% block body_notifications %}<div
                    id="notifications"></div>
              {% endblock body_notifications %}
```

Then we add, to the `footer_javascript_site` block, a slightly tweaked `send_notifications()`. Compared to our earlier code, instead of delaying five seconds, it delays five seconds plus two milliseconds per character of the message. This does not have a noticeably different effect for normal, short notifications, but it means that if a 60k Django error page is served up, you have more time to inspect the error. We could tweak it further so that above a threshold length, or on some other conditions, the notification is only dismissed by explicitly pressing a button, but we will stop here.

```
       <script language="JavaScript" type="text/javascript">
       function send_notification(message)
           {
```

```
$("#notifications").html("<p>" + message + "</p>");
setTimeout("$('#notifications').show('slow').delay(" + (5000 +
  message.length * 2) + ").hide('slow');", 0);
}
```

Our notifications area has several different messages, not all of which need to be visually labeled as errors, so we move from a red-based styling to one that is silver and grey in `static/css/style.css`:

```
#notifications
{
background-color: #c0c0c0;
border: 3px solid #808080;
display: none;
padding: 20px;
}
```

We call, on page load, `$.ajaxSetup()` to specify a default error handler, and also specify form submission via POST. This will need to be changed for deployment, but together this means that a valuable Django error page is displayed as a notification whenever an Ajax error occurs, which is a kind of "best of both worlds" solution for development.

```
$(function()
    {
    $.ajaxSetup(
        {
        error: function(XMLHttpRequest, textStatus, errorThrown)
            {
            send_notification(XMLHttpRequest.responseText);
            },
        type: "POST",
        });
    });
</script>
```

In the profile template, we will remove the containing `form` elements and the hidden inputs, and replace the contents of the `onchange` attributes. We will also rename the original `update_autocomplete()` to `update_autocomplete_handler()`, leaving it available should the originally intended approach work. The new `update_autocomplete()` will make the Ajax call, submitting the same information as the (now) `update_autocomplete_handler()`. We will remove the bit bucket `iframe`, although we leave the CSS in, in case a bit bucket is desired later on.

We are in a position technically to make one big paragraph out of several fields as we did originally, but breaking them into their own paragraphs was a fortunate change, and we will retain it.

The `Department` paragraph now looks like a cross between the previous two entries. It is its own paragraph, but the form is gone. There is an `onchange` attribute set, although its contents are different from earlier. It calls `update_autocomplete()` with an ID following the name convention and the present value of the `select`.

```
<p>Department:
    <select name="department" id="department" class="autocomplete"
      onchange="update_autocomplete(
            'Entity_department_{{ entity.id}}', this.value);">
        <option
        {% if not entity.department.id %}
            selected="selected"
        {% endif %}
         value="department.-1">None</option>
        {% for department in departments %}
            <option
              {% if department.id == entity.department.id %}
                  selected="selected"
              {% endif %}
              value="department.{{ department.id }}">
                    {{ department.name }}</option>
            {% endfor %}
    </select>
</p>
```

The `location` and `reports_to` areas follow suit:

```
<p>Location:
    <select name="location" id="location" class="autocomplete"
      onchange="update_autocomplete('Entity_location_{{ entity.id}}',
                            this.value);">
    <option
    {% if not entity.location.id %}
        selected="selected"
    {% endif %}
     value="location.-1">None</option>
    {% for location in locations %}
        <option
        {% if location.id == entity.location.id %}
            selected="selected"
        {% endif %}
            value="location.{{ location.id }}">
                    {{ location.identifier }}</option>
    {% endfor %}
      </select>
</p>
```

The `Reports to` field also follows suit:

```
<p>Reports to:
    <select name="reports_to" id="reports_to" class="autocomplete"
      onchange="update_autocomplete(
              'Entity_reports_to_{{ entity.id}}', this.value);">
  <option
  {% if not entity.reports_to.id %}
      selected="selected"
  {% endif %}
  value="reports_to_-1">None</option>
  {% for reports_to in reports_to_candidates %}
      <option
      {% if reports_to.id == entity.reports_to.id %}
          selected="selected"
      {% endif %}
      value="reports_to_{{ reports_to.id }}">
          {{ reports_to.name }}</option>
  {% endfor %}
    </select>
</p>
```

And that's it. We now have a working, and slightly more polished internally, implementation that supports autocomplete and in-place editing like the following.

For the autocomplete:

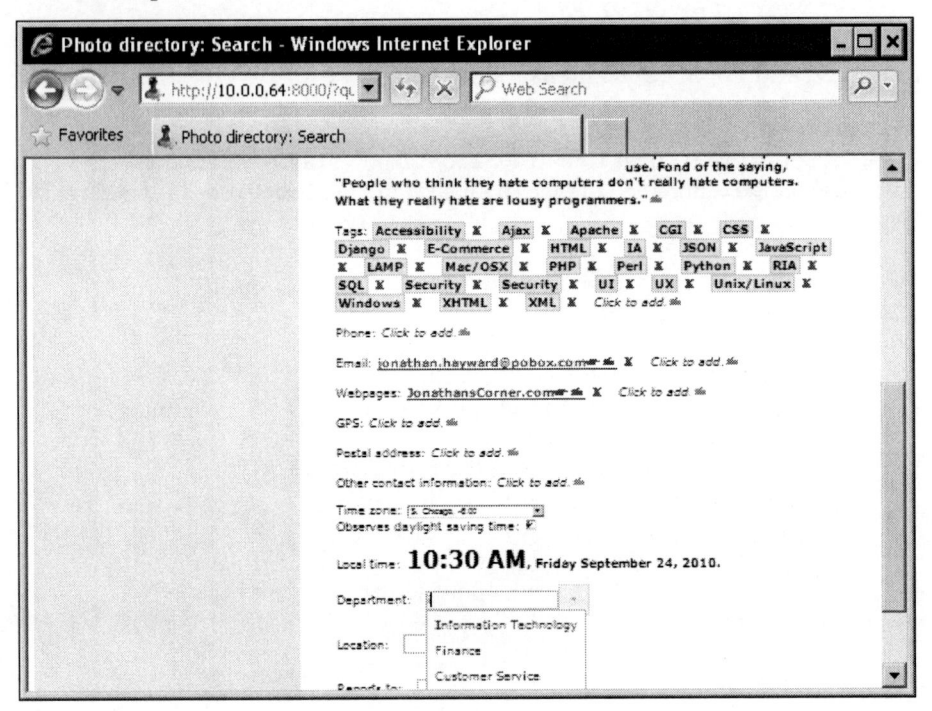

Or, for another of several examples of user input that was allowed, here is an in-place edit used to add a new email address.

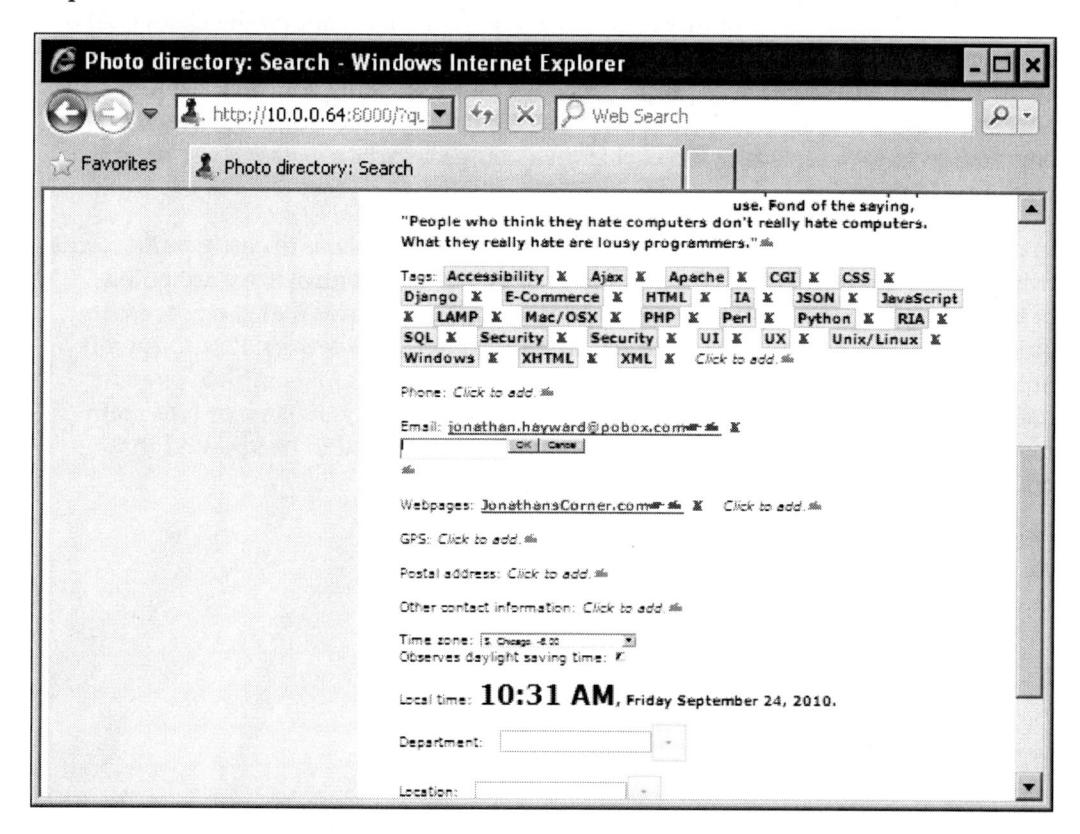

Summary

Again, we have moved in two different dimensions in this chapter. The first dimension is the obvious one: what we need on the client-side and server-side to get autocomplete working with jQuery UI. The second dimension has to do with creative problem solving when something goes wrong.

We have covered the nuts and bolts of jQuery UI's autocomplete, and where plugins can be obtained. We continue with the concept of "progressive enhancement," and a concrete example. We looked at what tools we have on the server-side and client-side to do this. We have continued to get our hands dirty with Django templating to build the desired pages.

We have covered the ideal case of setting up an event listener that will communicate with the server and keep it updated with pure Ajax, looked at DOM Level 0 and `iframe`-based alternatives on the client side, and further expanded the Django Ajax view on the server side so that it will accommodate autocomplete requests as well as the original edit-in-place requests. Once we had a working solution, we looked at how we could make it work better. We have also taken a cue from best practices in negotiation to look at getting the best from a computer when we can't get what we were first looking for.

In our next chapter, we will look at Django ModelForm or how to easily build forms from Django models. We have a great deal of power and control if we are going to build interfaces, but Django provides some built-in features that can get results quickly. Perhaps, for instance, your organization only has a few locations and it is not the best use of resources to build a fancy in-place edit/autocomplete page for data that is updated maybe once a month? Or perhaps you have one or two main models you need updated, and several more that don't need to be updated that often but do need to be available for editing?

Django ModelForms to the rescue!

8
Django ModelForm: a CSS Makeover

The Django admin interface provides a ready-made solution to the Create, Read, Update, and Delete operations. The idea is not that the Django admin interface is the only right way for your website to handle such operations, but rather that the chore of creating the same basic functionality is lifted off your shoulders. You can create the interface yourself for the kind of interface web developers find interesting, and leave the remaining chore to Django's admin interface. And Django's admin interface showcases ModelForm. We will be looking at the ModelForm that powers Django's admin interface, and at how we can add admin interface-like functionality wherever we want. In this chapter we will cover:

- Using ModelForm to get a "Hello, world!" ready-made form
- Styling ModelForm and giving a polished presentation
- Going under the hood and exploring additional customization
- ModelForm's limitations, where it is helpful, and where it is not
- Using CSS to take a raw initial appearance and give a visual transformation

Let's get started!

"Hello, world!" in ModelForm

Our application as it stands only allows Entities and Locations to be created from the Django admin interface. This may not be a problem. For some companies, it may make sense for one person or group of persons to shoulder that responsibility, while allowing "the rest of us" to keep the details of pages up to date.

However, some organizations may not want tiered update abilities. If the Entity model is used for anything employees want to keep track of, an organization may decide, "Secretaries do not need written pre-authorization from the CEO to order pencils." Without giving full admin interface privileges to all users, let's explore how we can use ModelForm to give the same kind of interface to let users add Entities and Locations. In some ways this interface may actually be nicer for creating a new user from scratch. Our in-place edit system works very gracefully for in-place, piecemeal editing, but if you want to specify most available fields, an old-fashioned form may be the best solution.

We start by making a ModelForm that in the Django documentation is said to "inherit" from our model. "Inherit" does not literally mean object-oriented inheritance, but describes something analogous. In our `models.py` file, we define two additional classes that in object-oriented fashion inherit from ModelForm, and in the ModelForm sense "inherit" from `Entity` and `Location` respectively. (If we have not done so, we add the appropriate `import` at the top.)

```
import django.forms

class EntityForm(django.forms.ModelForm):
    class Meta:
        model = Entity

class LocationForm(django.forms.ModelForm):
    class Meta:
        model = Location
```

Next we add views that check if a form has been submitted, and if it is valid, saves it. Then it populates a `RequestContext` and renders it to a response:

```
@login_required
def modelform_Entity(request):
    if request.method == u'POST':
        form = directory.models.EntityForm(request.POST)
        if form.is_valid():
            form.save()
    else:
        form = directory.models.EntityForm()
    variables = RequestContext(request,
        {
        u'form': form,
        u'title': u'Entity',
        })
    return render_to_response(u'modelform.html', variables)
```

```python
@login_required
def modelform_Location(request):
    if request.method == u'POST':
        form = directory.models.LocationForm(request.POST)
        if form.is_valid():
            form.save()
    else:
        form = directory.models.LocationForm()
    variables = RequestContext(request,
        {
        u'form': form,
        u'title': u'Location',
        })
    return render_to_response(u'modelform.html', variables)
```

We add entries to the `urlconf` in `urls.py` to create the models:

```
(ur'^create/Entity', views.modelform_Entity),
(ur'^create/Location', views.modelform_Location),
```

Lastly, we create a template, `modelform.html`, which will wrap the table contents provided:

```
{% extends "base.html" %}
{% block head_title %}{{ title }}{% endblock head_title %}
{% block body_header_title %}<h1>{{ title }}</h1>
{% endblock body_header_title %}
{% block body_main %}
<form action="" method="POST">
    <table>
        {{ form }}
        <tr>
            <th> </th>
            <td><input type="submit" /></td>
        </tr>
    </table>
</form>
{% endblock body_main %}
```

We can visit `http://127.0.0.1:8000/create/Entity`; this will bring up the following page:

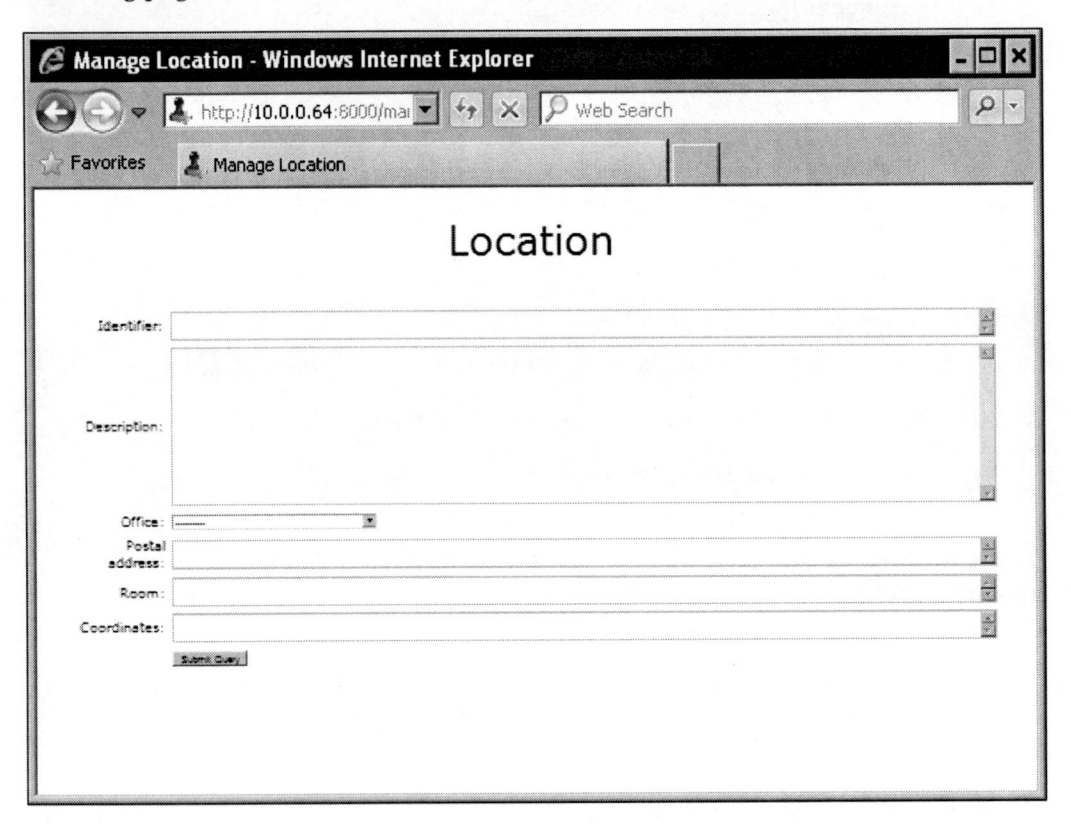

And now a logged-in user can create new Entities and Locations. We have achieved "Hello, world!" levels of functionality.

Expanding and customizing the example

As it stands now, our "Hello, world!" functionality works to create new Entities and Locations, but it does not provide the ability to look up an already-existing Entity or Location. Let's begin by updating the `urlpatterns` in `urls.py`. We change "create" to "manage", because part of "best practices" is to have well-chosen names, and while "create" accurately describes the link above, "manage" describes its broader ambit now. Though this is not necessary on a test system that no real users have seen, we should also perform any and all redirects so that any URL we have advertised ends up in the right place. Users should never visit a link you have sent them to before, and get an error page.

First, we update `urls.py` and replace the `create/Entity` and `create/Location` lines. We choose to be forgiving of a trailing slash left out, although a URL such as http://example.com/manage/Entity/12 would be slightly better to advertise than a URL like http://example.com/manage/Entity12. We enclose some of the information in parentheses so it can be sent as an argument to the views that deal with them.

```
(ur'^(create/Entity)', views.redirect),
(ur'^(create/Location)', views.redirect),
(ur'^manage/Entity/?(\d*)', views.modelform_Entity),
(ur'^manage/Location/?(\d*)', views.modelform_Location),
```

In `views.py`, we update the include section:

```
from django.http import HttpResponse, HttpResponseRedirect,
HttpResponsePermanentRedirect
```

Then we create a redirect view that permanently redirects the two URLs we want to redirect, and by default temporarily redirects to the homepage for anything else:

```
def redirect(request, original_url):
    if original_url == u'create/Entity':
        return HttpResponsePermanentRedirect(u'/manage/Entity')
    elif original_url == u'create/Location':
        return HttpResponsePermanentRedirect(u'/manage/Location')
    else:
        return HttpResponseRedirect(u'/')
```

We update `modelform_Entity()` and `modelform_Location()` to try and look an item up by integer primary key:

```
def modelform_Entity(request, id):
    if request.method == u'POST':
        form = directory.models.EntityForm(request.POST)
        if form.is_valid():
            form.save()
    else:
        try:
            form = directory.models.EntityForm(instance =
                directory.models.Entity.objects.get(pk = int(id)))
        except:
            form = directory.models.EntityForm()
    variables = RequestContext(request,
        {
        u'form': form,
        u'title': u'Entity',
        })
    return render_to_response(u'modelform.html', variables)
```

```
def modelform_Location(request, id):
    if request.method == u'POST':
        form = directory.models.LocationForm(request.POST)
        if form.is_valid():
            form.save()
    else:
        try:
            form = directory.models.LocationForm(instance =
                directory.models.Location.objects.get(pk = int(id)))
        except:
            form = directory.models.LocationForm()
    variables = RequestContext(request,
        {
        u'form': form,
        u'title': u'Location',
        })
    return render_to_response(u'modelform.html', variables)
```

We also clarify the template's title:

```
{% block head_title %}Manage {{ title }}{% endblock head_title %}
```

Customizing ModelForm pages' appearance

In order to observe the zero-one-infinity rule (either you don't allow something at all, or you allow at most one, or you allow as many as available resources support), we have used TEXT based, instead of VARCHAR based, fields. When you have a TEXT based field, Django assumes that you want the data to be large, and so it uses a textarea instead of a text input.

Before going further, I would like to address one question: why so much effort to compensate for Django's using a textarea here? The answer, in short, is that we are looking at a positive skill that is an asset to Ajax developers. Saying "There is no 'CSS' in 'Asynchronous JavaScript and XML,'" is somewhat like saying, "There is no 'JSON' in 'Asynchronous JavaScript and XML.'" It is true in a legalistic sense, but an Ajax developer who needs someone else to handle JSON has a liability and an Ajax developer who needs someone else to handle CSS is at a marked professional disadvantage. We take a lemon served to us by Django, namely that when you specify a TEXT database field Django hears a TEXTAREA in generated HTML, and see how far we can go to make lemonade from this lemon. The overall transformation is meant to broaden the list of bases covered and strengths this book developed it, and it does not stop at all, nor should it, once CSS rules are in place to address initially unwieldy TEXTAREA height. The intent is to provide a progressive transformation such as Edward Tufte offers in his now classic books such as *Envisioning Information*, and make the best of a good opportunity.

Django hearing TEXTAREA if you say TEXT means, for our models, that the forms use up more vertical space than they need to. We will use CSS to do much more than address just this issue. The page is marked up semantically while leaving any custom styling to the developers.

CSS styling does not have a direct way to specify how many rows or columns a `textarea` has—instead, `width` and `height` may be set. There are several units one can use; the best practice scales up or down if people change the font size. The `em` unit is one that is proportional to the font size, and if one is specifying a size, use `em` in preference to `px`/`pt`/`in`/`cm`. Also, depending on what HTML element you are using, a percentage based off that element may be calculated, browser-dependent, on the element's native size or on something else. Style an `h2` to be 80% tall and some browsers will give 80% of the base size of an unstyled `h2`, but still larger than unstyled text, while other browsers will give 80% of the size of unstyled text, meaning an `h2` that is smaller than both an unstyled `h2` and unstyled text. Specifying a value in `em`, like `1.5em` or `2em`, both avoids the accessibility issues of `px`/`pt`/`in`/`cm`, and mitigates against certain cross-browser headaches.

Before we start styling, our page looks like:

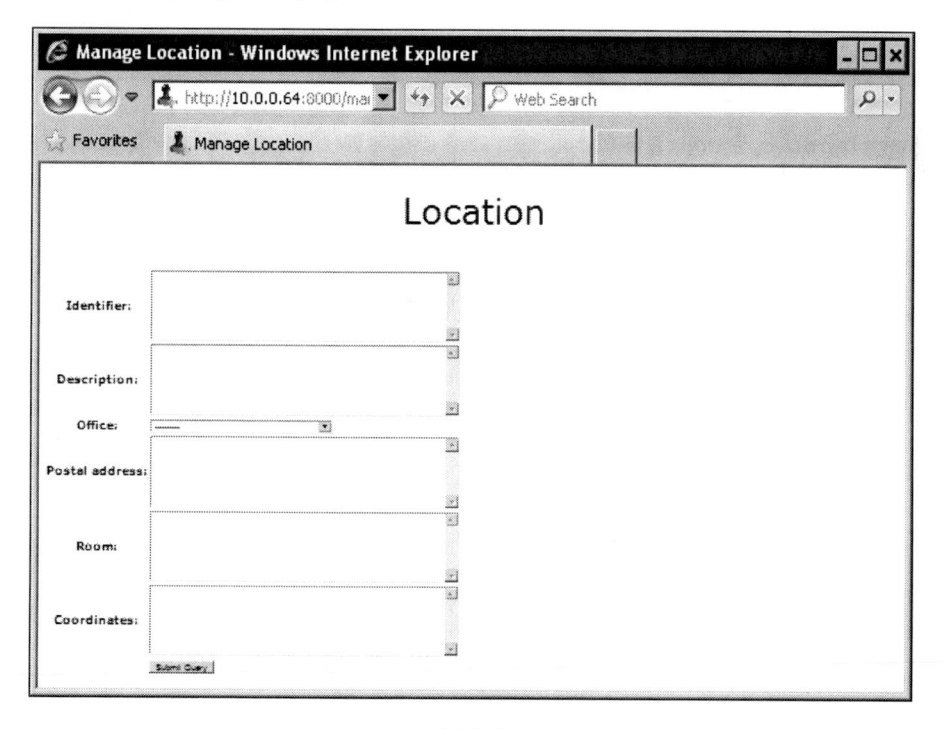

Let's start styling:

```
textarea
    {
    height: 1.5em;
    }
```

This lets much more fit on a single page as shown in the following:

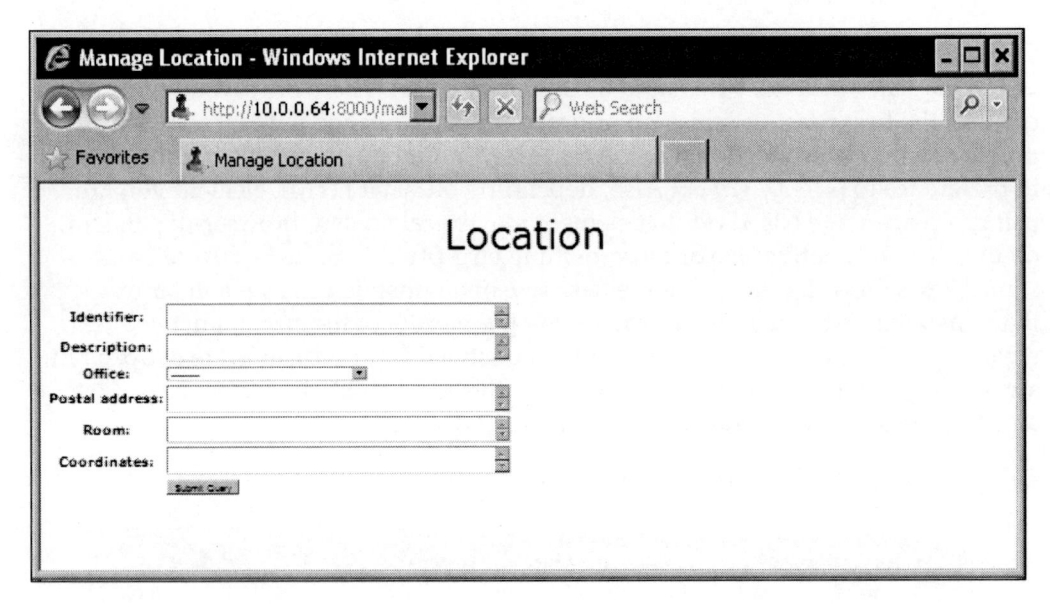

On a large monitor, there's a lot of screen real estate to the right of the text fields that isn't being used. Let's change that:

```
{% block head_css_page %}
<style type="text/css">
<!--

table
    {
    width: 99.9%;
    }

td
    {
    width: 99.9%;
    }

textarea
    {
```

[172]

```
     height: 1.5em;
     width: 99.9%;
     }

// -->
</style>
{% endblock head_css_page %}
```

In some browsers' default settings, `textarea` elements have a fixed-width font. The best practice on usability and accessibility grounds is to have a proportional sans-serif font; Verdana is a recommended choice ("Therefore, from a usability perspective, *the clear winner is Verdana*," `http://www.theinternetdigest.net/archive/websafefonts.html`). This is common practice because it is a best practice, and not perceived as a best practice because it is a common practice. If we update the `textarea` style:

```
textarea
    {
    font-family: Verdana, Arial, sans;
    height: 1.5em;
    width: 100%;
    }
```

It would appear different in Firefox, going to:

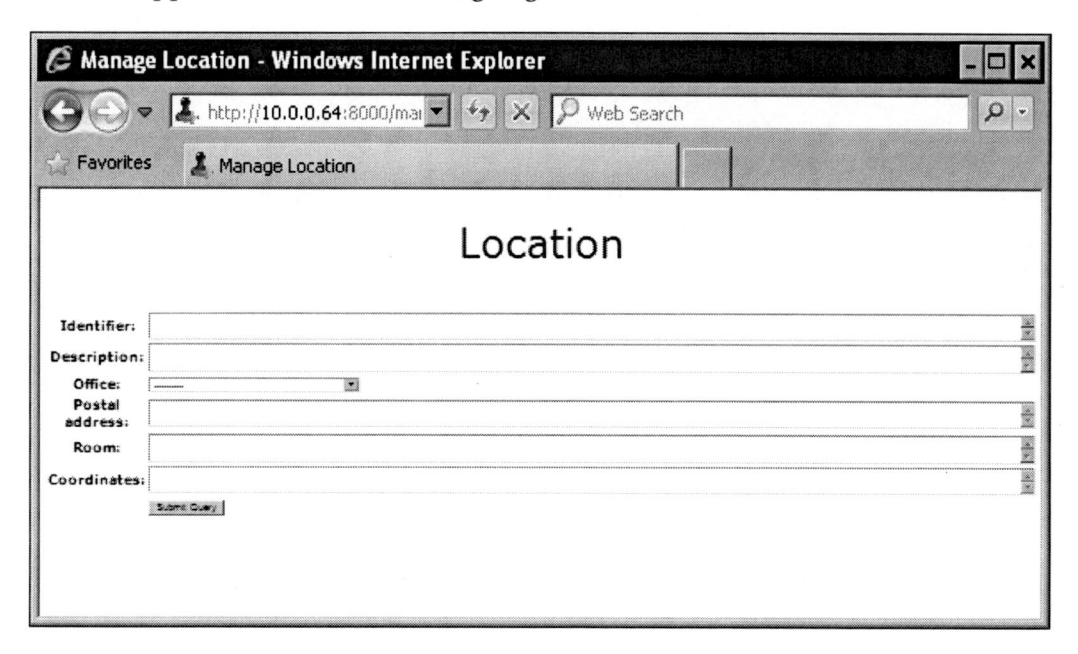

We add margins to the body to improve the effect at the right of the screen in particular:

```
body
    {
    padding-left: 40px;
    padding-right: 40px;
    }
```

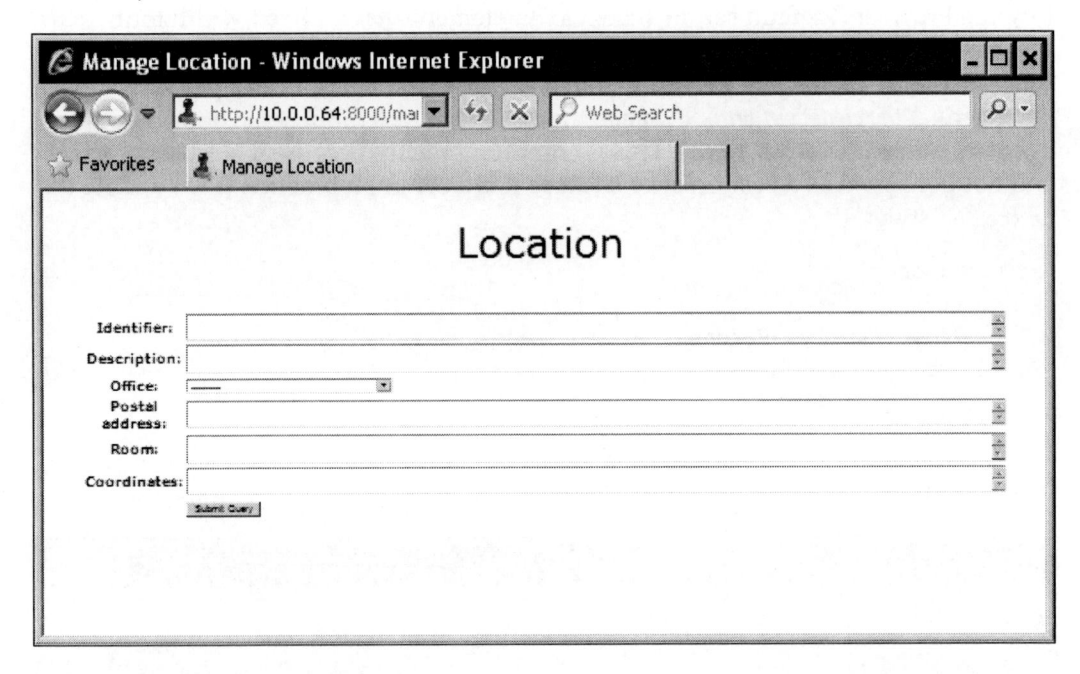

And we specify a `text-align` of `right`, instead of `center`, for the `th` elements Django ModelForm uses for labels. A `text-align` of `left` would also be an improvement, but not quite the same:

```
th
    {
    text-align: right;
    }
```

We now have a page that looks like the following:

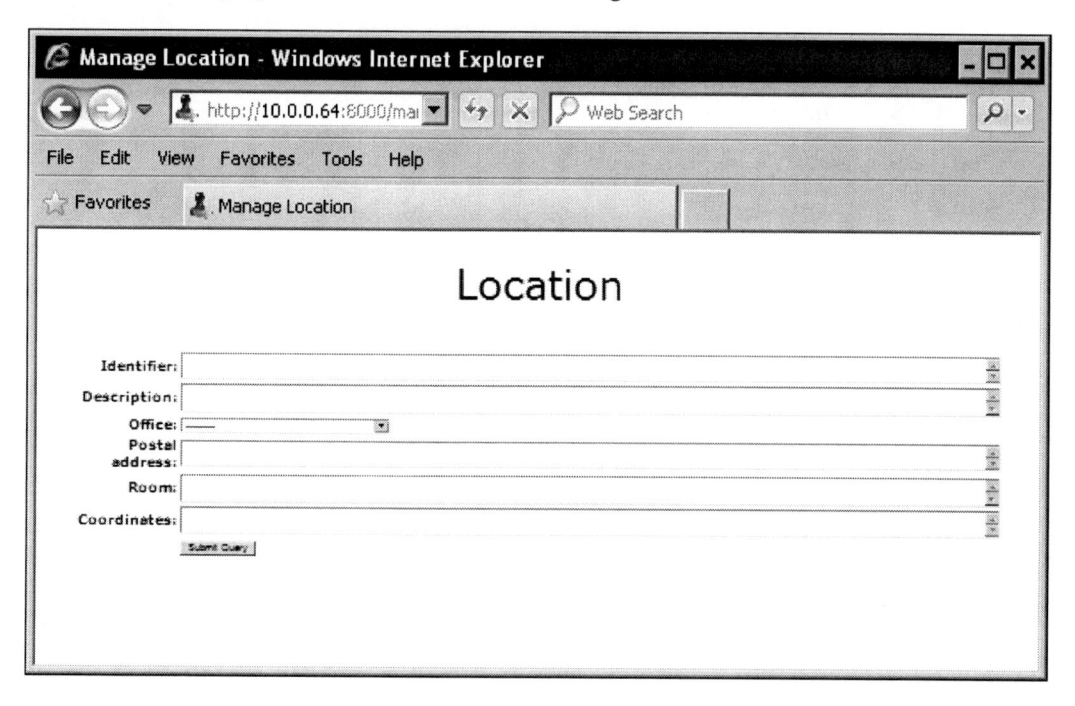

Now, there may be some fields that we want to be a bit longer: the **Description**, unlike the **Identifier** for instance, may be much longer than some other fields will normally be. The textarea elements have HTML IDs like id_description, so we can override that element's height:

```
textarea#id_description
    {
    height: 10em;
    }
```

This gives more screen real estate to the **Description**:

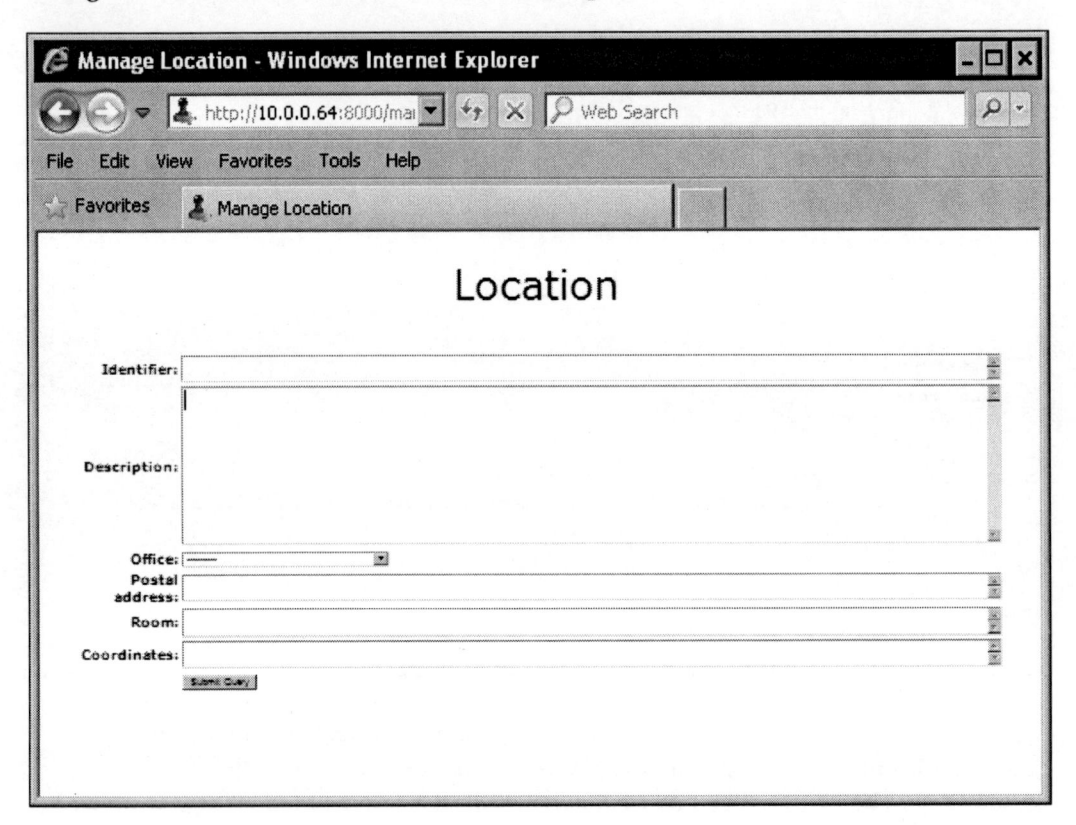

Right now we have bold for visual emphasis, but this is in the wrong place. Especially if people are going to use the form again and again, we should not draw their eyes to the labels, where the bold emphasis is now, but to the text that is input. Bold labels are standard practice, but whether this is the most usable standard practice is what is being disputed.

```
th
    {
    font-style: normal;
    font-weight: normal;
    text-align: right;
    }

textarea
    {
    font-family: Verdana, Arial, sans;
```

```
font-weight: bold;
height: 1.5em;
width: 100%;
}
```

There's a noticeable difference, but at this size the text in the `textarea` may be hard to read:

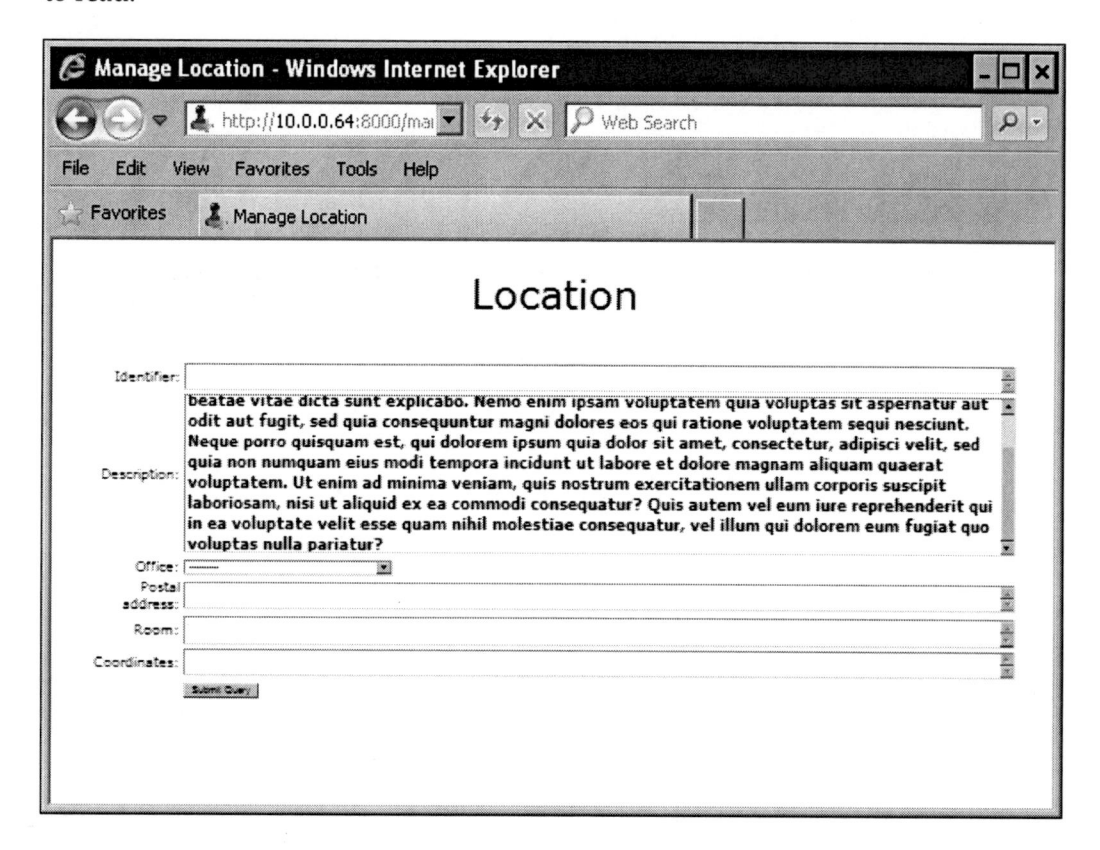

We can address this problem, and make the page easier to read, by slightly increasing the font size:

```
textarea
    {
    font-family: Verdana, Arial, sans;
    font-size: larger;
    font-weight: bold;
    height: 1.5em;
    width: 100%;
    }
```

This makes text in the `textarea` easier to read.

The borders are slightly more forceful than we need; a light touch would help:

```
textarea
    {
    border: 1px solid silver;
    font-family: Verdana, Arial, sans;
    font-size: larger;
    font-weight: bold;
    height: 1.5em;
    width: 100%;
    }
```

Now they are less of a distraction:

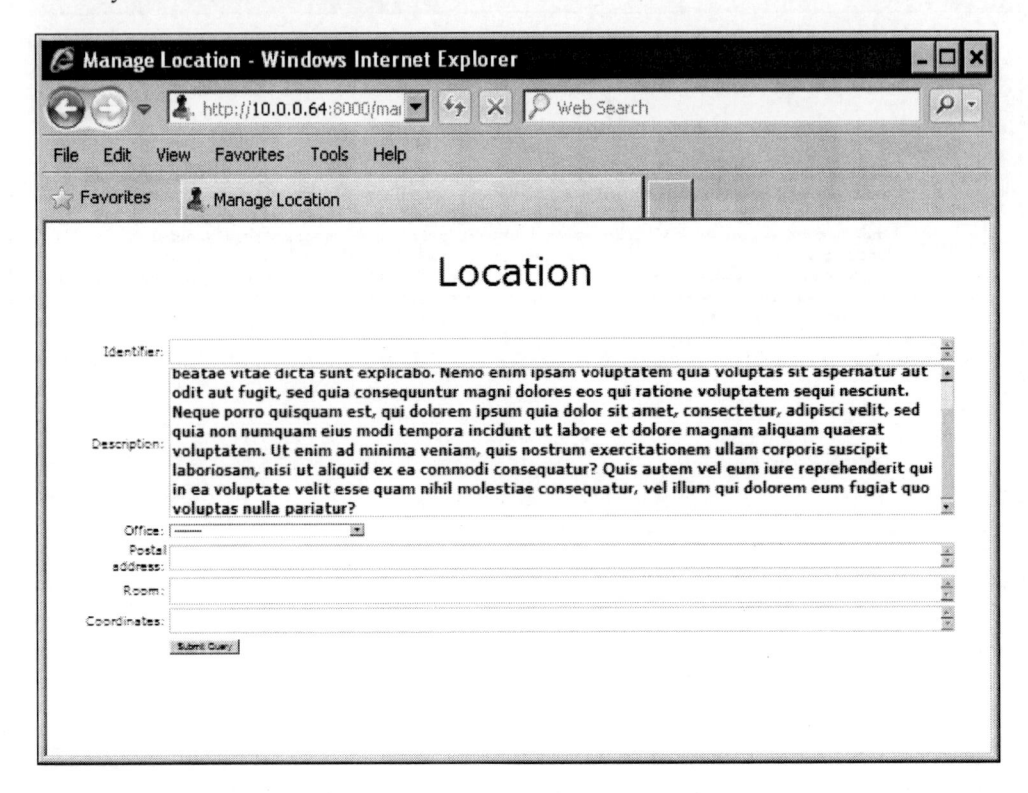

Now we will pay attention to the text `input` elements, which are as yet unstyled. For this form we could achieve comparable styling with CSS, as the page source shows what the HTML ID is for our text `input`, but this means that the solution is more brittle. Right now we have one template that works for both Entities and Locations, and we would ideally build open-ended functionality so that our solution works correctly for future expansion.

jQuery can do things that are CSS-like that CSS itself does not do very well, or rather that the top tier of CSS3 handles perfectly but which should not be relied on as available in CSS implementations for visitors' browsers, such as specify styles for all `input` elements of type `text`. And so, instead of hardcoding HTML ID's in the page-specific CSS, we will define a CSS class to apply to all text inputs:

```
input.text
    {
    border: 1px solid silver;
    font-size: larger;
    font-weight: bold;
    height: 1.5em;
    width: 100%;
    }
```

Then we use jQuery to apply that class to inputs of `type text`:

```
<script language="JavaScript" type="text/javascript">
<!--

    $("input:text").addClass("text");

// -->
</script>
```

One nicety to have is zebra striping. Slight visual emphasis helps prevent rows from blending and visually bleeding into each other. We define `even` and `odd` styles, although `even` is empty:

```
.even
    {
    }
.odd
    {
    background-color: #eeeeee;
    }
```

Then we run into one of the quirks of zero-based and one-based indices running into each other, namely, jQuery counts even and odd rows from zero rather than one, so the first row is even, the second row is odd, and so on. To remedy this behavior, we do a crossover in registering the styles in the JavaScript:

```
        $("tr:even").addClass("odd");
        $("tr:odd").addClass("even");
```

And now we have the following page:

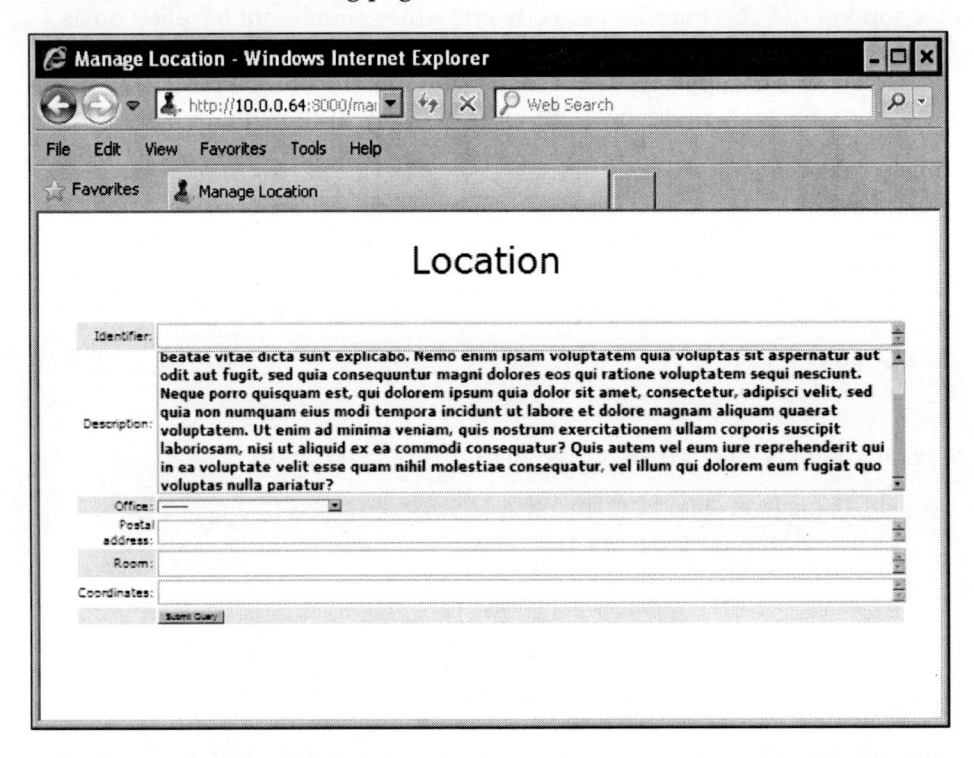

It would be nice to have muted zebra striping for the `textarea` elements and text `input` elements. So we define empty hooks for further CSS development so that maintainers will see what they need to customize and override even if we do nothing with it before maintainers have to deal with it:

```
.odd input
    {
    }
.odd textarea
    {
    }
.odd input
    {
    background-color: #f4f4f4;
    }
.odd textarea
    {
    background-color: #f4f4f4;
    }
```

There is a slight break visually between the table cells. This sort of thing is not enough to necessarily be noticed, but subtly distract people. We set the `table` element's `border-spacing` property to zero, and slightly pad `th` and `td`:

```
table
    {
    border-spacing: 0;
    width: 100%;
    }

td
    {
    padding: 4px;
    width: 100%;
    }

th
    {
    padding: 4px;
    font-style: normal;
    font-weight: normal;
    text-align: right;
    }
```

And that has taken us from an initial, unstyled appearance as shown:

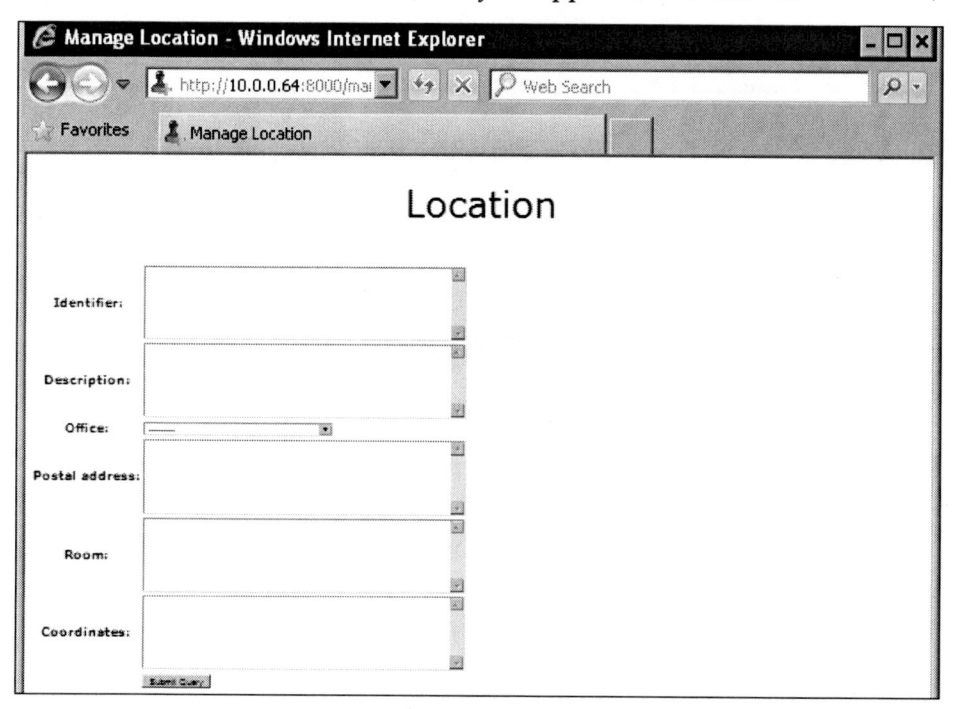

To a final result that can be seen and appreciated:

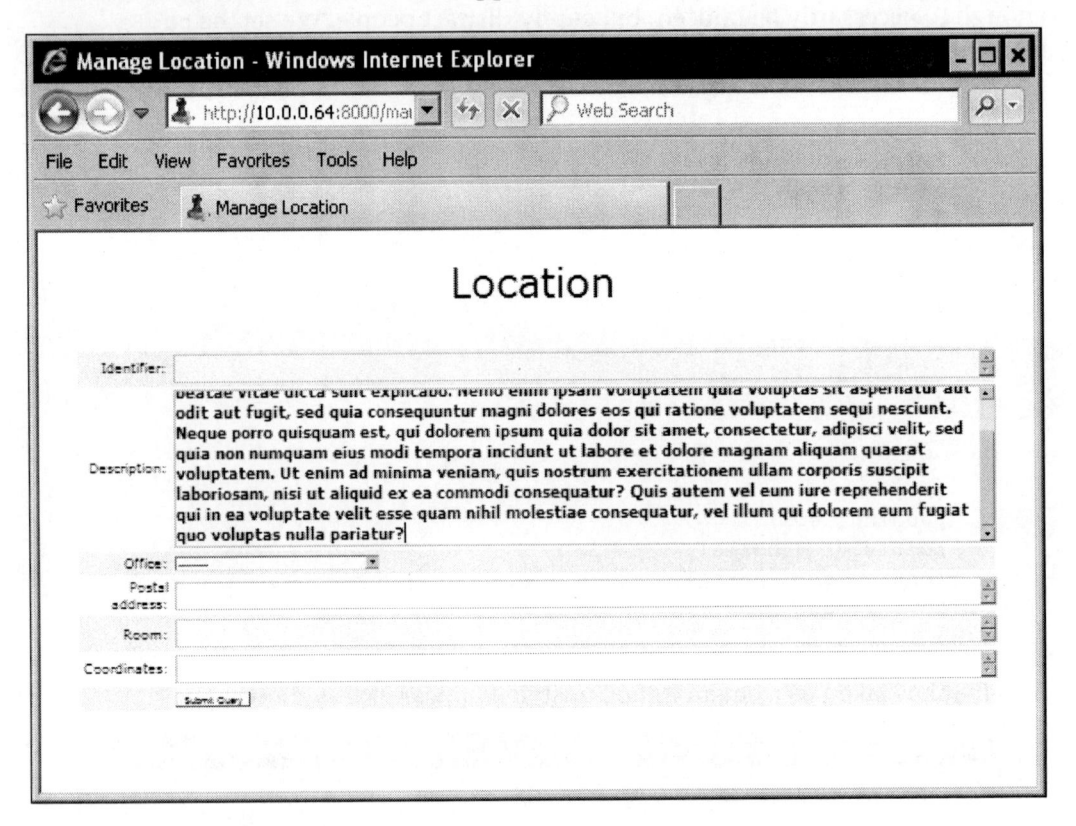

The interested reader who wants to know where the ideas came from is encouraged to read the works of Edward Tufte; *Envisioning Information* is a salient starting point. The makeover here is largely an imitation of the kind of makeover he fleshes out in his texts.

Going under ModelForm's hood

Django ModelForm is intended to allow a ready-made form, and its markup, to be easily styled. However, it is also intended to allow more server-side control if you want. We will leave our CSS and jQuery styling as they are, and go under the hood to customize the control.

You may or may not want all available fields to show up. Django supports both "opt-out" and "opt-in" approaches. Theoretically, one could use both, although it is not clear what kind of use case would make that desirable. Our Entity model has `active`, `department`, `description`, `image`, `homepage`, `honorifics`, `name`, `post_nominals`, `phone`, `publish_externally`, and `reports_to` fields. If we wished to allow anything but the homepage and image to be set, we could "opt-out" by setting:

```
class EntityForm(django.forms.ModelForm):
    class Meta:
        model = Entity
        exclude = (u'homepage', u'image')
```

Or we could "opt-in" by setting:

```
class EntityForm(django.forms.ModelForm):
    class Meta:
        model = Entity
        fields = (u'active', u'department', u'description', u'image',
                  u'homepage', u'honorifics', u'name',
                  u'post_nominals', u'phone', u'publish_externally',
                  u'reports_to')
```

By default, ModelForm displays fields in the order they were declared on the model. This usually has room for improvement. The best order for programmers to see is for code maintainability, and the best order for users to see will rarely be the same. We can use the "opt-in" approach, but specify another order to rearrange the fields:

```
class EntityForm(django.forms.ModelForm):
    class Meta:
        model = Entity
        fields = (u'name', u'honorifics', u'post_nominals',
                  u'description', u'homepage', u'phone',
                  u'department', u'reports_to', u'active',
                  u'publish_externally')
```

This rearranges the fields in a way that may make more sense than our alphabetical-like order.

The Django documentation tells of a number of other things one can do, such as customize how the data is cleaned, effectively having several forms on the same page, and so on. But we would best pause to listen to a "stupid" question.

An excellent "stupid" question: where's the e-mail slot?

You may have looked at the screenshots and asked, "Aren't Entities allowed to have e-mail addresses? I see phone numbers and a space for a homepage, but I don't see an e-mail address on the form." And that is a point worth pausing on.

The design decision was made to allow unlimited e-mail addresses, and, for purposes of illustration, only one homepage and/or phone. (For production purposes, only listing one phone number is a design flaw. It would be better to allow unlimited URLs and phone numbers, which can be done in the same basic way we allowed unlimited e-mail addresses.) The implementation, which we worked to seamlessly hide in our regular editing page, is that e-mail addresses are stored in their own models, which have a foreign key to an Entity. (Statuses are also handled that way, although we have not presently integrated them into the user interface.) Logically, the e-mails belong to the Entities, but the implementation is something like a legal fiction. E-mails are not fields on the Entities and the ModelForm has no way of knowing what the e-mail addresses (and, for production readiness, URLs and phone numbers, the latter of which should be stored with a description) are from the user's perspective.

We could change this behavior by allowing at most one e-mail address, which would allow e-mail to be handled gracefully by ModelForm. However, this would be a bad case of the tail wagging the dog. The question we should be answering is not "What can we do to best support implementation concerns?" but "What can we do to best support user needs?" (A clean, easy implementation is *usually* preferable to a hairy or involved implementation, but a hairy or involved implementation that serves user needs well is *always* preferable to a clean, easy implementation that serves user needs badly.)

And this means that ModelForm may not be the right solution for creating Entities. (But the solution we have developed works gracefully and appropriately for Locations.)

What we need to do for Entities is simply to create an **Add New** link. Let's add one at the top-right of both the **Search** and **Profile** pages. To do that, we update the beginning of `profile()` in `views.py`:

```
@login_required
def profile(request, id):
    if id == "new":
        entity = directory.models.Entity()
        entity.save()
        id = entity.id
```

```
        else:
            entity = directory.models.Entity.objects.get(pk = int(id))
            emails = directory.models.EntityEmail.objects.filter(
                              entity__exact = id).all()
```

We insert, just before the previous profile line in `views.py` the following:

```
(ur'^profile/(new)$', views.profile),
```

In this specific case we could place it anywhere on the list, but in some cases order matters because the first pattern that successfully matches a request is the one that is called.

Now we update the `base.html` template to have a hook for adding things at the top of the `body` tag:

```
{% block body %}<body>
        {% block body_preamble_site %}
        {% endblock body_preamble_site %}
        {% block body_preamble_section %}
        {% endblock body_preamble_section %}
        {% block body_preamble_page %}
        {% endblock body_preamble_page %}
```

We would like this **Add New** feature to be available both from the main search page and from profile pages. Right now both of these inherit directly from `base.html`. We will create an intervening template, `main.html`, which will include the link `main.html` has:

```
{% extends "base.html" %}
{% block body_preamble_section %}
<ul class="standard_links">
<li href="/profile/new">Add New</li>
</ul>
{% endblock body_preamble_section %}
```

We change `search.html` and `profile.html` to extend `main.html` rather than `base.html` directly:

```
{% extends "main.html" %}
```

We also add styling to `static/css/style.css`:

```
div.standard_links
    {
    font-weight: bold;
    margin-right: 15px;
    margin-top: 15px;
    text-align: right;
    }
```

This places a simple, nicely styled link at the top-right of the **Search** and **Profile** page. The **Search** page now looks like this:

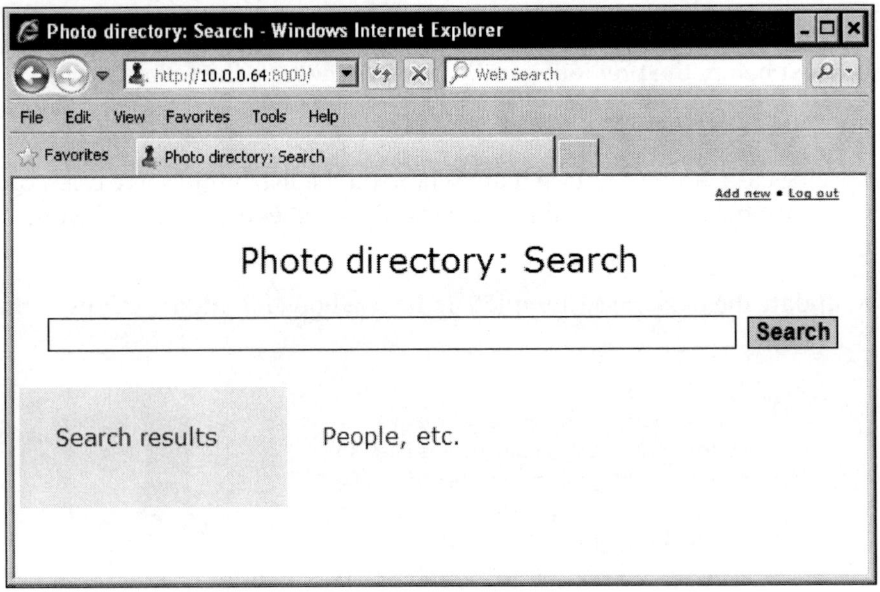
Photo directory: Search - Windows Internet Explorer
http://10.0.0.64:8000/
Web Search
File Edit View Favorites Tools Help
Favorites
Photo directory: Search
Add new • Log out
Photo directory: Search
Search
Search results
People, etc.

Following this link lets the user edit a new Entity, as shown:

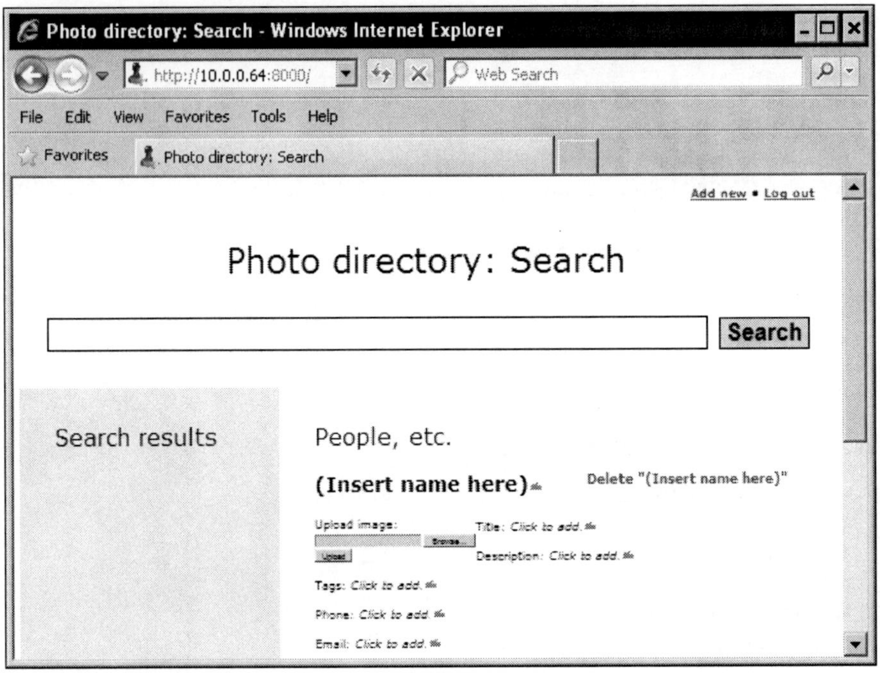
Photo directory: Search - Windows Internet Explorer
http://10.0.0.64:8000/
Web Search
File Edit View Favorites Tools Help
Favorites
Photo directory: Search
Add new • Log out
Photo directory: Search
Search
Search results
People, etc.
(Insert name here)
Delete "(Insert name here)"

Summary

Django ModelForm is very easy to use. If you have a model and want to let people edit its fields, without doing all the legwork of implementing things from scratch yourself, ModelForm lets you "cut to the chase," developing your own interfaces for the really interesting parts of your application, and falling back to ModelForm for the less interesting parts, particularly if you want to allow some of the Django admin interface functionality without having people in the admin interface itself. The markup it produces is good, semantic markup, and it is easily styled and customized in appearance. You can go under the hood and further customize what happens before it outputs the markup.

However, it is also limited: it seems not to offer a graceful way to handle cases like our e-mail address where we have used standard techniques to associate an unlimited number of e-mail addresses with one Entity. It would be possible to make a ModelForm page for Entities and another one for the e-mail address model, but the resulting implementation would be confusing to users, who can and should think of e-mail addresses as just one more piece of data you fill out for a person or department.

In this chapter, we have covered all the basics to get a "Hello, world!" ModelForm up and running. We have looked at how to take advantage of ModelForm's good markup to customize and style the appearance of the page to be easier and more powerful to use. We have explored the beginning of poking around under the hood to customize appearance. We have seen ModelForm's limitations, when to use it, and when it is not the best choice (because it does not handle some legal fictions gracefully). And in all this we have made a visual transformation by a CSS makeover.

Let's move on to database and search handling. Let's go!

9
Database and Search Handling

One early paradox that was discovered in the initial Web 2.0 buzz was that trying to be proactive and be more responsive by being prepared ahead of time ended up making applications *less* responsive, not more. The initial expectation that partial page updates would make more responsive applications met with a surprise when programmers made applications more like a desktop application and, initially at least, less responsive. The recommended best practice now is to be as lazy as possible.

In this chapter, we will:

- Start with a solution that demonstrates the easy AHAH (Asynchronous HTTP And HTML) technique, and plays to Django's strengths
- Demonstrate "graceful degradation" that allows our application to serve up read-only access with JavaScript turned off

Simply put, we will explore a solution with the responsiveness of an "as lazy as possible" solution. Behind the scenes, we will show how that solution showcases Django strengths.

Moving forward to an AHAH solution

Let's start with a "fewer moving parts" solution that will play to Django's strengths reasonably well. We will move on to a more in-depth solution, but some have said, "Every complex system that works is found to have evolved from a simple system that works," and we can make a relatively simple system that works well before we start trying to push the envelope of what the system can do.

Part of "graceful degradation" means making a solution that works without JavaScript. In our case we will make a modest goal of "read-only" functionality accommodated without JavaScript; that is, we will not be attempting graceful degradation that can update the data without JavaScript on. That job can be done with the Django admin interface, by registering all relevant models as editable, and adding a link, possibly enclosed in `<noscript>` tags, to update the database. While our directory is intended to be easily updated, the main use is read only.

For purposes of illustration, in previous chapters we required an Ajax login before the user could see any data. Now we will attempt a more user-friendly, and realistic, approach in which users may search and see profiles without logging in, but must log in to do anything that makes a change to the data. For organizations that do not want all users to be able to change any data, this offers a slightly finer granularity of access, by creating accounts *only* for people who should be allowed to make changes to the database. Others will have full-fledged access to search and view profiles; they just won't be able to make changes.

We are also updating the model/database schema by making expanded internal use of Entities to serve as Locations. That is, Locations are no longer their own Model; their work is now done by Entities.

When the user first loads the screen, it should look like the following:

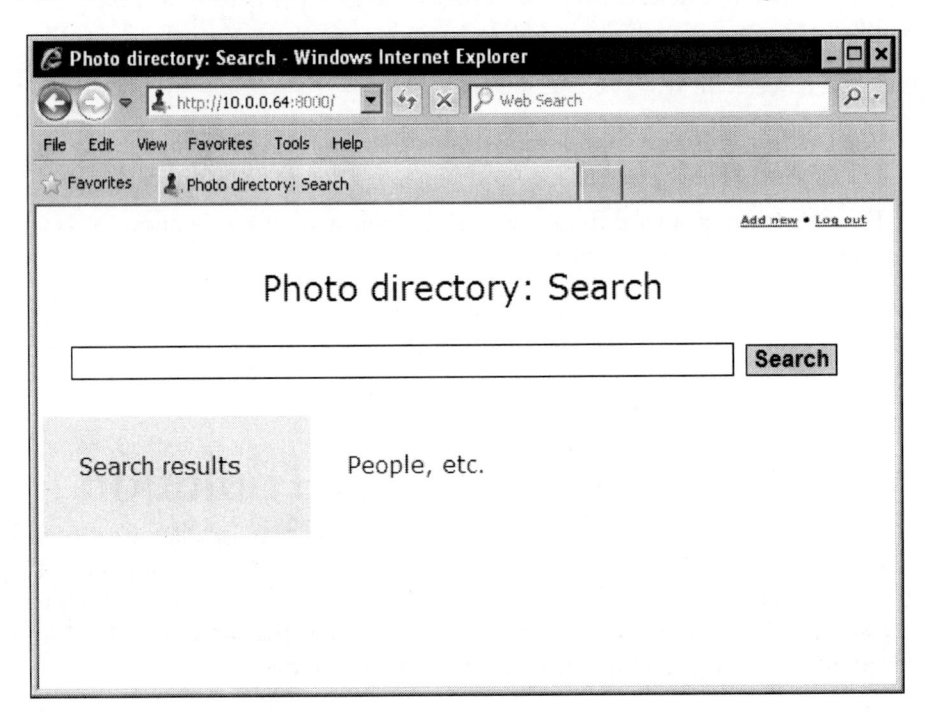

When the user has searched and loaded a profile, it should look like the following:

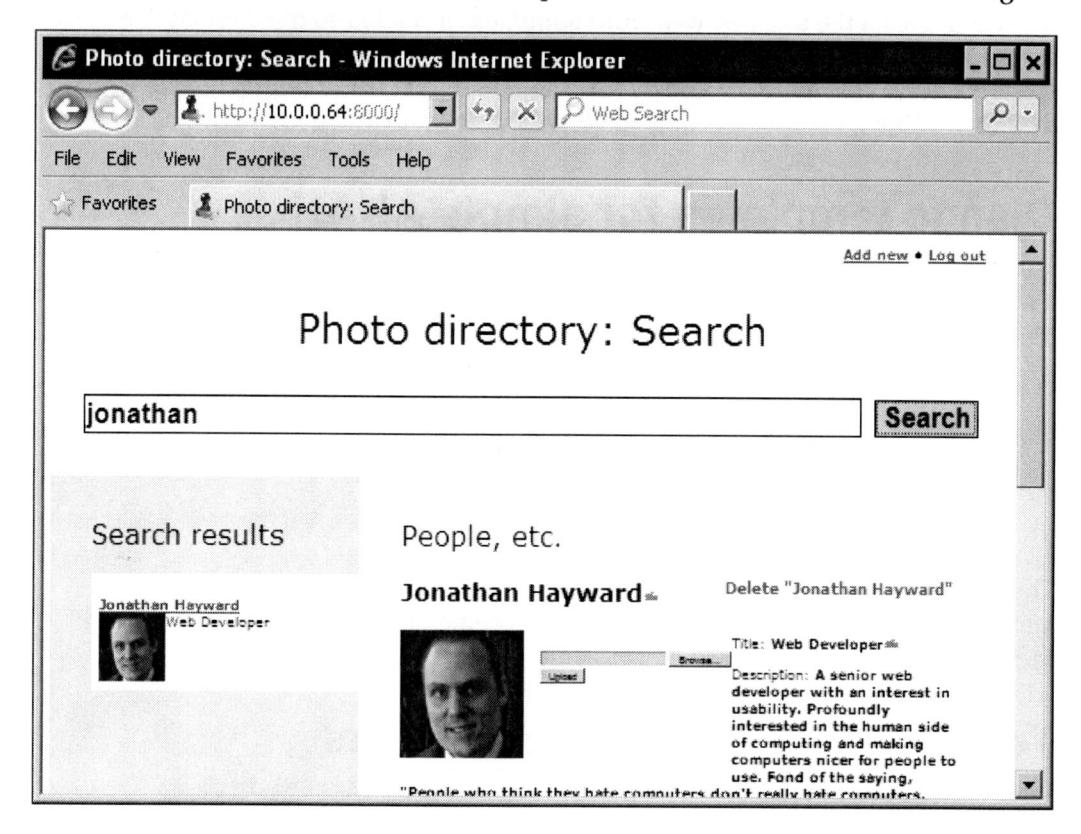

In both cases, the user's attention is drawn to three different areas of the page, each doing a different job. On a live computer, the left **Search results** area is a light blue, and the right **People, etc.** area is a light yellow. One accessibility note is to avoid using color to be the only way a piece of information is delivered, but we are following this guideline in what we are doing here because we are using color to offer additional emphasis to information that is delivered elsewhere. The bold red "✗", which could be replaced by a sprite in a production application for greater compatibility with Internet Explorer, is still a bold "✗" to the colorblind, and the light blue and light yellow differ slightly in value.

Non-colorblind designers wishing to see how something looks to the colorblind, may visit the web page filter at `http://colorfilter.wickline.org/`. In this case, one would expect people with different forms of colorblindness to perceive the slightly different values for the yellow and blue areas as slightly different shades of gray, if not slightly different colors. But even then, their job is to provide an additional underscore that says "Here on the left is one area of the screen doing one job, and here on the right is another area of the screen doing another job."

The breakdown we will use to accomplish this will be one parent template that hosts the search box at the top, and two child templates: a sidebar to the left that lists search results, and a larger template to the right that drills down to the details of one specific Entity. This interface allows users to retain their list of search results while they look at the specific result they have drilled down to at the moment.

Django templates for simple AHAH

"AHAH", or "Asynchronous HTML and HTTP", might be called Ajax lite and is a clean, lightweight variant of Ajax that fetches chunks of HTML and does not include intricate, surgical DOM manipulations.

We will be making three templates:

- A parent template for the whole page
- A template for search results
- A template to drill down to a specific result

The whole page template will be in `search.html` with the search results template in `search_internal.html` and the profile drill down template in `profile_internal.html`.

Templating for a list of search results

The **Search results** sidebar to the left, stored in `search_internal.html` is:

```
<h2>Search results</h2>
```

We also add to the CSS, to prevent wrapping in the middle of the h2 tags, which we never intend to wrap:

```
h2
    {
    white-space: nowrap;
    }
```

In addition, the perceptive reader may notice that this does not begin by extending `base.html`, or any other template. The reason for this is the template named `search_internal.html`, is a template to render *partial* web pages, and `base.html` is a template to render *whole* web pages. For what we are doing, we don't want a `header`, or a second `body` tag, or various other elements. Partial web page templates will be named `*_internal.html` and will not need to be based on `base.html`.

```
{% if first_portion %}
```

The view that will be using this template will hand it two, possibly empty, lists: `first_portion` and `second_portion`. In lieu of a full paging system, we will display a limited number of results, ten by default and like several other features configurable in the beginning of `settings.py`, and make an Ajax link to show the rest.

In addition, we will make an Ajax feature: when the user "mouses over" a search result, that profile is loaded. This makes for faster, lighter browsing, although old-fashioned clicking on links still works.

If the first portion is nonempty, that is, if the search turned up any results, the template loops through results and populates the query.

```
{% for result in first_portion %}

    <div class="search_result"
      onmouseover="PHOTO_DIRECTORY.load_profile(
                                   {{ result.id }});">
```

The following link is a classic example of a Hijaxed link. There is a link pointing to a URL, in this case RESTful, that quotes the query (escaped in the view), and the ID. The overall application will be designed so that loading that URL will render the desired page. Its `onclick` attribute is set to load the profile in the larger right pane for drilling down to individual results and returns `false` to prevent the default behavior. (One JavaScript gotcha is that you need to specifically return `false` to prevent the default behavior; you cannot return `0` or other "falsy" values and get the same result.)

There is another point to be made about URLs. Django is designed to flexibly allow the creation of attractive URLs like `http://example.com/2/test` where we have an effective URL of `http://example.com/?query=test&id=2`. And this is a carefully chosen feature, since users are more likely to bookmark the former than the latter. However, what we have chosen more directly correlates to "graceful degradation" form submission, and is more straightforward, especially in the case of queries containing characters that would need escaping. If you think you can improve on the "graceful degradation" URL handling, especially in a way that showcases one of Django's deliberately chosen features, go for it.

```
<p><a href="/?query={{ query }}&id={{ result.id }}"
    onclick="PHOTO_DIRECTORY.load_profile({{ result.id }});
    return false;" >{{ result.name }}</a><br />
```

Database and Search Handling

We will cover the CSS later on. The image class, `search_results`, is used to float the remainder of the paragraph that is the Entity's `description`, around the image.

```
{% if result.image %}
    <img class="search_results"
        src="/profile/images/{{ result.id }}" />
{% endif %}
{% if result.title %}
    {{ result.title }}{% if result.department.name %}
                    ,<br />{% endif %}
{% endif %}
{{ result.department.name }}
</p>
</div>

{% endfor %}
```

Having looped through the first portion of the search results, we forestall user puzzlement when a search turns up no results, by explicitly treating them with a simple note telling them why they do not see search results:

```
{% else %}
    <p><em>There were no matches to your search.</em></p>
{% endif %}
```

If the second "overflow" portion is non-empty, we add a JavaScript link (here, one that does not degrade gracefully) to show the additional results, and open a `div` that will initially be hidden, but still deliver them. This means that there will be a very slightly longer initial download for the user, but if the **Show all** link is clicked, it should work immediately without requiring a network request.

```
{% if second_portion %}
    <a class="show_additional_results"
    href="JavaScript:show_additional('results')"
    ><span class="emphasized">+</span> Show all</a>
    <div id="additional_results">
```

Now we loop through the second portion, doing the same thing for each result as with the first:

```
{% for result in second_portion %}

    <div class="search_result"
      onmouseover="PHOTO_DIRECTORY.load_profile(
                                    {{ result.id }});">
    <p><a href="/?query={{ query }}&id={{ result.id }}"
```

[194]

```django
                onclick="PHOTO_DIRECTORY.load_profile({{ result.id }});
                    return false;">{{ result.name }}</a><br />
            {% if result.image %}
                <img class="search_results"
                    src="/profile/images/{{ result.id }}" />
            {% endif %}
            {% if result.title %}
                {{ result.title }}{% if result.department.name %}
                        ,<br />{% endif %}
            {% endif %}
            {{ result.department.name }}
            </p>
            </div>

    {% endfor %}
```

We close the initially hidden `div`, and that's it for the template:

```django
        </div>
    {% endif %}
```

Template for an individual profile

Now we will be looking at how we keep the right, "drilldown individual profile" pane up to date. It is possible to surgically update individual elements within the `div`, and our code supports this to some degree. Jeditable is intended to do just that with in-place edits. If we are going to spend a lot of time making a micro-optimized solution, the first choice response may be to replace as little of the page as possible.

However, there are distinct advantages to a "fewest moving parts" solution that simply replaces the "drilldown individual profile" with a fresh pane generated by the server. The generated pane can be generated in a way that more directly plays to Django's strengths. There are major advantages to debugging also, fewer moving parts means fewer places bugs can creep in, and fewer places for them to hide because when there is something wrong, it will often be more obviously wrong, and "more obviously wrong" is much easier to debug than "sometimes appears faintly wrong."

`profile_internal.html` contains the line:

```html
<h2>People, etc.</h2>
```

Database and Search Handling

There is a link, which will be styled, to delete an Entity so that the interface supports full Create, Read, Update, and Delete operations.

```
<div class="deletion">
<span class="delete" id="Entity_{{ id }}">
Delete {{ entity.name }}</span>
</div>
```

Here we have a container, in this case an h2, that is marked up for in-line editing with Jeditable (http://www.appelsiini.net/projects/jeditable), by adding the class edit. It follows the naming convention: "Entity" and then the field ("name"), and then the entity's ID:

```
<h3 id="Entity_name_{{ id }}" title="Click to edit."
class="edit">{{ entity.name }}</h3>
```

The div uses the ajaxFileUpload plugin (http://www.phpletter.com/Our-Projects/AjaxFileUpload/). It displays an image, if there is one, and provides an Ajax file-uploading facility. It depends on the ajaxFileUpload code further down.

```
<div class="image">
    <form id="image_upload" name="image_upload"
      action="/ajax/saveimage/{{ id }}" method="POST"
      enctype="multipart/form-data">
       {% if entity.image_mimetype %}
           <img class="profile" src="/profile/images/{{ id }}" />
       {% else %}
           <div id="image_slot"></div>
           Upload image:<br />
       {% endif %}
       <button class="button" id="upload"
          onclick="return ajaxFileUpload({{ id }});">Upload</button>
    </form>
</div>
```

Now, with slight variations, we will go to Jeditable-based fields, those having CSS class edit, edit_rightclick, or edit_textarea, interspersed with deletion fields (✘ is the symbol "✘") handled by our own Ajax. First comes the title and description:

```
<p>Title: <strong id="Entity_title_{{ id }}" title="Click to edit."
  class="edit">{{ entity.title }}</strong></p>
<p>Description: <strong id="Entity_description_{{ id }}"
  title="Click to edit." class="edit_textarea">
{{ entity.description }}</strong></p>
```

After that come several similar, not particularly **DRY (Don't Repeat Yourself,** a Django mantra) sections. We iterate through all existing telephone numbers, displaying a **Click to edit** field with tooltip, and adding the deletion marker:

```
<p>Phone: <strong>
    {% for phone in phones %}
        <span id="Phone_{{ phone.id }}" class="edit"
          title="Click to edit.">{{ phone.number }}</span>
        <span class="delete"
          id="Phone_{{ phone.id }}">&#10008;</span>  
    {% endfor %}
```

Then, after the loop, we add a hook to add a new phone number:

```
<span class="edit" title="Click to add."
        id="Phone_new_{{ id }}"></span>
</strong></p>
```

E-mails and URLs are handled basically the same way, but `Click to edit` the way we did before would be undesirable because it would block the e-mail addresses and URLs functioning as a live link (which is how we would normally want them to function). Instead of using a regular click, we use the right click as the hook for editing. The CSS is similar but noticeably different in the marker it appends:

```
<p>Email: <strong>
    {% for email in emails %}
    <a id="Email_{{ email.id }}" class="edit_rightclick"
      title="RIGHT click to edit." href="mailto:{{ email.email }}"
      >{{ email.email }}</a>
    <span class="delete" id="Email_{{ email.id }}">&#10008;
    </span>  
    {% endfor %}
    <span class="edit" title="Click to edit."
        id="Email_new_{{ id }}"></span>
</strong></p>

<p>Webpages: <strong>
    {% for url in urls %}
        <a id="URL_url_{{ url.id }}" class="edit_rightclick"
          title="RIGHT click to edit."
          href="{{ url.url }}">{{ url.url }}</a>
        <span class="delete" id="URL_{{ url.id }}">&#10008;
        </span>  
    {% endfor %}
    <span class="edit" title="Click to add."
        id="URL_new_{{ id }}"></span>
</strong></p>
```

Database and Search Handling

The GPS coordinates are handled by a live link; Google maps will search by GPS coordinates, among many other kinds of queries, so this is a map link:

```
<p>GPS: <strong>
    {% if gps %}
        <a class="edit_rightclick" id="Entity_gps_{{ id }}"
           href="{{ gps_url }}">{{ gps }}</a>
    {% else %}
        <span class="edit" id="Entity_gps_{{ id }}"></span>
    {% endif %}
</strong></p>
```

Let's not forget the postal address:

```
<p>Postal address:
    <strong class="edit_textarea" title="Click to edit."
      id="Entity_postal_address_{{ id }}">
        {{ entity.postal_address }}</strong></p>
```

In terms of being future-proof and addressing business considerations, it can be very valuable to have a "catch-all" slot for other kinds of contact information. Right now there are existing forms of contact information that have not been listed, for instance a Skype ID, or IM addresses that are not identical to an e-mail address. It would be a very careless assumption to assume that the forms of contact information we have now are all we'll ever need. We can't guarantee a future-proof solution but listing a few forms of contact information that will probably stay around, and being sure to include a catch-all/wildcard slot, is almost certainly less wrong for the future than only listing what our organization uses today.

```
<p>Other contact information:
    <strong class="edit_textarea" title="Click to edit."
      id="Entity_other_contact_{{ id }}">{{ entity.other_contact }}
    </strong></p>
```

Tagging is a powerful value-added feature for a directory and is included in searches; it also provides an example of a many-to-many relationship. We iterate through an entity's tags in basically the same way we iterated through phone numbers, e-mail addresses, and URLs:

```
<p>Tags: <strong>
    {% for tag in tags %}
        <span class="tag">{{ tag.text }}</span>
        <span class="delete"
          id="tag_{{ id }}_{{ tag.id }}">&#10008;</span> 
    {% endfor %}
    <span class="edit" id="Entity_tag_new_{{ id }}"></span>
</strong></p>
```

For the `Department`, which is an Entity, we display its name as a hijaxed link to that Entity's profile:

```
<p>Department: <strong>
   <a href="/?query={{ query }}&id={{ entity.department.id }}"
      onclick="load_profile({{ entity.department.id }});
      return false;">{{ entity.department.name }}</a>  
```

We build up a `select`, and it is important here that the `select` defaults to the currently selected value and not whatever we happen to place first in our list. The `onchange` calls a function that saves the change and refreshes the profile:

```
<select name="department" id="department" class="autocomplete"
   onchange="PHOTO_DIRECTORY.update_autocomplete(
        'Entity_department_{{ id }}', 'department');">
```

First we manually create the `option` for no selected value:

```
<option
  {% if not entity.department %}
     selected="selected"
  {% endif %}
  value="department.-1">None</option>
```

Then we loop through the available entities for the options.

We may note as a known issue, and possible area for future enhancements, that the list of Entities is not trimmed to only present departments, locations, or bosses when those `select` elements are populated. It would be possible to add a checkbox below the `department/location/reports_to` paragraph saying that this Entity is available to populate those fields, but for now we will leave that as future room for enhancement.

```
    {% for department in entities %}
    <option
      {% if department.id == entity.department %}
          selected="selected"
      {% endif %}
      value="department.{{ department.id }}">
      {{ department.name }}</option>
    {% endfor %}
</select></strong></p>
```

The `location` and `reports_to` paragraphs are handled similarly:

```
<p>Location: <strong>
    <a href="/?query={{ query }}&id={{ entity.location.id }}"
         onclick="load_profile({{ entity.location.id }});
         return false;">{{ entity.location.name }}</a>  
    <select name="location" id="location" class="autocomplete"
      onchange="PHOTO_DIRECTORY.update_autocomplete(
              'Entity_location_{{ id }}', 'location');">
        <option
          {% if not entity.location %}
             selected="selected"
          {% endif %}
          value="location.-1">None</option>
        {% for location in entities %}
        <option
          {% if location.id == entity.location %}
              selected="selected"
          {% endif %}
          value="location.{{ location.id }}">
          {{ location.name }}</option>
        {% endfor %}
</select></strong></p>

<p>Reports to: <strong>
    <a href="/?query={{ query }}&id={{ entity.reports_to.id }}"
      onclick="load_profile({{ entity.reports_to.id }});
      return false;">{{ entity.reports_to.name }}</a>  
    <select name="reports_to" id="reports_to" class="autocomplete"
      onchange="PHOTO_DIRECTORY.update_autocomplete(
              'Entity_reports_to_{{ id }}', 'reports_to');">
        <option
          {% if not entity.reports_to %}
             selected="selected"
          {% endif %}
          value="reports_to.-1">None</option>
        {% for reports_to in entities %}
        <option
          {% if reports_to.id == entity.reports_to %}
              selected="selected"
          {% endif %}
          value="reports_to.{{ reports_to.id }}">
          {{ reports_to.name }}</option>
        {% endfor %}
</select></strong></p>
```

The `status` field is used as in Facebook or Twitter, as we have discussed earlier. This could be a very useful feature, but if it doesn't make sense in your corporate environment, then it should be disabled. It may be that this is the one field that consistently makes the database grow, and optimization concerns would eschew such fields, but we should recall Donald Knuth's observation, "Premature optimization is the root of all evil." And we should remember that our usual guesses before investigation and research, about why a system is having performance issues, are rarely correct. If this is an example of a feature that is not needed for performance reasons, this should be an observation corroborated by experiment.

We break the statuses up as we broke up search results, although with initial configuration we are only displaying the five most recent statuses:

```
<p>Status:</p>
<div class="edit_textarea" id="Status_new_{{ id }}"></div>
{% for status in first_statuses %}
<p>{{ status.text }}<br />
<span class="timestamp">{{ status.datetime }}</span></p>
{% endfor %}
{% if second_statuses %}
    <p><a class="show_additional_statuses"
    href="JavaScript:show_additional('statuses');"
    ><span class="emphasized">+</span> Show all</a></p>
    <div class="additional_statuses">
        {% for status in second_statuses %}
            <p>{{ status.text }}<br />
            <span class="timestamp">{{ status.datetime }}</span></p>
        {% endfor %}
    </div>
{% endif %}
```

Here we add CSS overrides, enclosed in a `noscript` tag. The CSS styling adds (dingbat) symbols after editable areas as a visual reminder that they can be edited by clicking; but if JavaScript is turned off, so is that functionality. So this little snippet removes the symbols:

```
<noscript>
    <style type="text/css">
        <!--
            .edit:after, .edit_textarea:after, .edit_rightclick:after
                {
                content: "";
                }
        // -->
    </style>
</noscript>
```

Views on the server side

We have the following views to service requests on the server side.

Telling if the user is logged in

We make a view to allow Ajax to test if the user is logged in. Because we have the `@ajax_login_required` decoator, we only need to write code to unconditionally state that the user is logged in, and then guard the view using the `@ajax_login_required` decorator:

```
@ajax_login_required
def ajax_check_login(request):
    output = json.dumps({ u'not_authenticated': False })
    return HttpResponse(output, mimetype = u'application/json')
```

A view to support deletion

The following view allows Ajax deletion of e-mail addresses, URLs, and so on, as well as Entities.

```
@ajax_login_required
def ajax_delete(request):
```

The many-to-many relationship in tagging requires special treatment:

```
        if request.POST[u'id'].lower().startswith(u'tag_'):
            search = re.search(ur'[Tt]ag_(\d+)_(\d+)',
            request.POST[u'id'])
            if search:
                entity = directory.models.Entity.objects.get(
                    id = int(search.group(1)))
                entity.tags.remove(directory.models.Tag.objects.get(
                    id = int(search.group(2))))
                entity.save()
```

Everything else, that is, every deletion of a model instance (including e-mail addresses and URLs as well as Entities), can be handled by the same method:

```
        else:
            search = re.search(ur'(.*)_(\d+)', request.POST[u'id'])
            if search:
                getattr(directory.models, search.group(1)).objects.get(
                    id = int(search.group(2))).delete()
```

In particular here, we log who made a deletion:

```
directory.functions.log_message(u'Deleted: ' +
  request.POST[u'id'] + u' by ' + request.user.username + u'.')
```

The response, which may feed back into the slot in the page, is an empty string:

```
return HttpResponse(u'')
```

These changes require an addition to the `urlpatterns` in `urls.py`. The full `urlpatterns` example given for the hybrid solution will work for the AHAH solution as well.

The AHAH view to load profiles

The AHAH view to load a profile returns a rendered XHTML fragment, not JSON. It is fairly simple:

```
def ajax_profile(request, id):
```

First it looks up and/or calculates values needed by the template:

```
entity = directory.models.Entity.objects.filter(id = int(id))[0]
if entity.gps:
    gps = entity.gps
elif entity.location and entity.location.gps:
    gps = entity.location.gps
else:
    gps = u''
if gps:
    gps_url = \
      u'http://maps.google.com/maps?f=q&source=s_q&hl=en&q=' \
      + gps.replace(u' ', u'+') + "&iwloc=A&hl=en"
else:
    gps_url = u''
```

Then it feeds those values to the template and renders it to a returned response:

```
return render_to_response(u'profile_internal.html',
  {
  u'entities': directory.models.Entity.objects.all(),
  u'entity': entity,
  u'first_statuses':
    directory.models.Status.objects.filter(
      entity = id).order_by(
        u'-datetime')[:directory.settings.INITIAL_STATUSES],
  u'gps': gps,
```

```
        u'gps_url': gps_url,
        u'id': int(id),
        u'emails': directory.models.Email.objects.all(),
        u'phones': directory.models.Phone.objects.all(),
        u'second_statuses':
          directory.models.Status.objects.filter(
            entity = id).order_by(
              u'-datetime')[directory.settings.INITIAL_STATUSES:],
        u'tags': entity.tags.all().order_by(u'text'),
        u'urls': directory.models.URL.objects.all(),
        })
```

Helper functions for the AHAH view for searching

First, we define a function to count, case-insensitive, the number of times a token appears in a string. The matching is whole word matching, so the string "they looked" would be matched by the query "they" or "looked" but not "look." We put this in `functions.py`, which now needs to have `import re` in its `import` section. The string to search for is the first argument, and the token to search for is the second argument:

```
def count_tokens(raw, query):
    result = 0
    try:
```

Note that this regular expression splits more or less on a non-word character, but a hyphen is treated as a word character. This means, in particular, that tagging, which uses this function, will count "customer-service" as one token, not two.

```
        tokens = re.split(ur'(?u)[^-\w]', raw)
    except TypeError:
        tokens = raw
    while u'' in tokens:
        tokens.remove(u'')
    try:
        matches = re.split(ur'(?u)[^-\w]', query)
    except TypeError:
        matches = query
    while u'' in matches:
        matches.remove(u'')
    for token in tokens:
        for match in matches:
            if token.lower() == match.lower():
                result += 1
    return result
```

Chapter 9

In addition, we define a weighted scoring function designed to estimate the relevance of an Entity to a query. If a search term appears in an Entity's name, there will be a very high score; if an Entity is tagged with the term, it will also be a high score, but lower; if it appears in the Entity's statuses, it will have some relevance but not nearly as high of a score.

The weighted scoring function is as follows. The scoring algorithm is simple: for the Entity provided, count how many times a keyword matches a relevant field associated with the Entity, and multiply it by a weight defined in settings.py. This provides a way to try to present the best matches first. It also resides in functions.py.

```
def score(entity, keywords):
    result = 0
    if entity.name:
```

In this case, long lines are broken up by adding a backslash (\) as the last character before a line is broken; the indentation by two spaces more is a matter of convention more than requirement, but makes for readability. There are some cases where a line may be broken without a backslash, such as where a parenthesis, curly brace, or square brace has been opened but not closed, in which case a backslash is permitted but unnecessary:

```
        result += count_tokens(entity.name, keywords) * \
          directory.settings.NAME_WEIGHT
    if entity.description:
        result += count_tokens(entity.description, keywords) *\
          directory.settings.DESCRIPTION_WEIGHT
    if entity.tags:
        for tag in entity.tags.all():
            result += count_tokens(tag.text, keywords) * \
              directory.settings.TAG_WEIGHT
    if entity.title:
        result += count_tokens(entity.title, keywords) * \
          directory.settings.TITLE_WEIGHT
    if entity.department:
        result += count_tokens(entity.department.name, keywords) * \
          directory.settings.DEPARTMENT_WEIGHT
    if entity.location:
        result += count_tokens(entity.location.name, keywords) * \
          directory.settings.LOCATION_WEIGHT
    for status in directory.models.Status.objects.filter(
      entity = entity.id):
        result += count_tokens(status.text, keywords) * \
          directory.settings.STATUS_WEIGHT
    return result
```

We have added, towards the top of our `settings.py`, the scoring weights and other custom settings for our photo directory:

```
DEBUG = True
TEMPLATE_DEBUG = DEBUG

DIRNAME = os.path.dirname(__file__)

# These are constants used in the template.
DELAY_BETWEEN_RETRIES = 1
INITIAL_RESULTS = 10
INITIAL_STATUSES = 5
SHOULD_DOWNLOAD_DIRECTORY = 1 # 1 or 0, BUT NOT True or False
SHOULD_TURN_OFF_HIJAXING = 0 # 1 or 0, BUT NOT True or False
# These are weightings used to determine importance in searches.
# The values provided are integer clean, but the code should work for the most
# part with floating point values.
DEPARTMENT_WEIGHT = 30
DESCRIPTION_WEIGHT = 30
LOCATION_WEIGHT = 10
NAME_WEIGHT = 70
STATUS_WEIGHT = 1
TAG_WEIGHT = 50
TITLE_WEIGHT = 50
```

This concludes what we add to `settings.py` to customize behavior of our application.

An updated model

Before we move on, our Entity model has evolved; now would be a good time to give the new Entity model. The changes are mostly straightforward, some fields have been deleted and others added, and we now have a `ManyToManyField`:

```
class Entity(models.Model):
    active = models.BooleanField(blank = True)
    department = models.ForeignKey(u'self', blank = True,
      null = True, related_name = u'member')
    description = models.TextField(blank = True)
    gps = GPSField()
    image_mimetype = models.TextField(blank = True, null = True)
    location = models.ForeignKey(u'self', blank = True, null = True,
      related_name = u'occupant')
    name = models.TextField(blank = True)
    other_contact = models.TextField(blank = True)
    postal_address = models.TextField(blank = True)
    publish_externally = models.BooleanField(blank = True)
    reports_to = models.ForeignKey(u'self', blank = True,
```

```
        null = True, related_name = u'subordinate')
    start_date = models.DateField(blank = True, null = True)
    tags = models.ManyToManyField(Tag)
    title = models.TextField(blank = True)
```

And that is the last thing before our AHAH search function.

An AHAH server-side search function

Without further ado, here is the Ajax search function. We determine the tokens in the query first:

```
def ajax_search(request):
    try:
        query = request.POST[u'query']
    except KeyError:
        try:
            query = request.GET[u'query']
        except KeyError:
            return HttpResponse(u'')
    tokens = re.split(ur'(?u)[^-\w]', query)
    while u'' in tokens:
        tokens.remove(u'')
```

Then we compile a list of candidates for inclusion in the search results. A candidate, in this context, is a two-item list containing an Entity and a starting relevance score of zero. Because we are trying to preserve Unicode sensitivity, and not all database backends play nice with Unicode case-insensitive regular expression matching, we handle all of this in Python, instead of dancing around database backend incompatibilities or needlessly restricting the reader's choices in database backends.

```
    candidates = []
    for candidate in directory.models.Entity.objects.all():
        candidates.append([candidate, 0])
```

Then, for each token, we weed out the candidates that don't match; that is, we have AND-based and not an OR-based handling of query terms. If a candidate does make the cut, its total score is increased by the total for that token.

```
    for token in tokens:
        new_candidates = []
        for candidate in candidates:
            if directory.functions.score(candidate[0], token) > 0:
                candidate[1] += directory.functions.score(
                    candidate[0], token)
                new_candidates.append(candidate)
        candidates = new_candidates
```

The candidates are sorted by score, from highest to lowest. We use an anonymous function, a `lambda` function, which returns the negative of `cmp` of the first item in an array: `cmp()` returns 1 if the first argument is greater (numerically or alphabetically), 0 if they are equal or equivalent, and -1 if the second argument is greater. We pass a `sort` argument that requests sorting from highest to lowest score. `candidates.sort()` can be passed a named or anonymous function, as long as the function takes two arguments and returns a comparison such as can be used to sort from lowest to highest (or highest to lowest).

```
candidates.sort(lambda a, b: -cmp(a[1], b[1]))
```

The data structure we hand off to the template is not our raw list of candidates; rather, we extract the `description`, `id`, whether or not an image should be displayed, and the `name` of the candidate.

```
export = []
for candidate in candidates:
    if candidate[0].image_mimetype:
        image = True
    else:
        image = False
    export.append(
        {
        u'department': name,
        u'description': candidate[0].description,
        u'id': candidate[0].id,
        u'image': image,
        u'name': candidate[0].name,
        u'title': candidate[0].title,
        })
```

Without tackling a full pagination solution, we display a configurable number of initial results in one area of the template, and then put the others in a hidden `div` that is displayed if the user clicks **Show all**.

```
first_portion = export[:directory.settings.INITIAL_RESULTS]
second_portion = export[directory.settings.INITIAL_RESULTS:]
return render_to_response(u'search_internal.html',
    {
    u'first_portion': first_portion,
    u'second_portion': second_portion,
    u'query': urllib.quote(query),
    })
```

Handling the client-side: A template for the main page

This template extends `base.html`, which contains all the JavaScript includes. This page contains a small amount of boilerplate JavaScript that goes with jQuery plugins, but is mostly custom JavaScript for our application.

We limit ourselves to one incursion into the global namespace above jQuery, namely `PHOTO_DIRECTORY`. We enclose our jQuery-using code in:

```
jQuery(function($)
    {
    /* Code enclosed here. */
    });
```

This allows us to freely reference `jQuery` as `$`, but still create code that can coexist with other libraries that use the `$` identifier for their own purposes. Why are we doing this in a test setup where no other libraries want to use `$`? There is a martial arts maxim, which could just as well be taken from musical instrument performance: "The way you practice is the way you will fight." The only time a martial artist or a musician really has a live choice about how well to perform is in practice; in the heat of performance the decision has already been made. So we follow this best practice, now while we have a choice about it, and not in a project when we will confidently use `$` and incur the wrath of another library. While we will be placing everything under the `PHOTO_DIRECTORY` namespace, we will not be using closures to try to lock down unintended access. If other people want to incorporate this code and use it for other purposes without editing its internals, we are leaving the door open.

We will be following a Whitesmith brace style, meaning that in code written from scratch we will indent four spaces and indent braces along with the code they go with:

```
function log(message)
    {
    try
        {
        console.log(message);
        }
    catch(error)
        {
        alert(message);
        }
    }
```

We will, when possible, place functions and lists of variable assignment in alphabetical order. The more functions or objects you have in a file (or the more functions you have in an object), the easier it is to find things if they are arranged in alphabetical order, or as alphabetical an order as constraints allow.

One surprising feature of this application, and one that is not generally expected, is that in this version all top-level page renderings come from a single template, `search.html`. This is an unexpected simplicity; ordinarily one would be managing multiple templates for different top-level page renderings, and Django template inheritance would be a more potent advantage. However, we will still see an example of template inheritance.

The `base.html` template now reads as follows. We open by defining an XHTML 1.0 doctype and `html` tag:

```
{% block dtd %}
  <!DOCTYPE html PUBLIC "-//W3C//DTD XHTML 1.0 Strict//EN"
  "http://www.w3.org/TR/xhtml1/DTD/xhtml1-strict.dtd">
{% endblock dtd %}
{% block html_tag %}
  <html xmlns="http://www.w3.org/1999/xhtml" xml:lang="en-US"
  lang="en-US">
{% endblock html_tag %}
```

Then we open the `head`. In some cases we define actual tags within hooks; in other cases we define hooks, the goal being to have more hooks rather than less to override.

```
{% block head %}<head>
    <title>{% block head_title %}{{ page.title }}
    {% endblock head_title %}</title>
    {% block head_favicon %}<link rel="icon"
    href="/static/favicon.ico" type="x-icon" />
    <link rel="shortcut icon" href="/static/favicon.ico"
    type="x-icon" />{% endblock head_favicon %}
    {% block head_meta %}
        {% block head_meta_author%}
        {% endblock head_meta_author %}
```

We specify a charset of `UTF-8`; without it, many Unicode characters are displayed inappropriately, and user-provided Unicode content will be garbled:

```
{% block head_meta_charset %}
  <meta http-equiv="Content-Type"
  content="text/html; charset=UTF-8" />
{% endblock head_meta_charset %}
```

```
{% block head_meta_contentlanguage %}
  <meta http-equiv="Content-Language" value="en-US" />
{% endblock head_meta_contentlanguage %}
```

We then define several tags, the meta description, keywords, and possibly refresh and robots tags are important even if they are not defined in this template. If search engine friendliness is at all a concern, you will want pages to define the meta description tag and possibly others.

```
        {% block head_meta_description %}
        {% endblock head_meta_description %}
        {% block head_meta_keywords %}
        {% endblock head_meta_keywords %}
        {% block head_meta_othertags %}
        {% endblock head_meta_othertags %}
        {% block head_meta_refresh %}
        {% endblock head_meta_refresh %}
        {% block head_meta_robots %}
        {% endblock head_meta_robots %}
    {% endblock head_meta %}
    {% block head_rss %}{% endblock head_rss %}
```

The best practice is to have one HTML or XHTML page, with one CSS hit at the top, and one JavaScript hit at the bottom. For development purposes, we do not yet concatenate and minify down to one hit. We define section and page CSS files for development; the principle again is that it is better to have more hooks than less.

```
    {% block head_css %}
        {% block head_css_site %}<link rel="stylesheet"
          type="text/css" href="/static/css/style.css" />
          <link rel="stylesheet" type="text/css"
          href="/static/css/smoothness/
          jquery-ui-1.8.2.custom.css" />
        {% endblock head_css_site %}
        {% block head_css_section %}
        {% endblock head_css_section %}
        {% block head_css_page %}{% endblock head_css_page %}
    {% endblock head_css %}
    {% block head_section %}{% endblock head_section %}
    {% block head_page %}{% endblock head_page %}
</head>{% endblock head %}
```

After adding more `header` hooks, we define multiple hooks in the main body of the page:

```
{% block body %}<body>
    {% block body_preamble_site %}
    {% endblock body_preamble_site %}
    {% block body_preamble_section %}
    {% endblock body_preamble_section %}
    {% block body_preamble_page %}
    {% endblock body_preamble_page %}
    <div id="sidebar">
    {% block body_sidebar %}{% endblock body_sidebar %}
    </div>
    <div id="content">
    {% block body_content %}
        <div id="header">
        {% block body_header %}
            {% block body_header_banner %}
            {% endblock body_header_banner %}
            {% block body_header_title %}<h1>
              {{ page.title }}</h1>
            {% endblock body_header_title %}
            {% block body_header_breadcrumb %}
               {{ page.breadcrumb }}
            {% endblock body_header_breadcrumb %}
        {% endblock body_header %}
        </div>
        {% block body_site_announcements %}
        {% endblock body_site_announcements %}
        {% block body_notifications %}
          <div id="notifications"></div>
        {% endblock body_notifications %}
        {% block body_main %}{% endblock body_main %}
    {% endblock body_content %}
```

Having placed those hooks in the `body` content, we define a `footer`. We leave room for a `breadcrumb` in two places, at the top and the bottom of the page; from a usability standpoint a `breadcrumb` is a minor feature but if it makes sense to provide one, you should at least leave the door open to one.

```
        </div>
        <div id="footer">
        {% block body_footer %}
            {% block body_footer_breadcrumb %}
              {{ page.breadcrumb }}
```

```
            {% endblock body_footer_breadcrumb %}
            {% block body_footer_legal %}
            {% endblock body_footer_legal %}
        {% endblock body_footer %}
        </div>
    </body>{% endblock body %}
```

We define a logical `footer`. In development we leave separate files for what we will concatenate and minify for development.

```
    {% block footer %}
        {% block footer_javascript %}
            {% block footer_javascript_site %}
              <script language="JavaScript" type="text/javascript"
                src="/static/js/jquery.js"></script>
              <script language="JavaScript" type="text/javascript"
                src="/static/js/jquery-ui.js"></script>
              <script language="JavaScript" type="text/javascript"
                src="/static/js/jquery.jeditable.js"></script>
              <script language="JavaScript" type="text/javascript"
                src="/static/js/ajaxfileupload.js"></script>
              <script language="JavaScript" type="text/javascript"
                src="/static/js/jquery.effects.fade.js"></script>
            {% endblock footer_javascript_site %}
            {% block footer_javascript_section %}
            {% endblock footer_javascript_section %}
            {% block footer_javascript_page %}
            {% endblock footer_javascript_page %}
        {% endblock footer_javascript %}
    {% endblock footer %}
</html>
```

We open the template we are working on by declaring it to extend `base.html`:

```
{% extends "base.html" %}
```

We define the block that populates the HTML title:

```
{% block head_title %}Photo directory: Search
{% endblock head_title %}
```

We override a (new) block in `base.html` to put something at the beginning of a page, and put a link to add a new Entity. This will be styled to appear at the top right of the page.

```
{% block body_preamble_page %}
<div id="body_preamble_page">
    <strong>
        <a href="/" onclick="PHOTO_DIRECTORY.add_new();
                    return false;">Add new</a>
    </strong>
</div>
{% endblock body_preamble_page %}
```

Now we will populate the main part of the page body.

```
{% block body_main %}
```

First, we define a semantically marked-up search form with a **query** and **submit** button. These will be styled to be fairly striking, and centered (with a little help from presentationally used jQuery to adjust things).

```
<h1>Photo directory: Search</h1>
<form name="search_form" id="search_form" action="/">
    <input type="text" name="query" id="query" value="{{ query }}" />
    <input type="submit" name="submit" id="submit" value="Search" />
</form>
```

We wrap the search results and Entity drilldown portions in two containing `div` elements, in order to facilitate styling:

```
<div class="outer_outer">
    <div class="outer">
```

If there are search results, we display them, but if there are no search results, we still populate the `div` with a heading. This means that when a user first visits a page and is getting acquainted, it is easier to recognize what the search results portion of the page is there for.

```
        <div id="search_results">
            {% if search_results %}
                {{ search_results }}
            {% else %}
                <h2>Search results</h2>
            {% endif %}
        </div>
```

[214]

We do the same thing with the Entity drilldown page. However, we have chosen a different label. For the purposes of development, there are benefits to using an abstract term: not "Person" but "Entity". The directory is first and foremost a directory to keep track of people, but a successful tool is one that is used in a way that its maker never imagined, and if this succeeds people will keep track of more than people. We both identify that this section of the page is for people, and that it may be used for other things, with an h2 labeling it as People, etc.:

```
<div id="profile">
    {% if profile %}
        {{ profile }}
    {% else %}
        <h2>People, etc.</h2>
    {% endif %}
</div>
        </div>
    </div>
```

This div is not displayed initially, but is used by jQuery UI to support Ajax logins.

```
<div id="login_form" title="Log in">
    <form>
        <fieldset>
            <label for="login">Login</label>
            <input type="text" name="login" id="login"
                class="text ui-widget-content ui-corner-all" /><br />
            <label for="password">Password</label>
            <input type="password" name="password" id="password"
                class="text ui-widget-content ui-corner-all" /><br />
        </fieldset>
    </form>
</div>
```

This is all that we will be putting in the main body area. We close this template block, and move on to the page-specific JavaScript block:

```
{% endblock body_main %}
{% block footer_javascript_page %}
<script language="JavaScript" type="text/javascript">
<!--
```

We enclose virtually all of our code in a `jQuery(function($) { ... });` wrapper, but the `PHOTO_DIRECTORY` namespace is declared outside so that it will be available in the global namespace and therefore visible to event handlers and the like.

```
var PHOTO_DIRECTORY = new Object();

jQuery(function($)
    {
```

Firefox's Firebug plugin is a powerful debugging tool, and it provides a `console.log()` function that is much better for diagnostic purposes than `alert()`. However, if your code tries to call `console.log()` when Firebug is not open, an error is thrown that may stop some of your JavaScript.

This means that if you forget and leave in a `console.log()` call that you were using when you were debugging, you can have code that will work for your debugging setup and break badly when a visitor tries to see it. It would be best of all not to leave in a `console.log()` call, but the following code provides a safety net, that is, if `console.log()` does not exist, we define it as a function that does nothing.

```
    try
        {
        console.log("Starting...");
        }
    catch(error)
        {
        console = function()
            {
            }
        console.log = console;
        }
```

We request that when the DOM is ready, the default values in jQuery's `.ajax()` call be set. Besides a default returned data type and form submission type, the global error handler does one other major service, namely, if the settings are set to debug mode, it extracts the `responseText` from the `XMLHttpRequest` and sends it in a notification.

This is important because in Ajax development, we will not necessarily see Django's error pages when there has been a server error. This is unfortunate because they often provide information that is helpful for debugging. This is a way that Ajax development can have access to a helpful Django development feature.

We only do this if settings.DEBUG is true. However helpful a good error page may be to developers, including one in this way is needlessly confusing and intimidating to users. If debug mode is off, a short and simple message is sent:

```
$(function()
    {
    $.ajaxSetup(
        {
        datatype: "json",
        error: function(XMLHttpRequest, textStatus, errorThrown)
            {
            if (XMLHttpRequest.responseText)
                {
                {% if settings.DEBUG %}
                    PHOTO_DIRECTORY.send_notification(
                        XMLHttpRequest.responseText);
                {% else %}
                    PHOTO_DIRECTORY.send_notification(
                        "There was error handling your request.");
                {% endif %}
                }
            },
        type: "POST",
        });
    });
```

The following is boilerplate code provided for use with jQuery UI's autocomplete:

```
(function( $ ) {
    $.widget( "ui.combobox", {
        _create: function() {
            var self = this;
            var select = this.element.hide(),
                selected = select.children( ":selected" ),
                value = selected.val() ? selected.text() : "";
            var input = $( "<input>" )
                .insertAfter( select )
                .val( value )
                .autocomplete({
                    delay: 0,
                    minLength: 0,
                    source: function( request, response ) {
                        var matcher = new RegExp(
                            $.ui.autocomplete.escapeRegex(
                                request.term), "i" );
                        response( select.children(
```

```
            "option" ).map(function() {
                var text = $( this ).text();
                if ( this.value && ( !request.term ||
                  matcher.test(text) ) )
                    return {
                        label: text.replace(
                        new RegExp(
                        "(?![^&;]+;)(?!<[^<>]*)(" +
                        $.ui.autocomplete.escapeRegex(
                        request.term) +
                        ")(?![^<>]*>)(?![^&;]+;)",
                        "gi"), "<strong>$1</strong>"
                         ),
                         value: text,
                         option: this
                    };
            }) );
        },
        select: function( event, ui ) {
        PHOTO_DIRECTORY.update_autocomplete_handler(
            event, ui);
            ui.item.option.selected = true;
            //select.val( ui.item.option.value );
            self._trigger( "selected", event, {
                item: ui.item.option
            });
        },
        change: function( event, ui ) {
         PHOTO_DIRECTORY.update_autocomplete_handler(
            event, ui);
            if ( !ui.item ) {
                var matcher = new RegExp( "^" +
                $.ui.autocomplete.escapeRegex(
                    $(this).val() ) + "$", "i" ),
                    valid = false;
                select.children(
                "option" ).each(function() {
                    if ( this.value.match(
                      matcher ) ) {
                        this.selected = valid = true;
                        return false;
                    }
                });
                if ( !valid ) {
                    // remove invalid value,
                    // as it didn't match anything
                    $( this ).val( "" );
```

```
                            select.val( "" );
                            return false;
                        }
                    }
                }
            })
            .addClass(
             "ui-widget ui-widget-content ui-corner-left" );

        input.data( "autocomplete" )._renderItem = function(
        ul, item ) {
            return $( "<li></li>" )
                .data( "item.autocomplete", item )
                .append( "<a>" + item.label + "</a>" )
                .appendTo( ul );
        };

        $( "<button> </button>" )
            .attr( "tabIndex", -1 )
            .attr( "title", "Show All Items" )
            .insertAfter( input )
            .button({
                icons: {
                    primary: "ui-icon-triangle-1-s"
                },
                text: false
            })
            .removeClass( "ui-corner-all" )
            .addClass( "ui-corner-right ui-button-icon" )
            .click(function() {
                // close if already visible
                if ( input.autocomplete( "widget" ).is(
                   ":visible" ) ) {
                    input.autocomplete( "close" );
                    return;
                }

                // pass empty string as value to search for,
                // displaying all results
                input.autocomplete( "search", "" );
                input.focus();
            });
        }
    });
})(jQuery);
```

Here we define several variables that will be used. The `id` provided by the view may be empty if no page has been specified; we have an example of giving a default value in the templating engine. The variable will be initialized to a JavaScript `null` value if no (nonempty) `id` has been provided.

```
PHOTO_DIRECTORY.current_profile = {{ id|default:"null" }} ;
PHOTO_DIRECTORY.database_loaded = false;
PHOTO_DIRECTORY.last_attempted_function = null;
PHOTO_DIRECTORY.logged_in = false;
PHOTO_DIRECTORY.DELAY_BETWEEN_RETRIES =
    {{ settings.DELAY_BETWEEN_RETRIES }};
PHOTO_DIRECTORY.SHOULD_DOWNLOAD_DIRECTORY =
    {{ settings.SHOULD_DOWNLOAD_DIRECTORY }};
PHOTO_DIRECTORY.SHOULD_TURN_OFF_HIJAXING =
    {{ settings.SHOULD_TURN_OFF_HIJAXING }};
```

Here is the function that requests a new Entity instance and pulls up its profile for editing:

```
PHOTO_DIRECTORY.add_new = function()
    {
    $.ajax({
        success: function(data, textStatus, XMLHttpRequest)
            {
            if (PHOTO_DIRECTORY.check_authentication(data))
                {
                PHOTO_DIRECTORY.load_profile(data[0].pk);
                }
            else
                {
```

While this functionality is not available everywhere across the program, `PHOTO_DIRECTORY.last_attempted_function` is used for a callback on successful login. On successful login, it will be called if non-null.

```
                PHOTO_DIRECTORY.last_attempted_function =
                    PHOTO_DIRECTORY.add_new;
                PHOTO_DIRECTORY.offer_login();
                }
            },
        url: "/ajax/new/Entity",
        });
    }
```

The following is boilerplate code provided for the `ajaxFileUpload` plugin, homepage at http://www.phpletter.com/Our-Projects/AjaxFileUpload/:

```
PHOTO_DIRECTORY.ajax_file_upload = function()
    {
    //starting setting some animation when the ajax starts
    // and completes
    $("#loading")
    .ajaxStart(function()
        {
        $(this).show();
        })
    .ajaxComplete(function()
        {
        $(this).hide();
        });
    /*  preparing ajax file upload
        url: the url of script file handling the
            uploaded files
        fileElementId: the file type of input
                    element id and it will be the index of
                    $_FILES Array()
        dataType: it support json, xml
        secureuri:use secure protocol
        success: call back function when the ajax complete
        error: callback function when the ajax failed

                */
    $.ajaxFileUpload(
        {
        url: '/ajax/saveimage/' +
            PHOTO_DIRECTORY.current_profile,
        secureuri: false,
        fileElementId: 'image',
        dataType: 'json',
        success: function(data, status)
            {
            if (!PHOTO_DIRECTORY.check_authentication(data))
                {
                PHOTO_DIRECTORY.offer_login();
                }
            },
        });
    return false;
    }
```

The following function is intended to check authentication on data returned by the server. On the server the `@ajax_login_required` decorator intercepts the request and, if the user is not logged in, returns JSON of `{"not_authenticated": true}`. This function and `check_login()` both save their findings in `PHOTO_DIRECTORY.logged_in`.

```javascript
PHOTO_DIRECTORY.check_authentication = function(parsed_json)
    {
    if (parsed_json == '{"not_authenticated": true}')
        {
        PHOTO_DIRECTORY.logged_in = false;
        return false;
        }
    try
        {
        if (parsed_json.not_authenticated)
            {
            PHOTO_DIRECTORY.logged_in = false;
            return false;
            }
        else
            {
            PHOTO_DIRECTORY.logged_in = true;
            return true;
            }
        PHOTO_DIRECTORY.logged_in = true;
        return true;
        }
    catch(error)
        {
        PHOTO_DIRECTORY.logged_in = false;
        return false;
        }
    }
```

`check_login()` serves a similar purpose but does not need to be supplied with any data or arguments:

```javascript
PHOTO_DIRECTORY.check_login = function()
    {
    var result = $.ajax({
        success: function(data, textStatus, XMLHttpRequest)
            {
            if (PHOTO_DIRECTORY.check_authentication(data))
                {
```

```
                PHOTO_DIRECTORY.logged_in = true;
                }
            else
                {
                PHOTO_DIRECTORY.logged_in = false;
                }
            },
        url: "/ajax/check_login",
        });
    }
```

A function to hide additional search results or statuses, beyond the limited number that are initially displayed, would go something like the following:

```
PHOTO_DIRECTORY.hide_additional = function(name)
    {
    $(".show_additional_" + name).hide();
    $("#additional_" + name).show("slow");
    }
```

The following is a function to load the currently selected profile, if there is one:

```
PHOTO_DIRECTORY.load_current_profile = function()
    {
    if (PHOTO_DIRECTORY.current_profile)
        {
        $("#profile").load("/ajax/profile/" +
            PHOTO_DIRECTORY.current_profile,
            PHOTO_DIRECTORY.register_update);
        }
    else
        {
        $("#profile").load("");
        }
    }
```

A function to load an Entity's profile with a specified ID is shown below:

```
PHOTO_DIRECTORY.load_profile = function(id)
    {
    PHOTO_DIRECTORY.current_profile = id;
    if (PHOTO_DIRECTORY.current_profile)
        {
        $("#profile").load("/ajax/profile/" +
            PHOTO_DIRECTORY.current_profile,
            PHOTO_DIRECTORY.register_update);
```

```
            }
        else
            {
            $("#profile").html("");
            }
    }
```

If people upload their own photos, some of them will likely be rather large. This proportionally scales down all images belonging to, say, img.profile that are above a maximum width in pixels, to that maximum width.

The following function may be called before an image has loaded; in that case, its width() may be 0, in which case the function sets a timeout to wait a configurable number of milliseconds and retry:

```
PHOTO_DIRECTORY.limit_width = function(css_class, limit)
    {
    $(css_class).each(function(index, element)
        {
        if ($(element).width() == 0)
            {
            setTimeout("PHOTO_DIRECTORY.limit_width('" +
                    css_class + "', " + limit + ");",
                    PHOTO_DIRECTORY.DELAY_BETWEEN_RETRIES);
            }
        if ($(element).width() > limit)
            {
            var height = Math.ceil($(element).height() * limit /
                $(element).width());
            $(element).width(limit);
            $(element).height(height);
            }
        });
    }
```

We place a wrapper around the code to display the login screen:

```
PHOTO_DIRECTORY.offer_login = function()
    {
    $("#login_form").dialog("open");
    }
```

The following code, when run, will hide the `select` elements of class `autocomplete`, displaying an autocomplete text field. The commented-out line shows the hidden `select` elements:

```
PHOTO_DIRECTORY.register_autocomplete = function()
    {
    $(".autocomplete").combobox();
    /*
    $(".autocomplete").toggle();
    */
    }
```

This function enables inline editing and deletion for fields where in-place editing is desired. We can prepare a field for this by following the naming convention where an HTML ID of `Entity_name_1` means "on the Entity of primary key 1, the field name," and adding `edit` or another CSS class to enable editing, and making sure this function is called.

The following function registers editables and elements otherwise needing to have Ajax functionality added:

```
PHOTO_DIRECTORY.register_editables = function()
    {
```

Items of class `delete` are set to send a request for the server to delete that item, and then make a request to reload a fresh profile. This reloading the profile as a unit, instead of trying to keep track of surgical updates, makes for fewer moving parts with less complex debugging.

```
$(".delete").each(function(index, item)
    {
    var id = item.id;
    $(item).click(function()
        {
        $.ajax(
            {
            data:
                {
                id: id,
                },
            datatype: "html",
            success: function(data)
                {
```

If the user comes back as logged in, the profile is reloaded; if the user is not logged in, a "reload the profile next" note is set, and a login screen is offered. (The login screen offers an escape hatch in case the user is not interested enough to want to log in, and we should not assume that our application is important enough to all of our users that it will be worth logging in.)

```
                if (PHOTO_DIRECTORY.check_authentication(
                  data))
                    {
                    PHOTO_DIRECTORY.reload_profile();
                    }
                else
                    {
                    PHOTO_DIRECTORY.last_function_called =
                        PHOTO_DIRECTORY.reload_profile;
                    PHOTO_DIRECTORY.offer_login();
                    }
                },
            url: "/ajax/delete",
            });
        });
    });
```

The .edit class, as compared to delete, has a similar overall structure. Its URL is different (/ajax/save instead of /ajax/delete), and it is based on Jeditable, filling out the details of a Jeditable call instead of doing everything from scratch.

```
        $(".edit").editable("/ajax/save",
            {
            callback: function(data)
                {
                if (PHOTO_DIRECTORY.check_authentication(data))
                    {
                    PHOTO_DIRECTORY.reload_profile();
                    }
                else
                    {
                    PHOTO_DIRECTORY.last_function_called =
                        PHOTO_DIRECTORY.reload_profile;
                    PHOTO_DIRECTORY.offer_login();
                    }
                },
            cancel: "Cancel",
            submit: "OK",
            });
```

The .edit_rightclick class is basically the same as .edit, and works in basically the same way. The chief difference is that it uses the contextmenu/right-click event instead of the regular (usually left) click for e-mail addresses and URLs where the desired behavior is not to initiate editing on a click as .edit is set to do, but to let the normal click behavior occur when the user clicks, and then intercept the contextmenu event (specified explicitly) to allow editing on a right-click.

```
$(".edit_rightclick").editable("/ajax/save",
    {
    cancel: "Cancel",
    callback: function(data)
        {
        if (PHOTO_DIRECTORY.check_authentication(data))
            {
            PHOTO_DIRECTORY.reload_profile();
            }
        else
            {
            PHOTO_DIRECTORY.last_function_called =
               PHOTO_DIRECTORY.reload_profile;
            PHOTO_DIRECTORY.offer_login();
            }
        },
    event: "contextmenu",
    submit: "OK",
    tooltip: "Right click to edit.",
    });
```

Here we have another variation on the theme: instead of a text input for ordinarily small fields, we allow a textarea for what may often be a much larger chunk of data:

```
$(".edit_textarea").editable("/ajax/save",
    {
    cancel: "Cancel",
    callback: function(data)
        {
        if (PHOTO_DIRECTORY.check_authentication(data))
            {
            PHOTO_DIRECTORY.reload_profile();
            }
        else
            {
            PHOTO_DIRECTORY.last_function_called =
               PHOTO_DIRECTORY.reload_profile;
```

```
                PHOTO_DIRECTORY.offer_login();
                }
            },
        rows: 5,
        submit: "OK",
        tooltip: "Click to edit.",
        type: "textarea",
        });
    }
```

This is a convenience method that calls several things that should be called after the page has been updated. If the settings.py says that link Hijaxing should be turned off, the "graceful degradation" option will become the default.

```
PHOTO_DIRECTORY.register_update = function()
    {
    PHOTO_DIRECTORY.limit_width("img.profile", 150);
    PHOTO_DIRECTORY.limit_width("img.search_results", 80);
    PHOTO_DIRECTORY.register_editables();
    PHOTO_DIRECTORY.register_autocomplete();
    if (PHOTO_DIRECTORY.SHOULD_TURN_OFF_HIJAXING)
        {
        $("a").removeAttr("onclick");
        // This link needs to be hijaxed:
        $("#add_new").click(function()
            {
            PHOTO_DIRECTORY.add_new();
            return false;
            });
        }
    }
```

The following function reloads the current profile. This can be called after an edit to ensure a fresh and correct page.

```
PHOTO_DIRECTORY.reload_profile = function()
    {
    PHOTO_DIRECTORY.tables_loaded = 0;
    PHOTO_DIRECTORY.load_current_profile();
    }
```

The following function hijaxes the search function:

```
PHOTO_DIRECTORY.search = function()
    {
    $("#search_results").load("/ajax/search?query=" +
```

```
            escape(document.search_form.query.value),
            PHOTO_DIRECTORY.register_update);
    }
```

The following function displays notifications to the user. The `setTimeout()` call is used so that the function will return immediately, and jQuery calls are made to fade it in, wait, and fade it out. The delay involved is five seconds plus two milliseconds per character in the message; in production, this should make very little difference, but if a detailed Django error page is served up, it will stay around for much longer.

```
    PHOTO_DIRECTORY.send_notification = function(message)
        {
        $("#notifications").html("<p>" + message + "</p>");
         clearTimeout($('#notifications').data('showTimeout'));
        $('#notifications').data('showTimeout',
           setTimeout((function(message)
              {
              return function ()
                  {
                  $('#notifications').show('slow').delay((5000 +
                     (message.length * 2))).hide('slow');
                  };
              })(message), 0);
        }
```

The following is a function to show additional search results or statuses. It hides the link that says **Show all**:

```
    PHOTO_DIRECTORY.show_additional = function(name)
        {
        $(".show_additional_" + name).hide();
        $("#additional_" + name).show("slow");
        }
```

The following function is intended to be called with preset arguments by the event handler for a select used in autocompletes:

```
    PHOTO_DIRECTORY.update_autocomplete = function(id, html_id)
        {
        var value = $("#" + html_id).val();
        $.ajax({
           data:
              {
              id: id,
              value: value,
              },
```

```
            url: "/ajax/save",
        });
    PHOTO_DIRECTORY.reload_profile();
    }
```

The following function is intended to serve as an event handler by the autocomplete fields themselves:

```
    PHOTO_DIRECTORY.update_autocomplete_handler = function(event, ui)
        {
        var split_value = ui.item.value.split(".");
        var field = split_value[0];
        var id = split_value[1];
        $.ajax({
            data:
                {
                id: "Entity_" + id + "_" +
                    PHOTO_DIRECTORY.current_profile,
                value: field,
                },
            url: "/ajax/save",
            });
        PHOTO_DIRECTORY.reload_profile();
        }
```

The following setup function should be called as soon as the document's DOM is ready.

```
    $(function()
        {
        if (!PHOTO_DIRECTORY.SHOULD_TURN_OFF_HIJAXING)
            {
            $("#search_form").submit(function(event)
                {
                PHOTO_DIRECTORY.search();
                return false;
                });
            }
        $("#query").width($(window).width() - 240);
```

A dialog is created for the login form; it is not initially used, but it is available for `offer_login()`. The button makes an Ajax login call.

```
        $("#login_form").dialog({
            autoOpen: false,
            height: 300,
```

```
            width: 350,
            modal: true,
            buttons:
                {
                'Log in': function()
                    {
                    $.ajax({
                        data:
                            {
                            "login": document.getElementById(
                                    "login").value,
                            "password": document.getElementById(
                                    "password").value,
                            },
                        datatype: 'text',
```

On a successful login attempt, we notify the user, and if a function has been registered as the last attempted function before attempting login, that function was called. This provides for some continuity after the interruption of a login request to resume the prior workflow.

```
                        success: function(data, textStatus,
                          XMLHttpRequest)
                            {
```

On login, we notify the user, load the database, and call any function registered as what the user was attempting before login.

```
                            if (data)
                              {
                              PHOTO_DIRECTORY.send_notification(
                                "You have successfully logged " +
                                "in and can now make changes.");
                              PHOTO_DIRECTORY.load_database();

                              $(".ui-dialog").hide();
                              $(".ui-widget-overlay").hide();
                              PHOTO_DIRECTORY.register_update();
                              if (
                              PHOTO_DIRECTORY.last_attempted_function)
                                  {
                              PHOTO_DIRECTORY.last_attempted_function();
                                  }
                              }
                            else
```

```
                        {
                          PHOTO_DIRECTORY.send_notification(
                            "Your login was not successful.");
                        }
                      },
                  url: "/ajax/login",
```

That takes us to the end of the setup. We perform a couple of housekeeping calls and wind down:

```
                            close: function(){},
                          });
                      },
                    },
                });
            PHOTO_DIRECTORY.check_login();
            PHOTO_DIRECTORY.register_update();
        });


    });
// -->
</script>
{% endblock footer_javascript_page %}
```

And that's it.

Let's take a look at some of the CSS referred to earlier.

CSS for styling the directory

This is the stylesheet we use to style things, adding emphasis to some and de-emphasizing other things. If we want to deliver a good, working system that is graceful to use, saying "There is no 'CSS' in 'Asynchronous JavaScript and XML'" is the same kind of legalistic error as saying, "There is no 'JSON' in 'Asynchronous JavaScript and XML.'" CSS can be used for aesthetics that do not correlate to the functionality of the core system, but the difference to usability and usefulness between practical use of CSS and impractical (or no) CSS is substantial. CSS will be treated here like JavaScript and other technologies as ways to deliver practical usefulness.

The following links show initially hidden search results or statuses that are important and are emphasize them:

```
a.hide_additional_statuses, a.hide_additional_results
    {
    font-weight: bold;
    }

a.show_additional_statuses, a.show_additional_results
    {
    font-weight: bold;
    }
```

Not presently in use, this is intended for a non-displayed `iframe` to send unwanted submissions to:

```
.bitbucket, #bitbucket
    {
    display: none;
    }
```

This is a usability-related choice of fonts; Verdana in particular reads very well on the screen, and it looks larger.

Note that we are not making a common web design mistake of choosing Verdana for its usability, and then cancelling out some of its usability benefits by shrinking it to free up more screen real estate.

```
body
    {
    font-family: Verdana, Arial, sans;
    }
```

The following is for the links at the upper right-hand corner of the page:

```
#body_preamble_page
    {
    text-align: right;
    margin-right: 30px;
    margin-top: 15px;
    }
```

These are the initially hidden `div` elements with "extra" search results or statuses if there are more than will be displayed initially. (The parameters for how many search results or statuses are displayed are modifiable in `settings.py`.)

```css
div#additional_statuses, div#additional_results
    {
    display: none;
    }
```

The the following `div` is for the link to delete a whole Entity:

```css
div.deletion
    {
    float: right;
    margin-right: 20px;
    }
```

An entity's description, postal address, status, or other editable fields are specified as `textarea`. Here and with other fields, we do the opposite of having a bold label and plaintext content: we leave the label with the default appearance and font weight, and make the content itself bold:

```css
div.edit_textarea
    {
    font-weight: bold;
    }
```

The `:after` pseudo-class will be used to display Unicode symbols as a cue that fields are user editable. This specifies that they will not be in bold.

```css
div.edit_textarea:after
    {
    font-weight: normal;
    }

div.image
    {
    float: left;
    }
```

We use semantic markup and style with CSS even when we want a table-like display.

```css
div.outer
    {
    display: table-row;
    }
```

```
div.outer_outer
    {
    display: table;
    width: 100%;
    }

div.search_result
    {
    display: table;
    margin-bottom: 20px;
    padding-right: 50px;
    width: 100%;
    }

div.search_result:hover
    {
    background-color: #ffffc0;
    }
```

Links in a search result `div` will be Entities' names, and will pull up their profiles.

```
div.search_result a
    {
    font-weight: bold;
    }
```

The following is used for the **Add new** link, and we will add below a **Bad network connection** link:

```
div.standard_links
    {
    font-weight: bold;
    margin-right: 15px;
    margin-top: 15px;
    text-align: right;
    }
```

We add a symbol showing a hand with a pen, grayed to lighten its visual effect, but larger to be easier to see. This will appear as HTML entities belonging to the relevant CSS classes.

```
.edit:after, .edit_textarea:after
    {
    color: #808080;
    content: "✍"; /* The symbol, not ASCII encoding, of &#9997; */
    font-size: larger;
    }
```

We add a similar, but not identical, markup to the end of links, which are edited by right-clicking. There are two symbols as we added a finger pointing right, and the symbol is a darker shade of grey. These do not make a perfect solution, and it would be wrong to expect users to automatically infer what the tooltip says: **Right-click to edit**. However, they provide a distinct and distinctive visual cue, and even if they are not perfect, they make the interface easier to remember and use.

```
.edit_rightclick:after
    {
    color: #404040;
    content: "☞✎"; /* The symbols, not ASCII encodings, of &#9755;
                 and then &#9997; */
    text-decoration: none;
    font-size: larger;
    }

img.profile
    {
    float: left;
    margin-bottom: 20px;
    margin-right: 20px;
    }
```

h1 and h2 tags are made to be large, but the emphasis of being bold is taken away, to be given instead to the search query, profile data, and similar tags. This develops a theme introduced earlier: labels are not emphasized; real content is made bold.

```
h1
    {
    font-size: 3em;
    font-weight: normal;
    margin-bottom: 50px;
    text-align: center;
    }

h2
    {
    font-size: 2em;
    font-weight: normal;
    }

h3
    {
    font-size: 1.8em;
    }
```

```css
img.search_results
    {
    float: left;
    }
```

The markup used for the Ajax login is hidden immediately.

```css
#login_form
    {
    display: none;
    }
```

Notifications have a yellow background and grey border. This is striking and catches the eye, and we intentionally are not using red as not all notifications are errors and we do not want to imitate the error dialog that says, "Error: The operation completed successfully." (Not to mention that computers make some people nervous and a bright red error message has needless force.)

```css
#notifications
    {
    background-color: #ffff80;
    border: 3px solid #808080;
    display: none;
    padding: 20px;
    }
```

The profile has a light blue background, while the search results have a light yellow background and the search bar itself has a plain white background. These backgrounds are not specifically intended for aesthetics, but to visually mark out how the screen is divided into different areas doing different jobs. The purpose is to add (helpful) redundancy in the signals provided about where the user is and what things the user can do.

```css
#profile
    {
    background-color: #ffffc0;
    display: table-cell;
    height: 100%;
    padding: 50px;
    width: 100%;
    }
```

Database and Search Handling

Especially for an empty profile, it is nice to have a little more padding at the bottom than the top. This accomplishes that slight aesthetic touch.

```css
#profile h2
    {
    margin-top: 0;
    }

.search_result
    {
    padding: 10px;
    padding-right: 0px;
    }

.search_result:hover
    {
    background-color: #ccccff;
    }

#search_results
    {
    background-color: #ddddff;
    display: table-cell;
    height: 100%;
    padding: 50px;
    padding-right: 0px;
    width: 32%;
    }

#search_results h2
    {
    margin-top: 0;
    }
```

The following is the `span` that is used to delete an added URL, e-mail address, and so on from an Entity:

```css
span.delete
    {
    color: #aa0000;
    font-size: larger;
    font-weight: bold;
    }
```

```
span.emphasized
    {
    font-size: larger;
    }

span.placeholder
    {
    font-style: italic;
    font-weight: normal;
    }
```

We style `tag` elements to look slightly distinctive compared to the rest of the application:

```
span.tag
    {
    background-color: #dddddd;
    border: 1px solid silver;
    padding-left: 3px;
    padding-right: 3px;
    }
```

The timestamp below a status is displayed, but it is visually downplayed, as usually the status is the important thing to read.

```
span.timestamp
    {
    font-size: smaller;
    color: #808080;
    }
```

We also use more usable fonts in a `textarea`. We style `textarea` elements to have a reasonable height (CSS requires a hack if it is to be used to allow for direct specification of a number of rows in a `textarea`), and to be as wide as they can.

```
textarea
    {
    font-family: Verdana, Arial, sans;
    font-size: larger;
    height: 5em;
    width: 100%;
    }
```

The input for the user query is large, and is given bold emphasis:

```
#query
    {
    border: 2px solid black;
    font-size: 2em;
    font-weight: bold;
    margin-bottom: 50px;
    padding: 2px;
    width: 80%;
    }

#search_form
    {
    margin-left: 40px;
    }

#submit
    {
    border: 2px solid black;
    font-size: 2em;
    font-weight: bold;
    margin-left: 10px;
    }
```

The following is boilerplate CSS for a `div` used to dim the screen in Ajax modal forms, including our Ajax login functionality:

```
.ui-widget-overlay
    {
    background: #000000;
    -ms-filter:"progid:DXImageTransform.Microsoft.Alpha(Opacity=50)";
    filter: alpha(opacity=50);
    opacity: .5;
    position: absolute;
    top: 0;
    bottom: 0;
    left: 0;
    right: 0;
    z-index: 1000;
    }
```

Our updated urlpatterns

Our `urlpatterns`, for the example AHAH solution above and for the fuller client-side database example solution below, are as follows:

```
urlpatterns = patterns(u'',
    (ur'^$', directory.views.homepage),
    (ur'^accounts/login/$', u'django.contrib.auth.views.login'),
    (ur'^admin/', include(admin.site.urls)),
    (ur'^ajax/check_login', directory.views.ajax_check_login),
    (ur'^ajax/delete', directory.views.ajax_delete),
    (ur'^ajax/download/(Email|Entity|Phone|Status|Tag|URL)',
       directory.views.ajax_download_model),
    (ur'^ajax/login', directory.views.ajax_login_request),
    (ur'^ajax/new/Entity', directory.views.new_Entity),
    (ur'^ajax/profile/(\d+)', directory.views.ajax_profile),
    (ur'^ajax/saveimage/(\d+)', directory.views.saveimage),
    (ur'^ajax/save', directory.views.save),
    (ur'^ajax/search', directory.views.ajax_search),
    (ur'^(create/Entity)', directory.views.redirect),
    (ur'^(create/Location)', directory.views.redirect),
    (ur'^manage/Entity/?(\d*)', directory.views.modelform_Entity),
    (ur'^manage/Location/?(\d*)',
       directory.views.modelform_Location),
    (ur'^profile/images/(\d+)', directory.views.image),
    (ur'^profile/(new)$', directory.views.profile_new),
    (ur'^profile/(\d+)$', directory.views.profile_existing),
)
```

And that is the last of the code we need!

We now have, on the server-side and client-side, all the pieces in place for a complete system that includes some best practices. We can tinker and extend it, but we have a complete working system now.

Summary

We have now covered all the bases for a simple, AHAH solution, and most of the time this will be best. However, there is more that we can do. In general, lazy programming and lazy network access that pulls as little as possible and does so as late as possible is the solution of choice and works better than a premature proactive solution that seems to be the root of all evil.

In our next chapter we will cover further customization and development. Let's go!

10
Tinkering Around: Bugfixes, Friendlier Password Input, and a Directory That Tells Local Time

One of the great joys of programming is not when we are trying to get the bare essentials basically working, but when the system is working as a whole, and we start to ask, "What about this? What about that?" One positive sense of the term "hacking" can refer to this tinkering, and it can be a joy to tinker with an already working system to see what enhancements are possible. Here we will tinker with the system and make some minor tweaks and two slightly more major enhancements. We will cover:

- Minor bugfixes and enhancements
- A more usable input solution for passwords
- Telling an (approximate) local time for other people we are working with, who may be in different time zones

Let's dig in.

Minor tweaks and bugfixes

Good tinkering can be a process that begins with tweaks and bugfixes, and snowballs from there. Let's begin with some of the smaller tweaks and bugfixes before tinkering further.

Setting a default name of "(Insert name here)"

Most of the fields on an Entity default to blank, which is in general appropriate. However, this means that there is a zero-width link for any search result which has not had a name set. If a user fills out the Entity's name before navigating away from that page, everything is fine, but it is a very suspicious assumption that all users will magically use our software in whatever fashion would be most convenient for our implementation.

So, instead, we set a default name of "(Insert name here)" in the definition of an Entity, in `models.py`:

```
name = models.TextField(blank = True,
  default = u'(Insert name here)')
```

Eliminating Borg behavior

One variant on the classic Singleton pattern in **Gang of Four** is the **Borg** pattern, where arbitrarily many instances of a Borg class may exist, but they share the same dictionary, so that if you set an attribute on one of them, you set the attribute on all of them. At present we have a bug, which is that our views pull all available instances. We need to specify something different. We update the end of `ajax_profile()`, including a slot for time zones to be used later in this chapter, to:

```
        return render_to_response(u'profile_internal.html',
          {
          u'entities': directory.models.Entity.objects.filter(
            is_invisible = False).order_by(u'name'),
          u'entity': entity,
          u'first_stati': directory.models.Status.objects.filter(
            entity = id).order_by(
              u'-datetime')[:directory.settings.INITIAL_STATI],
          u'gps': gps,
          u'gps_url': gps_url,
          u'id': int(id),
          u'emails': directory.models.Email.objects.filter(
            entity = entity, is_invisible = False),
          u'phones': directory.models.Phone.objects.filter(
            entity = entity, is_invisible = False),
          u'second_stati': directory.models.Status.objects.filter(
            entity = id).order_by(
              u'-datetime')[directory.settings.INITIAL_STATI:],
          u'tags': directory.models.Tag.objects.filter(entity = entity,
            is_invisible = False).order_by(u'text'),
```

```
          u'time_zones': directory.models.TIME_ZONE_CHOICES,
          u'urls': directory.models.URL.objects.filter(entity = entity,
            is_invisible = False),
        })
```

Likewise, we update `homepage()`:

```
        profile = template.render(Context(
          {
          u'entities':
            directory.models.Entity.objects.filter(
              is_invisible = False),
          u'entity': entity,
          u'first_stati': directory.models.Status.objects.filter(
            entity = id).order_by(
              u'-datetime')[:directory.settings.INITIAL_STATI],
          u'gps': gps,
          u'gps_url': gps_url,
          u'id': int(id),
          u'emails': directory.models.Email.objects.filter(
            entity = entity, is_invisible = False),
          u'phones': directory.models.Phone.objects.filter(
            entity = entity, is_invisible = False),
          u'query': urllib.quote(query),
          u'second_stati':directory.models.Status.objects.filter(
            entity = id).order_by(
              u'-datetime')[directory.settings.INITIAL_STATI:],
          u'time_zones': directory.models.TIME_ZONE_CHOICES,
          u'tags': directory.models.Tag.objects.filter(
            entity = entity,
            is_invisible = False).order_by(u'text'),
          u'urls': directory.models.URL.objects.filter(
            entity = entity, is_invisible = False),
          }))
```

Confusing jQuery's load() with html()

If we have failed to load a profile in the main `search.html` template, we had a call to `load("")`. What we needed was:

```
      else
        {
        $("#profile").html("");
        }
```

```
$("#profile").load("")
```
loads a copy of the current page into the `div` named `profile`. We can improve on this slightly to "blank" contents that include the default header:

```
            else
            {
                $("#profile").html("<h2>People, etc.</h2>");
            }
```

Preventing display of deleted instances

In our system, enabling undo means that there can be instances (Entities, Emails, URLs, and so on) which have been deleted but are still available for undo. We have implemented deletion by setting an `is_invisible` flag to `True`, and we also need to check before displaying to avoid puzzling behavior like a user deleting an Entity, being told **Your change has been saved**, and then seeing the Entity's profile displayed exactly as before.

We accomplish this by a specifying, for a Queryset `.filter(is_invisible = False)` where we might earlier have specified `.all()`, or adding `is_invisible = False` to the conditions of a pre-existing filter; for instance:

```
def ajax_download_model(request, model):
    if directory.settings.SHOULD_DOWNLOAD_DIRECTORY:
        json_serializer = serializers.get_serializer(u'json')()
        response = HttpResponse(mimetype = u'application/json')
        if model == u'Entity':
            json_serializer.serialize(getattr(directory.models,
                model).objects.filter(
                    is_invisible = False).order_by(u'name'),
                ensure_ascii = False, stream = response)
        else:
            json_serializer.serialize(getattr(directory.models,
                model).objects.filter(is_invisible = False),
                ensure_ascii = False,
                stream = response)
        return response
    else:
        return HttpResponse(u'This feature has been turned off.')
```

In the main view for the profile, we add a check in the beginning so that a (basically) blank result page is shown:

```
def ajax_profile(request, id):
    entity = directory.models.Entity.objects.filter(id = int(id))[0]
    if entity.is_invisible:
        return HttpResponse(u'<h2>People, etc.</h2>')
```

One nicety we provide is usually loading a profile on mouseover for its area of the search result page. This means that users can more quickly and easily scan through drilldown pages in search of the right match; however, there is a performance gotcha for simply specifying an `onmouseover` handler. If you specify an `onmouseover` for a containing `div`, you may get a separate event call for every time the user hovers over an element contained in the `div`, easily getting 3+ calls if a user moves the mouse over to the link. That could be annoying to people on a VPN connection if it means that they are getting the network hits for numerous needless profile loads.

To cut back on this, we define an initially `null` variable for the last profile moused over:

```
PHOTO_DIRECTORY.last_mouseover_profile = null;
```

Then we call the following function in the containing `div` element's `onmouseover`:

```
PHOTO_DIRECTORY.mouseover_profile = function(profile)
    {
    if (profile != PHOTO_DIRECTORY.last_mouseover_profile)
        {
        PHOTO_DIRECTORY.load_profile(profile);
        PHOTO_DIRECTORY.last_mouseover_profile = profile;
        PHOTO_DIRECTORY.register_editables();
        }
    }
```

The relevant code from `search_internal.html` is as follows:

```
<div class="search_result"
  onmouseover="PHOTO_DIRECTORY.mouseover_profile(
    {{ result.id }});"
  onclick="PHOTO_DIRECTORY.click_profile({{ result.id }});">
```

We usually, but not always, enable this mouseover functionality; not always, because it works out to annoying behavior if a person is trying to edit, does a drag select, mouses over the profile area, and reloads a fresh, non-edited profile. Here we edit the Jeditable plugin's source code and add a few lines; we also perform a second check for if the user is logged in, and offer a login form if so:

```
/* if element is empty add something clickable
   (if requested) */
if (!$.trim($(this).html())) {
    $(this).html(settings.placeholder);
}
```

```
            $(this).bind(settings.event, function(e) {

                $("div").removeAttr("onmouseover");
                if (!PHOTO_DIRECTORY.check_login())
                    {
                    PHOTO_DIRECTORY.offer_login();
                    }
                /* abort if disabled for this element */
                if (true === $(this).data('disabled.editable')) {
                    return;
                }
```

For Jeditable-enabled elements, we can override the placeholder for an empty element at method call, but the default placeholder is cleared when editing begins; overridden placeholders aren't. We override the placeholder with something that gives us a little more control and styling freedom:

```
        // publicly accessible defaults
            $.fn.editable.defaults = {
                name        : 'value',
                id          : 'id',
                type        : 'text',
                width       : 'auto',
                height      : 'auto',
                event       : 'click.editable',
                onblur      : 'cancel',
                loadtype    : 'GET',
                loadtext    : 'Loading...',
                placeholder: '<span class="placeholder">
                              Click to add.</span>',
                loaddata    : {},
                submitdata  : {},
                ajaxoptions: {}
            };
```

All of this is added to the file `jquery.jeditable.js`.

We now have, as well as an `@ajax_login_required` decorator, an `@ajax_permission_required` decorator. We test for this variable in the default postprocessor specified in `$.ajaxSetup()` for the `complete` handler. Because Jeditable will place the returned data inline, we also refresh the profile.

This occurs after the code to check for an undoable edit and offer an undo option to the user.

```
            complete: function(XMLHttpRequest, textStatus)
                {
                var data = XMLHttpRequest.responseText;
```

```
            var regular_expression = new RegExp("<!-" +
              "-# (\\d+) #-" + "->");
            if (data.match(regular_expression))
                {
                var match = regular_expression.exec(data);
                PHOTO_DIRECTORY.undo_notification(
                  "Your changes have been saved. " +
                  "<a href='JavaScript:PHOTO_DIRECTORY.undo(" +
                  match[1] + ")'>Undo</a>");
                }
            else if (data == '{"not_permitted": true}' ||
              data == "{'not_permitted': true}")
                {
                PHOTO_DIRECTORY.send_notification(
                  "We are sorry, but we cannot allow you " +
                  "to do that.");
                PHOTO_DIRECTORY.reload_profile();
                }
            },
```

Note that we have tried to produce the least painful of clear message we can: we avoid both saying "You shouldn't be doing that," and a terse, "bad movie computer"-style message of "Access denied" or "Permission denied."

We also removed from that method code to call `offer_login()` if a call came back not authenticated. This looked good on paper, but our code was making Ajax calls soon enough that the user would get an immediate, unprovoked, modal login dialog on loading the page.

Adding a favicon.ico

In terms of minor tweaks, some visually distinct `favicon.ico` (http://softpedia.com/ is one of many free sources of `favicon.ico` files, or the favicon generator at http://tools.dynamicdrive.com/favicon/ which can take an image like your company logo as the basis for an icon) helps your tabs look different at a glance from other tabs. Save a good, simple favicon in `static/favicon.ico`. The icon may not show up immediately when you refresh, but a good favicon makes it slightly easier for visitors to manage your pages among others that they have to deal with. It shows up in the address bar, bookmarks, and possibly other places.

This brings us to the end of the minor tweaks; let us look at two slightly larger additions to the directory.

Handling password input in a slightly different way

Our first addition has to do with password inputs. The traditional style of password input leaves plenty of room for second guessing about "Did I hit this key hard enough? Did I mistype something?" Logging in and specifying your password the traditional way ranks up with CAPTCHA as the hardest part of the form for regular users (apart from any disability issues).

What we will do, then, is present a regular text input for the default (users can click on **Hide password** for the old-school password input), and work a little Ajax to let the users switch. We will have two inputs, and when one of them receives a keydown or keyup event, its data is copied to the other. Only one of them, and only one link, will be visible at a time. In our `style.css` we have:

```css
#new_password_hidden, #password_hidden
    {
    display: none
    }

#show_new_password, #show_password
    {
    display: none;
    }
```

In the template, we expand the markup for the login and create account forms:

```html
<div id="login_form" title="Log in">
    <form>
        <fieldset>
            <label for="login">Login</label><br />
            <input type="text" name="login" id="login"
              class="text ui-widget-content ui-corner-all" /><br />
            <label for="password">Password</label><br />
            <input onkeyup="PHOTO_DIRECTORY.field_sync(
              'password_visible', 'password_hidden');"
              onkeydown="PHOTO_DIRECTORY.field_sync(
              'password_visible', 'password_hidden');"
              autocomplete="off" type="text" name="password_visible"
                id="password_visible"
                class="text ui-widget-content ui-corner-all" />
            <input onkeyup="PHOTO_DIRECTORY.field_sync(
              'password_hidden', 'password_visible');"
              onkeydown="PHOTO_DIRECTORY.field_sync(
              'password_hidden', 'password_visible');"
```

```html
                    type="password" name="password_hidden"
                    id="password_hidden"
                    class="text ui-widget-content ui-corner-all" /><br />
                <a id="hide_password" name="hide_password"
                    href="JavaScript:PHOTO_DIRECTORY.hide_element(
                    'password');">Hide password</a>
                <a id="show_password" name="show_password"
                    href="JavaScript:PHOTO_DIRECTORY.show_element(
                    'password');">Show password</a>
            </fieldset>
        </form>
    </div>
    <div id="create_account" title="Create account">
        <form>
            <fieldset>
                <label for="new_username">Account name</label><br />
                <input type="text" name="new_username" id="new_username"
                    class="text ui-widget-content ui-corner-all" /><br />
                <label for="new_email">Email</label><br />
                <input type="text" name="new_email" id="new_email"
                    class="text ui-widget-content ui-corner-all" /><br />
                <label for="new_password">Password</label><br />
                <input onkeyup="PHOTO_DIRECTORY.field_sync(
                    'new_password_visible', 'new_password_hidden');"
                    onkeydown="PHOTO_DIRECTORY.field_sync(
                    'new_password_visible', 'new_password_hidden');"
                    autocomplete="off" type="text"
                    name="new_password_visible" id="new_password_visible"
                    class="text ui-widget-content ui-corner-all" />
                <input onkeyup="PHOTO_DIRECTORY.field_sync(
                    'new_password_hidden', 'new_password_visible');"
                    onkeydown="PHOTO_DIRECTORY.field_sync(
                    'new_password_hidden', 'new_password_visible');"
                    type="password" name="new_password_hidden"
                    id="new_password_hidden"
                    class="text ui-widget-content ui-corner-all" /><br />
                <a id="hide_new_password" name="hide_new_password"
                    href="JavaScript:PHOTO_DIRECTORY.hide_element(
                    'new_password');">Hide password</a>
                <a id="show_new_password" name="show_new_password"
                    href="JavaScript:PHOTO_DIRECTORY.show_element(
                    'new_password');">Show password</a>
            </fieldset>
        </form>
    </div>
```

With this change, we also change the `search.html` file's reference to `document.getElementById("password").value` to `document.getElementById("password_visible").value`.

`field_sync()` copies data from one specified form element to another:

```
PHOTO_DIRECTORY.field_sync = function(from, to)
    {
    $("#" + to).val($("#" + from).val());
    }
```

`hide_element()` and `show_element()` feed their argument into toggling visibility for several elements:

```
PHOTO_DIRECTORY.hide_element = function(name)
    {
    $("#hide_" + name + ".#" + name + "_visible").hide();
    $("#show_" + name + ".#" + name "_hidden").show();
    }
```

And with the last arguments reversed:

```
PHOTO_DIRECTORY.show_element = function(name)
    {
    $("#hide_" + name + ".#" + name + "_visible").show();
    $("#show_" + name + ".#" + name "_hidden").hide();
    }
```

In our HTML markup for the inputs of type text, we specified `autocomplete="off"`, which is an important housekeeping detail to exclude the password from the list of form elements that are quietly recorded whether the user wants it that way or not.

And that completes this usability enhancement.

A directory that includes local timekeeping

We live in a world where we can deal with people in many different time zones, and sometimes it would be nice to know what time it is for the other person.

The solution here is an approximate solution that can run aground on the intricacies of Daylight Saving Time. Readers wishing for a more accurate solution may find an Ajax use of the Python module `pytz` on the backend (http://pytz.sourceforge.net/) to be more accurate in handling Daylight Saving Time. All the world's time zones amount to a lot of nooks and crannies, and a server-side database allows a finer granularity than a quick client-side solution. However, even an approximate client-side solution can be helpful in knowing, "What time of day is it for the other person?"

First of all, we define a choice for a time zone. (Note that we are using strings rather than decimals for offsets; pure decimals had implementation issues and produced results that JavaScript did not recognize as equal.)

```
TIME_ZONE_CHOICES = (
  (None, "Select"),
  ("1.0", "A: Paris, +1:00"),
  ("2.0", "B: Athens, +2:00"),
  ("3.0", "C: Moscow, +3:00"),
  ("4.0", "D: Dubai, +4:00"),
  ("4.5", "-: Kabul, +4:30"),
  ("5.0", "E: Karachi, +5:00"),
  ("5.5", "-: New Delhi, +5:30"),
  ("5.75", "-: Kathmandu, :5:45"),
  ("6.0", "F: Dhaka, +6:00"),
  ("6.5", "-: Rangoon, +6:30"),
  ("7.0", "G: Jakarta, +7:00"),
  ("8.0", "H: Kuala Lumpur, +8:00"),
  ("9.0", "I: Tokyo, +9:00"),
  ("9.5", "-: Adelaide, +9:30"),
  ("10.0", "K: Sydney, +10:00"),
  ("10.5", "-: Lord Howe Island, +10:30"),
  ("11.0", "L: Solomon Islands, +11:00"),
  ("11.5", "-: Norfolk Island, +11:50"),
  ("12.0", "M: Auckland, +12:00"),
  ("12.75", "-: Chatham Islands, +12:45"),
  ("13.0", "-: Tonga, +13:00"),
  ("14.0", "-: Line Islands, +14:00"),
  ("-1.0", "N: Azores, -1:00"),
  ("-2.0", "O: Fernando de Norohna, -2:00"),
  ("-3.0", "P: Rio de Janiero, -3:00"),
  ("-3.5", "-: St. John's, -3:50"),
  ("-4.0", "Q: Santiago, -4:00"),
  ("-4.5", "-: Caracas, -4:30"),
  ("-5.0", "R: New York City, -5:00"),
  ("-6.0", "S: Chicago, -6:00"),
  ("-7.0", "T: Boulder, -7:00"),
  ("-8.0", "U: Los Angeles, -8:00"),
  ("-9.0", "V: Anchorage, -9:00"),
  ("-9.5", "-: Marquesas Islands, -9:30"),
  ("-10.0", "W: Hawaii, -10:00"),
  ("-11.0", "X: Samoa, -11:00"),
  ("-12.0", "Y: Baker Island, -12:00"),
  ("0.0", "Z: London, +0:00"),
)
```

We expand the Entity definition to include a time zone slot, along with a checkmark for whether Daylight Saving Time is observed:

```
class Entity(models.Model):
    active = models.BooleanField(blank = True)
    department = models.ForeignKey(u'self', blank = True, null =
      True, related_name = u'member')
    description = models.TextField(blank = True)
    gps = GPSField()
    image_mimetype = models.TextField(blank = True, null = True)
    is_invisible = models.BooleanField(default = False)
    location = models.ForeignKey(u'self', blank = True, null = True,
      related_name = u'occupant')
    name = models.TextField(blank = True,
      default = u'(Insert name here)')
    observes_daylight_saving_time = models.BooleanField(
      blank = True, default = True)
    other_contact = models.TextField(blank = True)
    postal_address = models.TextField(blank = True)
    publish_externally = models.BooleanField(blank = True)
    reports_to = models.ForeignKey(u'self', blank = True,
      null = True, related_name = u'subordinate')
    start_date = models.DateField(blank = True, null = True)
    time_zone = models.CharField(max_length = 5, null = True,
      choices = TIME_ZONE_CHOICES)
    title = models.TextField(blank = True)
    class Meta:
        permissions = (
          ("view_changelog", "View the editing changelog"),
        )
```

Then we expand the `profile_internal.html` template to allow selection of time zone and Daylight Saving Time observance:

```
<p>Time zone:
    <select name="time_zone" id="time_zone"
      onchange="PHOTO_DIRECTORY.update_autocomplete(
      'Entity_time_zone_{{ id }}', 'time_zone');">
        {% for time_zone in time_zones %}
            <option value="{{ time_zone.0 }}"
                {% if time_zone.0 == entity.time_zone %}
                    selected="selected"
                {% endif %}
            >{{ time_zone.1 }}</option>
        {% endfor %}
```

```
        </select><br />
Observes daylight saving time: <input type="checkbox"
  name="observes_daylight_saving_time"
  id="observes_daylight_saving_time"
  onchange="PHOTO_DIRECTORY.update_autocomplete(
    'Entity_observes_daylight_saving_time_{{ id }}',
    'observes_daylight_saving_time');"
  {% if entity.observes_daylight_saving_time %}
    checked="checked"
  {% endif %}
  /></p>
```

And in addition, we add hooks to be filled out with the local time:

```
{% if entity.time_zone != None %}
<p>Local time:
<span id="local_time_zone">{{ entity.time_zone }}</span>
<span id="local_time"></span></p>
{% endif %}
```

The `local_time_zone` span is hidden:

```
#local_time_zone
    {
    display: none;
    }
```

Its purpose is to let Ajax fetch the Entity's time zone. In `search.html`, we expand the `register_update()` to set the clock:

```
      PHOTO_DIRECTORY.register_update = function()
          {
          PHOTO_DIRECTORY.limit_width("img.profile", 150);
          PHOTO_DIRECTORY.limit_width("img.search_results", 80);
          PHOTO_DIRECTORY.register_editables();
          PHOTO_DIRECTORY.register_autocomplete();
          if (!PHOTO_DIRECTORY.SHOULD_TURN_ON_HIJAXING)
              {
              $("a").removeAttr("onclick");
              // This link needs to be hijaxed:
              $("#add_new").click(function()
                  {
                  PHOTO_DIRECTORY.add_new();
                  return false;
                  });
              }
```

Tinkering Around: Bugfixes, Friendlier Password Input, and a Directory That Tells Local Time

One gotcha has to do with Daylight Saving Time: some places observe daylight saving time, some places don't, and if you don't take it into account, it's an easy way to be wrong by an hour about the other party's local time.

JavaScript offers no explicit facility to tell if our local time includes Daylight Saving Time. One way to tell if we have Daylight Saving Time right now is by looking at our offset from UTC and seeing if it is the same as the January 1 offset. If the two offsets are different then we are in Daylight Saving Time.

```
if ($("#local_time_zone").html())
    {
    var date = new Date();
    var profile_offset = -parseFloat(
      $("#local_time_zone").html()) * 3600000;
    var january_offset = new Date(date.getFullYear(), 0,
      1).getTimezoneOffset() * 60000;
    var our_offset = date.getTimezoneOffset() * 60000;
    if (our_offset != january_offset)
        {
        if (document.getElementById(
          "observes_daylight_saving_time").checked)
            {
            profile_offset -= 60 * 60 * 1000;
            }
        }
    PHOTO_DIRECTORY.update_clock(our_offset - profile_offset,
      PHOTO_DIRECTORY.current_profile);
    }
}
```

And we define the `update_clock` function. First it checks to see if the profile it was registered with is the current profile, and if not, we bail out:

```
PHOTO_DIRECTORY.update_clock = function(offset, id)
    {
    if (id != PHOTO_DIRECTORY.current_profile)
        {
        return;
        }
```

Then we make an adjusted date, "fudged" to give us values for the Entity's local time, and build human-friendly display output for it.

```
var adjusted_date = new Date(new Date().getTime() + offset);
var days = ["Sunday", "Monday", "Tuesday", "Wednesday",
  "Thursday", "Friday", "Saturday"];
```

```
var months = ["January", "February", "March", "April",
  "May", "June", "July", "August", "September", "November",
  "December"];
var ampm = "AM";
var hours = adjusted_date.getHours()
if (hours > 11)
    {
    hours -= 12;
    ampm = "PM"
    }
if (hours == 0)
    {
    hours = 12;
    }
var formatted_date = "<strong>" + hours + ":";
if (adjusted_date.getMinutes() < 10)
    {
    formatted_date += "0";
    }
formatted_date += adjusted_date.getMinutes() + " " + ampm;
formatted_date += "</strong>, ";
formatted_date += days[adjusted_date.getDay()] + " ";
formatted_date += months[adjusted_date.getMonth()] + " ";
formatted_date += adjusted_date.getDate() + ", ";
formatted_date += adjusted_date.getFullYear();
$("#local_time").html(formatted_date + ".");
```

An example of the formatted output this produces is "**12:01** PM, January 1, 2001."

Lastly, before closing, we set the clock to update again in a second, to keep the displayed value fresh.

```
setTimeout("PHOTO_DIRECTORY.update_clock(" + offset + ", " +
  id + ")", 1000);
}
```

In the code to dynamically build a profile, we add, after **Other contact information** and before **Department**, fields to build the equivalent of what we added to `profile_internal.html` earlier:

```
result += "<p>Other contact information: <strong ";
result += "class='edit_textarea' " +
  "title='Click to edit.' " +
  "id='Entity_other_contact_" + id + "'>" +
  entity.fields.other_contact + "</strong></p>\n";
```

```
            result += "<p>Time zone: ";
            result += "<select name='time_zone' id='time_zone'";
            result += "onchange=
                'PHOTO_DIRECTORY.update_autocomplete(
                \"Entity_time_zone_{{ id }}\", \"time_zone\");'>";
            {% for time_zone in time_zones %}
                result += "<option value='{{ time_zone.0 }}'>";
                result += "{{ time_zone.1 }}</option>\n";
            {% endfor %}
            result += "</select><br />\n";
            result += "Observes daylight saving time: ";
            result += "<input type='checkbox' ";
            result += "name='observes_daylight_saving_time' ";
            result += "id='observes_daylight_saving_time' ";
            result += "onchange=
                'PHOTO_DIRECTORY.update_autocomplete(";
            result += '"Entity_observes_daylight_saving_time_';
            result += id;
            result += '", "observes_daylight_saving_time");';
            result += "'";
            if (entity.fields.observes_daylight_saving_time)
                {
                result += " checked='checked'";
                }
            result += " /></p>";
            if (entity.fields.time_zone)
                {
                result += "<p>Local time:";
                result += "<span id='local_time_zone'>";
                result += entity.fields.time_zone;
                result += "</span>
                    <span id='local_time'></span></p>";
                }
            result += "<p>Department: <strong>";
```

The code fails to select the Entity's time zone; we remedy that after `build_profile()` is called:

```
    PHOTO_DIRECTORY.load_profile = function(id)
        {
        PHOTO_DIRECTORY.current_profile = id;
        if (PHOTO_DIRECTORY.SHOULD_TURN_ON_HIJAXING)
            {
            try
                {
```

```
            $("#profile").html(PHOTO_DIRECTORY.build_profile(id));
            if (PHOTO_DIRECTORY.entities[id].fields.time_zone !=
              null)
                {
                $("#time_zone").val(
                    PHOTO_DIRECTORY.entities[id].fields.time_zone);
                }
            PHOTO_DIRECTORY.register_update();
```

We add a bit of styling:

```
#local_time
    {
    font-weight: bold;
    }

#local_time strong
    {
    font-size: 2em;
    }
```

And with that, we have a clear local time slot in our profile:

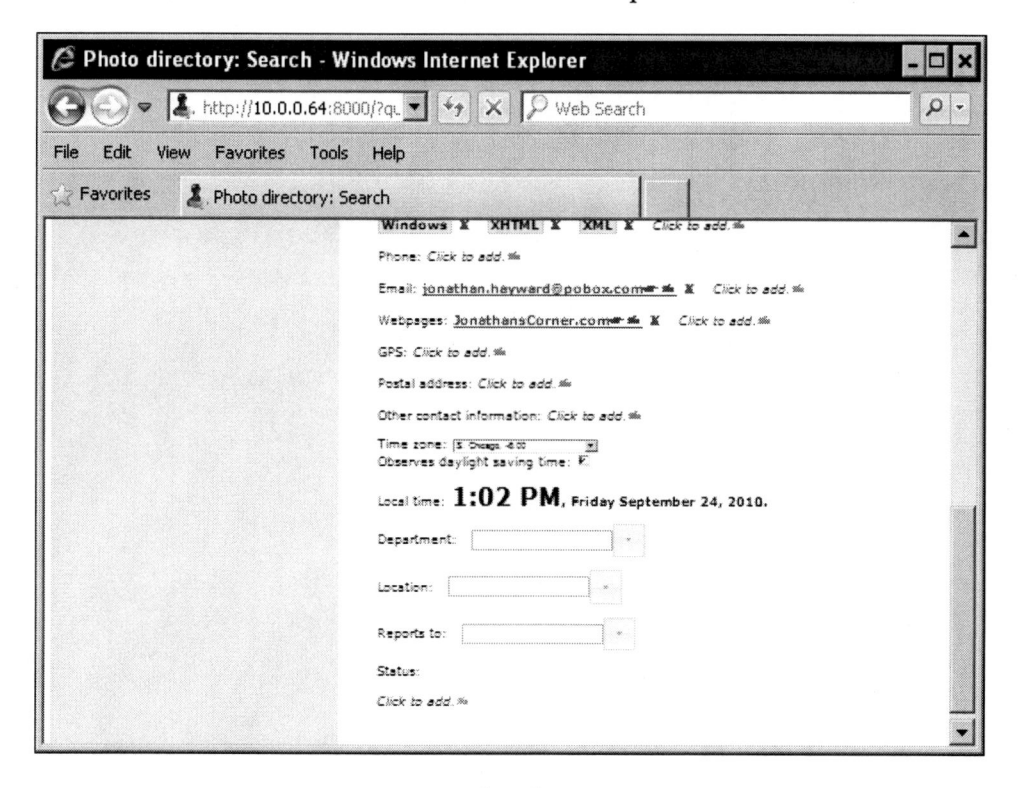

Summary

We have covered some tinkering and tweaks, and bugfixes along the way. Our directory has fewer rough spots! These include: updating the code to handle deletion correctly after we have added undoing and we retain some "deleted" items in the database, tweaking a standard plugin to enhance its behavior, improving a basic widget in terms of its usability, and adding a good first pass at a world time zone "What's their local time?" slot on the profile.

Let us continue to take a look at usability itself in the next chapter.

11
Usability for Hackers

The heart of software craftsmanship is writing code that is usable to programmers, including the author re-reading his own code in six months.

In this chapter we will look at usability concerns that make a user interface make sense to non-programmers. Certain kinds of math loom large in algorithms, and cultural anthropology looms large in good usability. We will look at anthropology as it relates to usability, and move from theory to practice.

In this chapter we will discuss:

- Anthropology as the foundation of usability
- Anthropologists' strengths that Django hackers are likely to share
- An example of an anthropology-based technique and the surprise it brought an investigator
- Why focus groups are deprecated for usability research
- Anthropology as a way of breaking up a seemingly simple and straightforward thing and understanding it through multiple cultural explanations
- How to apply this foundation to observing users as they deal with an interface
- How good usability observation is like solving a hard bug
- Examples of other background elements we can turn to our advantage in usability observation
- Liabilities that this book's readership may need to compensate for
- What the main tools for usability testing are and when they should be used
- Usability as the soul of what is Pythonic
- Further reading and resources

This chapter takes a little step further back than some of the others, and there is a lot there, but it is interesting material. Let's dig in!

Usability begins with anthropology… and Django hackers have a good start on anthropology

If you're reading this text, there's a good chance that you are already halfway to being an anthropologist.

> Note: for the purposes of this chapter, 'anthropology' is used to refer to cultural anthropology. Other anthropological disciplines exist (for example, biological or physical anthropology, linguistic anthropology, and archaeology), but it is cultural anthropology and its techniques which are most directly relevant here.

How could an author know that you are probably at least half an anthropologist? Let's turn the question around. Why are you reading this book at all? **Visual Basic .NET** has enormous marketing muscle behind it, possibly eclipsing the marketing budgets for all open source technologies put together. Guido van Rossum holds a dim view of marketing, as does much of the Python community. **Monster.com** lists three thousand Visual Basic positions, almost five thousand .NET positions, but only one thousand Python positions. Why are you reading a Django book when you could be reading a title like *Completely Master Visual Basic in Thirty Seconds or Less*?

You are probably a hacker. It does not matter if you were mortified when you found out the preferred JavaScript technique to create an object with fields that aren't globally accessible variables, or if you wince when you hear of a devious way to get technology to do things that shouldn't be possible, or if you have no desire to be considered a 133t hax0r. You're probably a hacker. The classic **How to Become a Hacker** (http://www.catb.org/~esr/faqs/hacker-howto.html) for the most part outlines things that have a very obvious relationship to being a hacker: attitudes towards technical problem solving, or learning an open source Unix, learning to program and contribute to the web, and so on and so forth. Towards the end there is a particularly interesting section, because on the surface it looks completely beside the point. The section is titled **Points for Style** and mentions learning to write well, reading in science fiction, training in martial arts, meditation, music (preferably obscure), and wordplay. Other things could be added: avoiding mainstream TV or having arcane hobbies and interests, for instance, so that in a social context hackers may ask each other questions about obscure hobbies as a rough social equivalent to, "What's your favorite TV show?"

Not that any of these is necessary to be a hacker, but together these common trends point to a personality profile that can learn the anthropological style of observation relevant to usability work much more easily than the general public, or even Joe Professional Programmer who regards learning new technologies as a necessary evil rather than a joy, works in Visual Basic .NET after being swayed by advertising, goes home and watches TV after work, has probably never heard of ThinkGeek, and would probably rather do gift shopping at Walmart even if that programmer does know of ThinkGeek.

All of this is to say that the culture surrounding you is not, to you, like water to a fish. It is a basic fact of life that you don't automatically share the perspective of others. Cross-cultural experience or ethnic minority status may accentuate this, but this is true even if you're not (regarded as) a minority. And this kind of experience provides a very good foundation for anthropological ways of understanding exactly how you are not a user and users don't think like you.

Anthropological usability techniques

There are a number of anthropology-based techniques that apply in usability. They include card sorting, discussed below, and also activities such as observing users try to use your site, eyetracking "heatmap" studies, cognitive walkthroughs, and so on. http://www.usabilityfirst.com/usability-methods/ shows some standard techniques, although it lists focus groups without the standard warning. Focus groups, as will be discussed, are cargo cult anthropology. They are considered harmful when used for usability instead of marketing research, and are for that matter considered harmful by some of the more savvy market researchers who are realizing that to understand your audience you need the best anthropology has to offer.

An introductory example: card sorting

One basic challenge for organizing a site's information architecture is the taxonomy, or way of breaking things down. If one is asked for an example of a good taxonomy, one example par excellence is the biological taxonomy that organizes all the way from kingdoms down to species or subspecies and varieties. And indeed that is one kind of taxonomy, but it is not the only possibility. If one is asked to break down a list of a fork, spoon, plate, bowl, soup, and macaroni and cheese, one obvious way is to put the fork and spoon together as cutlery, the plate and bowl together as dishware, and the soup and macaroni and cheese together as food. But this is not the only basic way, and it can make sense to put the fork, plate, and macaroni and cheese together as representing one complete option, and the spoon, bowl, and soup together as representing another basic option.

Stores and websites that have adopted the latter approach, such as a gardening store or website that organizes its products according to the type of garden a customer is trying to make and what the customer is trying to do, see a significant increase in sales. Even biology could use other complementary technologies: a taxonomy that classified organisms according to both ecosystems and their roles within their ecosystems and ecological subsystems could say something very valuable that the eighteenth century classification wouldn't.

In terms of websites, an information architecture that corresponds to the organization's org chart is never a helpful choice. Even when we are talking about an intranet intended only for organizational insiders, one section or subsite for each department is not the right choice. A better option would be to support workflow and design around the tasks that employees will be doing with the intranet.

What is the best information architecture? That is not a question to answer by looking something up in a book or even thinking it out. It is something that we should work out based on what we observe doing research, even if we also read and need to do a bit of thinking. And this is the best practice across the board for usability.

One valuable exercise to help guide information architecture design is called card sorting. In this exercise, we get a stack of index cards, perhaps 3 x 5, and write the individual names of different pieces of functionality the website should offer, trying to name things neutrally so that the names do not have common terms suggesting how certain parts belong together. Then we shuffle and lay out the cards, and individually ask subjects (people who will participate in an experiment and who are not insiders, whether employees of your organization or of an external website, or information technology professionals) to organize them so that cards that belong together are put in the same stack.

Then we note which cards have been placed together, thank the subject, and move on to the next person.

On looking through the notes, we may see a few things. First, not all people think the same. We will likely see some breakdowns that are very similar, but there will likely be two or more breakdowns as fundamentally divergent as our breakdowns of the fork, spoon, plate, bowl, soup, and macaroni and cheese. Second, there will probably be a breakdown that simply catches us off guard. And this is good; it means the exercise is working.

After doing this, we can go about looking for a preferably standard information architecture that will gracefully serve the major ways we observed of breaking things down.

Focus groups: cargo cult research for usability

With an eye to how to best approach observation, we would like to take a moment to talk about Coca-Cola's blunder with "New Coke" and explain why focus groups—bringing in a group of people and asking them what they want—are deprecated as a recipe to make products that look good on paper but don't wear well in normal use. For those of you who don't remember the uproar some years back, the Coca-Cola company announced that it was switching to a new and improved formula, and there was massive public outlash from people who wanted the old Coke back. (Now the company sells both the old formula as Coke Classic and the new formula as Coke II, and Coke Classic is vastly more popular.)

Why would the Coca-Cola company announce it was terminating its cash cow? The answer is that it did naïve marketing research, ran taste tests, and asked members of the public which they would choose: the formula today sold as Coke Classic, or the formula today sold as Coke II. The rather clear answer from the taste tests was that people said they would rather have the new formula, and it was a clear enough answer that it looked like a sensible course of action to simply drop the second-best formula. It was not until everybody could see that the Coca-Cola company had given itself a PR black eye that the company woke up to a baseline observation in anthropology: *the horse's mouth is a vastly overrated source of information*. Most anthropological observations, including the kinds relevant to usability, are about paying close attention to what people do, and not being too distracted by their good faith efforts to explain things that are very hard to get right.

Anthropological observation: the bedrock of usability

The first step in understanding your users is to wake up to how something that goes without saying to the entire development team can be unknown to your users. The first step to that is waking up to how many ways there can be to see one clear, simple situation.

More than one way to see the same situation

The kind of observation needed is probably closest to the anthropological technique of participant observation, except that instead of participating in using software or a website, we are observing others as they use software. Half the goal is to understand how the same thing can be observed differently. To quote from James Spradley's *Participant Observation*, which is an excellent resource:

> One afternoon in 1973 I came across the following news item in the Minneapolis Tribune:
>
>> Nov. 23, 1973. Hartford, Connecticut. Three policemen giving a heart massage and oxygen to a heart attack victim Friday were attacked by a crowd of 75 to 100 people who apparently did not realize what the policemen were doing. Other policemen fended off the crowd of mostly Spanish-speaking residents until an ambulance arrived. Police said they tried to explain to the crowd what they were doing, but the crowd apparently thought they were beating the woman.
>>
>> Despite the policemen's efforts the victim, Evangelica Echevacria, 59, died.
>
> Here we see people using their culture. Members of two different groups observed the same event but their interpretations were drastically different. The crowd used their cultural knowledge (a) to interpret the behavior of the policemen as cruel and (b) to act on the woman's behalf to put a stop to what they perceived as brutality. They had acquired the cultural principles for acting and interpreting things this way through a particular shared experience.
>
> The policemen, on the other hand, used their cultural knowledge (a) to interpret the woman's condition as heart failure and their own behavior as life-saving effort and (b) to give her cardiac massage and oxygen. They used artifacts like an oxygen mask and ambulance. Furthermore, they interpreted the actions of the crowd in an entirely different manner from how the crowd saw their own behavior. The two groups of people each had elaborate cultural rules for interpreting their experience and for acting in emergency situations, and the conflict arose, at least in part, because these cultural rules were so different.

Before making my main point, we would simply like to comment that the Spanish-speaking crowd's response makes a *lot* more sense than it would first seem. It makes a lot of sense even on the assumption that the crowd did in fact understand the police officer's explanation that they "apparently did not understand." What the article explicitly states is that the police officers were using an oxygen mask, and that is a device that needs to be pressed against a person's face and necessarily cover the same parts of a person's face one would cover to try to cause suffocation. If you are not expecting something like that, it looks awfully strange. (At best!)

Furthermore, although we might not know whether this actually happened, it is standard operating procedure to many emergency medical technicians and paramedics who perform CPR to cut off the person's top completely, palpate to the best place to place one's hands, and mark the spot with a ball-point pen. This may or may not have happened here, but if it did, it is appropriate enough for neighbors to view it as an extreme indignity. Lastly, although today's best practices in CPR are more forceful than was recommended in the past, "heart massage" is a technical term that does not refer to anything like softly kneading a friend's shoulder. People who do CPR regularly say they crack ribs all the time: cracking ribs may not be desirable on its own, but if a responder is doing good CPR with enough force to be effective, breaking a patient's ribs is considered entirely normal and *not* a red flag that CPR is being done inappropriately or with excessive force.

Furthermore, the woman's age of 59 raises the question of osteoporosis. Racism is almost certainly a factor in the community's memories; the community had quite probable stories circulating of bad treatment by police officers and possible police brutality. We know that the police *tried* to explain what they were doing, but if many of us saw police apparently trying to suffocate a member of our community, possibly saw an offensive indignity in that a senior's shirt and underwear had been cut away, and saw an officer keep on forcefully shoving down on her chest and probably heard ribs crackling with every shove, it would take quite some convincing, and almost a reprehensible gullibility, for the bystanders to believe the other officers who tried to explain, "No, really, we're trying to help her!"

[
For reasons that follow, we should be very wary of saying that she probably would have survived if *only* the crowd hadn't intervened. We shall view this example from a historical point of view, that is, the information presented here was the medical opinion of the times.
]

We may pause to note that neither group, nor apparently the authors of the newspaper article or anthropology text, appears to grasp how the situation would be viewed by a doctor. "Heart massage" is now more commonly known as "Cardiopulmonary *resuscitation*" or CPR, *resuscitation* being an otherwise obscure synonym for *resurrection* or returning from the dead. In French religious language, for instance, *resuscitation* is the term one uses for Christ returning to life after death on a cross. There is, to the purist, some fundamental confusion in the marketing-style slogan, "CPR saves lives." Clinically and legally, it was thought that death occurs when a person's heart stops beating. If a person is still alive, and if there is any chance of saving the person's life, then CPR is both premature and inappropriate.

> The **Uniform Determination Of Death Act**, United States (1981): An individual who has sustained either (1) irreversible cessation of circulatory and respiratory functions, or (2) irreversible cessation of all functions of the entire brain, including the brain stem, is pronounced death.

Once a person has entered a state of "cardiac arrest," which meant *death* (historically), then there might be a possibility of getting that person back by cardio-pulmonary resuscitation, even if that is a long shot. CPR at its very best is a third as effective as a heart beating normally, and even under ideal conditions can only slow deterioration to give the emergency room perhaps a 5% to 10% chance of getting the person back. And that is assuming that ideal conditions are possible: in reality ideal conditions do not happen. Though most people giving CPR do not have to deal with a crowd interpreting their efforts as assault, hoping to deliver perfect CPR is like hoping to become a good enough coder that one need not contend with debugging. Eric Raymond implicitly showed great maturity as a programmer by saying he was dumbfounded when his first attempt at Python meta-programming worked without debugging. The person who does CPR in a public setting will contend not only with the difficulties of CPR itself, but an "uh-oh squad", bystanders who second-guess one's efforts and create a social dynamic like that of giving a speech to an audience of hecklers.

Now there is no question of blows or physical restraint when it comes to the idea of CPR or cardiac massage as a way to save lives that is apparently shared by the newspaper article author, the anthropology author, and possibly the police. And the medical view is that CPR is "only indicated in the case of cardiac arrest," meaning that it is premature and inappropriate unless a person has already died, but can preserve a remote chance of getting a patient back after the patient has crossed the threshold of clinical death. Emergency room doctors who view CPR as slowing deterioration and holding onto a slender chance of getting someone back will be quite grateful for CPR performed by police officers and other members of the general public who view CPR as a skill which saves lives. But the understanding is still fundamentally different, and differences like this come up in how computer interfaces are understood: differences you will want and need to appreciate.

Applying this foundation to usability

The core of usability testing is designing some sample tasks, asking users to do them, and observing, as a fly on the wall, *without helping*. If you can record sessions, great; if not, a notepad, notebook, or netbook works well. (The advantage of recording sessions is that almost invariably people will say, "There is no way the user could have that much trouble with our design," and a five-minute video of a user looking everywhere on the page but where users are intended to look, is worth a thousand arguments.) Usually studying five users is sufficient.

There is a saying in customer service of, "The customer is always right." One may read the cautionary tale of a salesperson who kept on winning arguments with customers and somehow never closed a sale. And the principle is very simple. A customer who is wrong is to be treated as a valued customer as well as a customer who is right, and whether our customer is right or wrong, we treat each customer as a valued customer. Unless we are talking about an abusive customer, in which case it is appropriate to draw a line in the sand, we don't send a message of "I'm right, you're wrong."

That is *not* what we are talking about when we say, "The user is always right." Anyone who teaches programmers or remembers what it was like to begin programming remembers hearing, "There's no way the computer can be right! The computer has to be running my code wrong, or the compiler isn't working right, or SQL's lying to me again!" And it is a slow and at times painful lesson that the computer is in fact (almost) always right, that no matter how right your code seems, or how certain you are, if your code is not working, it is because you did something you did not intend, and your code will begin working when you find out how your code does not obviously say what you think it does, and adjust that part of your code. Bugs in libraries and (more rarely) compilers and interpreters do exist, but one important threshold has been crossed when a programmer stops blaming the tool for confusing bugs and begins to take responsibility personally.

And in the same sense that the computer is always right, and not the sense that the customer is always right, the user is always right about how users behave. If the user interacts with the user interface and does something counterproductive, this means the same sort of thing as code doing something counterproductive if it has been compiled. The user, who is always right, has identified an area where the interface needs improvement. The user should be regarded as "always right" just as the computer should be regarded as "always right," and when the user is wrong, that is good information about where the user interface has problems.

I could say that the only thing we really need to do at all is observe the user. But observing the user includes a major challenge: it includes the major task of grasping things that violate our assumptions. The task is something like first encountering how JavaScript's support for object-oriented programming includes objects and inheritance, but without classes, first coming to a scripting language and asking, "When does integer overflow occur?" and being told, "Your question does have an answer, but it matters less than you might think," or the experience of a novice programmer who posted to a forum, "How do I turn off all the annoying compiler warnings I'm getting?" and was extremely frustrated to have more than one guru say, "You want to beg your compiler to give you as many warnings as you can get, and treat all warnings as errors."

It was a deft move for Google to give Chrome a single search and URL bar, but the main reason may not be the one you think. Searching was heavily enough used that Firefox made life easier for many users by adding a second bar to the right of the URL bar so that we could search without first pulling up the Google homepage. For heavy users, simplifying the URL bar and the search bar into one full-width piece is the next refinement. But this is not the main reason why it was deft for Google to give Chrome a unified search/URL bar, or at very least not the only reason.

My own experience helping others out with their computers has revealed that something obvious to us has been absolutely non-existent in their minds. Perhaps you have had the experience, too, of telling someone to enter something in a page's text field, and they start typing it in the URL bar, or vice versa typing a URL into a page's search field. What this unearths is that something that is patently obvious to web designers is not obvious to many web users. "Here is an important, impenetrable dividing line, and all the chrome above that line belongs to the browser, and everything below that line (above the bottom chrome, and excluding any scroll bars) belongs to the website." This division of labor is obvious enough to most web designers that only experience could teach them that there are some people who don't understand it. But the real world has many users who do not have any such concept, and behaviors like typing search terms in the URL bar (years before Chrome was available) are clues to "This is something that is out there."

And if you think, "OK, but users are more sophisticated now," you might go through your website's search logs and see how many website addresses you can see. It will not be nearly as many as ordinary search terms, but have you ever wondered where the addresses to MySpace and porn sites in your search logs come from?

Culture shock is a fundamental reality of when things go contrary to your expectations. Most of us experience small amounts of culture shock in our day-to-day living and much greater amounts if we travel to another country or do something else. The three examples given earlier, of classless objects in JavaScript, integer overflow in scripting languages as not terribly important, and asking for a more draconian handling of warnings are examples of culture shock in relation to technologies. As a rule of thumb, if you are not experiencing culture shock from your user observations, you are not deriving full benefit from them, and you do not understand your users well enough to make the fullest improvements to the design. To put it more forcefully, if you aren't experiencing culture shock from your user observations, that's because you're taking a shower with your raincoat on.

It's just like (hard) debugging

We would like to make one closing parallel to debugging. There are several types of debugging we are not talking about; for instance, a missing close parenthesis causes an immediate error that makes it fairly quick work to find out what is wrong and what line of code it is. A traceback can also provide an excellent starting point for quick and effective debugging. Although debugging a failed unit test may not be quite so easy, a unit test is not just a tool to say that something is wrong, somewhere; it is a tool that should point a finger, and usually narrow the search field significantly. And many other bugs that are neither syntax errors nor resolved with the help of unit tests are still easy enough to fix that we need not be terribly aware of them. When we think of debugging, we may only think of the few hard bugs rather than the majority of bugs which better programmers resolve without really thinking about it, like we turn on light switches on entering a darkened room, or unzip a coat outdoors when the day warms up, without giving the matter too much conscious thought or vividly remembering that we do this. (This is, incidentally, somewhat of an ethnographic observation of good programmers.)

What we are talking about, as hard bugs, are bugs where you go through every investigative tool you can think of, and still cannot pin down what is going on. (This may include a relatively small proportion of bugs that also generate tracebacks or unit test failures.) Observing the bug seems like observing, not a miniature ship in a bottle, but a ship in a seamless glass sphere. There's no way you can tell that the ship could have gotten in there, but it is quite clear that the ship in fact is in a glass container that has no openings that you can imagine the ship getting in through.

Isaac Asimov said, "The most exciting sound in science is not, '*Eureka!*' [I've found it!], but 'That's funny,'" and the history of science bears him out. Today, X-rays are widely known among scientifically literate people to be a very high-energy, short-wavelength radiation belonging to the same spectrum as visible light, but it was not always so; the name "X-rays" is itself a holdover from when they were a fascinating and mysterious phenomenon, with the "X" in "X-rays" referring to something unknown. It was known that they were radiation of some sort, but they passed through some opaque material and in general did not fit into anything people had a conceptual place for.

In the middle of efforts to understand this mystery, there was one physicist who stumbled upon a golden clue that X-rays might be something like light He left unexposed photographic plates near a source of X-rays, and upon using and developing them, observed that they had all been partially exposed. His response, however, was to contact the photographic supply company and demand that they replace the photographic plates as defective. As Winston Churchill observed, "Man will occasionally stumble over the truth, but most of the time he will pick himself up and continue on."

In debugging, hard bugs, the kind that remain unresolved after we have investigated all the usual suspects, are rarely solved because we go looking for the right error and find exactly what we expected to find. With the analogy of the ship in the sphere, it is more like deciding there has to be some kind of concealed seam from gluing or otherwise sealing an aperture big enough to allow the ship to enter, at least in pieces. After looking the glasswork over, using magnifying glasses and lights, and still finding no trace of a seam, you stop ignoring something you had noticed along the way: the ship itself appeared surprisingly glossy. When you stop to look at the ship for a second, you realize that it is not made of the wood and cloth you expected (and that it appears to be at first glance), but as far as you can tell is shaped out of colored glass. And, after doing a little more research, you learn of a glassblower who makes colored glass ships and forms seamless glass spheres around them. In this case, you were not wrong in saying there was no seam. There is still no way that such a thing could have been crafted at room temperature, and there is in fact no ultra-subtle seam that you failed to notice in your efforts to find the seam to an aperture through which the ship could have been inserted at room temperature, even in pieces. But that's not the point. The ship in a globe was made at glassblowers' temperatures, and there it is possible to create a seamless sphere around a colored glass ship.

Hard bugs are debugged successfully when you learn to stop upon stumbling over the truth. And the same is true in the anthropological side of usability techniques: some things you can know to look for, and find, but the much more important competency is to recognize when you have stumbled over the truth, and stop and pay attention to something you don't know to look for.

Almost all of the difference between doing user observation badly and doing it well hinges on learning to recognize when you have stumbled over the truth.

Lessons from other areas

Opportunities to learn, and sharpen, core anthropological competencies for usability are all around us. We need, in many cases, simply to open our eyes, *and transfer what we have learned from one area to another.*

Live cross-cultural encounters

Learning and observing in cross-cultural encounters is an excellent way to learn how to pick up cues the way a user interface developer needs to. There are two basic cross-cultural encounters we recommend as particularly valuable. The first of these, as it takes shape in the U.S., is to spend time volunteering with an English as a Second Language program and tutor on computer basics. Or find out if you can tutor in classes at your local library. (If possible, work in an adult computer class that has seniors and not too many young people.) This may or may not be the most pleasant experience, but it is one of the most valuable. I remember one experience where I was working with a Sudanese refugee, quite possibly an escapee of genocide against Christians, who had just had his life uprooted under presumably traumatic circumstances and was learning to deal with living in the U.S. all at once, which would quite probably be traumatic in itself. I remember, in particular, one moment when we had very slowly typed a word or two in a word processor, and ticked the button to close a document, and were staring at a dialog box asking if we wanted to save the document before closing. And I remember a slow dawning realization that not only did he not know the quite substantial cultural concepts involved in recognizing that this was how culturally one asks a question, expecting an answer in the form of a click on one of two areas of the screen to answer **Yes**, **No**, or "*Mu*" (**Cancel**). But the question itself, "Do you want to save this document before closing?" was a question that did not exist at all in his culture, and even if I spoke his native language I would probably not be able to explain the question in terms that would make any sense to him. That was probably my most difficult teaching experience, and the one where I have the most doubts about whether I succeeded in teaching anything at all. But it was a profoundly valuable experience to me, and helped me see how things could "go without saying" to me but be baffling to others.

The second of these two cross-cultural encounters is whatever you already have. Few if any of us have no cross-cultural encounters; whether one is ethnically or (a)religiously a majority or a minority, an immigrant or a native citizen of one's country, or considering face-to-face encounters or Internet connections, most of us have at least some experience in cross-cultural encounters. The differences are there; if you have learned something from cross-cultural encounter, the experience can help you more readily recognize the cues you need to recognize.

History

While we are wary of reducing history to merely an apparatus to understand the cultures of previous times, most historians arrive at a fairly deep understanding of a culture that is not their own, and may arrive at a sensitivity to the ways, all too easy to ignore, in which historical texts veto modern assumptions. There was an experiment in which a question concerning Abraham Lincoln and a number of historical primary sources was given to a number of elementary school teachers, plus one historian of Lincoln, and a historian whose specialties were unrelated. During the time of the experiment, the elementary school teachers started with a wrong conceptual framework that imposed today's basic categories on the texts, and did not progress to anything better.

The historian of Lincoln started with a highly accurate conceptual framework and very quickly arrived at the answer. But what is particularly interesting is the other historian, who was trained as a historian but had little directly relevant knowledge of Lincoln. He started with the same conceptual framework as the non-historians, but by the end he had corrected his framework to the point of reaching where the Lincoln historian had started.

This latter historian is perhaps the most interesting, not because he was not initially right, but because he was self-correcting. Even though his starting framework was no better than the school teachers, he was sufficiently able to adjust his perspective from cues based on the text so that he reached the framework the Lincoln historian started with. And, one would imagine, the Lincoln historian would have had a similar self-correcting sensitivity to the texts had he been asked the same kind of question about a historical setting he did not initially understand.

Getting history right is relevant to us in two ways. First, you or I understand one, or perhaps many, other cultures more or less well. Second, when you or I trip over a clue that is wrong, we can stop and learn from it, instead of hoping it will go away. Both of these strengths are a powerful foundation to usability.

Old books and literature

Books can be a very good place to sharpen anthropological competencies through meeting other cultures. However, we might clear the ground of some distractions if it is tempting to say, "But I meet other cultures in all my favorite books! I'm an avid reader of science fiction and fantasy."

All science fiction is not created equal in terms of cultural encounter. There is a marked difference between reading Heinlein's *Stranger in a Strange Land* and watching *Star Trek*. Heinlein understood both culture and culture shock, and though his book only treats one alien culture, it is written to create culture shock in the reader, and challenge us in assumptions we didn't know we had. "*Whaaa – ?* They can't *do* that!" is a normal and intended reaction to several parts of the book. In *Star Trek*, there are many races, but culture shock in the viewer is almost non-existent even when the plot is intended to surprise. To put it more pointedly, the average American's culture shock from watching years of *Star Trek* is probably much less than the average American student's culture shock from a few months' experience in a foreign exchange program, perhaps less than the culture shock in the first month of that program. By comparison with a live encounter with another human culture, the alien races in *Star Trek* have less their own alien cultures than a shared personality profile we can already relate to even when we don't like it.

Likewise, not all fantasy is created equal. J.R.R. Tolkein and C.S. Lewis were both Oxford-educated medievalists who knew medieval literature intimately. The genre of fantasy that appeared in their wake, if you have seriously read medieval literature, seems by comparison like the opening rant in the movie *Dungeons & Dragons*, where a supposedly medieval character gives an impassioned "Miss America" speech about how horrible it is that the realm's government is unlike a U.S.-style democracy. Today's genre fantasy reads like the story of Westerners from our time who happen to be wearing armor. By contrast, in *The Chronicles of Narnia* some of the characters are indeed from the twentieth century, but in terms of how the story is put together there is something a bit medieval, and not individualist, about their characterization.

If our cultures' science fiction and fantasy are not the best place to be challenged by another encounter, and to develop that kind of sensitivity, where can we go? One obvious response is to look to be challenged by books like the *Dao De Jing* and the *Bhagavad-Gita*. Those are both excellent places to look to be challenged, but if we assume that we can be challenged by the *Bhagavad-Gita* but not Plato, we are selling both of them short. Plato's image of climbing out of the cave with its shadows and looking at the sun is something that a Hindu commentator on the *Bhagavad-Gita* can quite easily relate to, and in a certain sense Plato has more in common with that kind of Hinduism than with his disciple Aristotle.

How does one read a text to see what one can pick up culturally? Consider the following text:

> QUANTUM THEORY, THE. *As recently as the opening years of the present century the vast majority of physicists still regarded Newton's dynamical laws as something established for all time. And they were not without solid grounds for this faith. Many phenomena were indeed known, chiefly those which may be classed under the heading radiation, for example, black body radiation and line spectra, which refused to accommodate themselves to any sort of theory founded on Newtonian principle. But it was generally believed that such phenomena would, sooner or later, be completely accounted for without any departure from the classical principles of physics. Even the theory of relativity developed by Lorentz, Einstein, Minkowski and their successors was regarded only as a widening or generalization of the Newtonian basis of physics. It was the culmination of classical physical theory. These phenomena we now believe, cannot be accounted for on the basis of classical physical theory, whether Newtonian or Einsteinian. The first act of sacrilege was committed by Max Planck, until recently professor of theoretical physics at the University of Berlin, about the end of the year 1900, when he initiated the quantum theory. One of the problems engaging the attention of physicists during the closing years of the last century was that of the radiation from a black body...*

> *The reconciliation of these two aspects of the phenomenon, namely the independence of the energy of the ejected photo-electrons and the intensity, on the one hand, and the wave character of the radiation on the other, constitutes one of the most formidable problems which physical science has ever encountered...*

Now we would like to make a couple of points. We could, for instance, have chosen an interminable fight narrative from a medieval Arthurian legend to say, "We look on Arthurian legends as mysterious tales of wonder. Did you know that a large portion of those legends is actually quite dull to the modern reader?" Some readers may be wondering, "This is a scientific article, not a cultural area where anything goes." But, even if science is not a domain where anything goes, there are cultural issues here, and it may be possible to date the article by cultural markers as well as by values given for physical constants. (Based on details further on in the text, Avogadro's number appears to be given as 6.06×10^{23}, not today's 6.022×10^{23}, and the unit of electrical charge is reported in the text to have current values consistent with initial measurements, despite the fact that the initial reported experimental value was erroneous and subsequent experimenters fudged until it was found acceptable to report what is now believed to be the correct value.)

In the quoted text, there are two significant markers that date the text as showing significant cultural difference from how things are viewed today.

A physicist or philosopher today would say that Newtonian physics, Einsteinian physics, quantum physics, and for that matter superstring theory are fundamentally irreconcilable on an ontological plane but happen to predict the same behaviors for the kind of experiments one would expect of a high school physics lab: the predicted results for each of these theories are vastly smaller than even a top-notch experimental physicist doing high school experiments could possibly observe. But the reasons behind those differences are irreconcilable, like the difference between saying "You see this OS behavior because it is running natively on your computer," and "You see this OS behavior because it is being emulated under virtualization with several levels of indirection that are extremely slippery to understand." The behavior predicted is interchangeable, but the reasons proposed for the behavior are fundamentally irreconcilable. Furthermore, this is not just true if one compares quantum physics with Einsteinian or Newtonian physics; it is also true if one compares Einsteinian with Newtonian physics: to today's take on things, it is a bit astonishing to say, "on the basis of classical physical theory, whether Newtonian or Einsteinian." The usual way of presenting things in a physics class today is to present Einstein's theory of relativity as the first in a stream of foundational upsets after Newton reigned unchallenged and apparently eternally established for centuries. Today we would expect to need to dig a bit to find more examples of Einstein's theory referred to as a further expansion developing Newton, which should still be considered "classical physical theory."

The second quoted paragraph refers to how light (and, it may be mentioned, practically everything else as seen in quantum theory) behaves as a particle when treated in some ways and as a wave when treated in others. This duality has since hit the rumor mill well enough that a favorite illustration from science in theology programs is how light exists as both a particle and a wave, which reflects the extent to which the duality of light as particle and wave remains unresolved but is no longer regarded as, "one of the most formidable problems that physical science has ever encountered."

Our point is not to deride the article, which is written at a higher level of sophistication and detail than, for instance, Wikipedia. Apart from its certitude in the existence of an "aether," slightly surprising in light of the fact that the Michelson-Morley experiment dates to 1887 and the article refers to 1900 as a past year, its picture of quantum physics portrays the same core science one would expect of a physics text today. But, even in physics, which is not in any sense a field where just anything goes, culture is present, and for that matter in this article the cultural cues alone are most likely sufficient for an historian of twentieth century physics to closely date it.

This kind of cue is what you can practice learning in reading old books, and this kind of cue is what you need to be able to pick up in observing for good user interface development.

The way you observe that a user does not share an understanding that is obvious to you is by the same kind of cue that can clue you in that a text doesn't share an understanding that is obvious to you.

The last other area: whatever you have

Whatever else you have is probably a resource you can draw on. Do you love birding? Birding is a hobby of observation. Do you do martial arts, for instance? A common theme in martial arts is harmony between opponents, and if you can attune yourself to a sparring partner, you should be able to attune yourself to a user. Comedy or performing arts? You are not a good comedian if you are insensitive to your audience. Have you made a lot of mistakes, and learned from them, or at least *started* to learn? Wonderful news! (Are you an amateur or professional anthropologist? *That* one does not need explaining!) There is some connection between any two areas of life; let other skills support and strengthen your usability work.

Understanding the user

Do we best understand the user by sitting off by ourselves and speculating how a user would look, think, and act about our interface? Let us take a look at what may be a very familiar lesson to expert programmers, however unreal it may seem to novices.

A lesson from optimization

Knuth said, for the novice programmer, "Do not optimize," and to experts only, "Optimize later." Always writing for optimization is a recipe for bad, unreadable code, and for that matter slow code, compared to code written for clarity that is later optimized using that clarity. And Knuth also said, "Premature optimization is the root of all evil."

In one production system I was working on, I wrote one search with the realization that the implementation I was using was extremely inefficient, and had to deliberately refrain from optimizing it, to leave for later. When the whole system was put together, it took a couple of seconds longer than was acceptable, and I began mentally gearing up to optimize the inefficient search. Before doing so, I did some testing, and found to my surprise that my inefficient search implementation took very little time to run, and when I began mapping things out, found the root problem. I had called a poorly chosen method, and with that choice made a purely preventable network call, and that network call took a few seconds. When that problem was fixed, the remaining code ran at an acceptably fast rate for even the largest accounts.

This story is my own version of something that keeps on being retold in the programming literature: "Our system was running slowly, and we had reasonable ideas about what was going on here, but our reasonable ideas were wrong. We didn't know what the real problem was until we dug into some observation."

This basic lesson in optimization is a fundamental phenomenon in usability as well. We will have reasonable ideas about what the usability issues are, and our reasonable ideas will be wrong. We won't know what the real issues are until we dig into some observation.

What's wrong with scratching an itch, or you are not your user

The open source community is largely driven by scratching itches, but scratching a programmer's itch is a terrible way to approach user interface design.

The story is told of a program used in an office where a popup window appeared and said, "Type mismatch." And the secretary obediently typed M-I-S-M-A-T-C-H, a perfectly appropriate user response to an inappropriate error message. (This kind of thing shows up in many more subtle ways, some of which are not so obviously wrong.)

Designing a user interface that makes sense to someone who understands its inner workings, and designing a user interface that makes sense to its intended audience, are not the same thing. A mechanic's understanding of how a car starts is very elaborate and detailed, but a user should be able to get by thinking, "I turn the key and press the gas, and the car starts" without necessarily thinking anything about what is under the hood. If users need to understand what's under the hood to operate the car, the car needs improvement.

Worst practices from the jargon file

The **Jargon File** defines the extremely pejorative "PEBKAC" as:

> [Abbrev., "Problem Exists Between Keyboard And Chair"] Used by support people, particularly at call centers and help desks. Not used with the public. Denotes pilot error as the cause of the crash, especially stupid errors that even a luser could figure out. Very derogatory. Usage: 'Did you ever figure out why that guy couldn't print?' 'Yeah, he kept canceling the operation before it could finish. PEBKAC'. See also ID10T. Compare pilot error, UBD.

And the particular example is unfortunately revealing of an attitude user interface people need to avoid like the plague.

It is common enough in computer programs to have modal dialog boxes; the humble JavaScript `alert("Hello, world!");` is one of innumerable ways to get them. And what they mean from an ordinary non-technical user perspective is, "A box popped up, probably one that you do not want and may not understand. What is even more annoying is that it is blocking your work; you can't continue what you are doing until you get rid of it." And so an entirely appropriate way to deal with these annoyances is to get rid of them as quickly as possible.

The example given in the Jargon File's definition of "PEBKAC" is:

> 'Did you ever figure out why that guy couldn't print?' 'Yeah, he kept canceling the operation before it could finish. PEBKAC.'

For a long time, at least, attempting to print from a GUI gave something that looked like a modal dialog box, but for this "modal dialog lookalike," there is one important difference in behavior. When you click on the button to make it go away, it destroys your print job. This is not a case of a problem existing between the user's keyboard and chair. It is a case of a problem existing between the user interface designer's keyboard and chair. PEBKAC.

To pick on the jargon file a little more, "Drool-proof paper" is defined as:

> *Documentation that has been obsessively dumbed down, to the point where only a cretin could bear to read it, is said to have succumbed to the "drool-proof paper syndrome" or to have been "written on drool-proof paper." For example, this is an actual quote from Apple Computer's LaserWriter manual: "Do not expose your LaserWriter to open fire or flame."*

Let's ignore the fact that this sounds less like a technical writer trying to be easy to understand, than corporate legal counsel trying to ward off ambulance chasers.

There is a very user-hostile attitude here: the basic idea that if your system is too difficult for your users to understand, the users must be too stupid, and making something user-friendly is a matter of stretching to meet people you should not have to cater to. Stories and terms like this circulate among programmers. We might suggest that terms like these, for your software's audience, are little, if any, better than a racial slur. They reflect an attitude we do not need.

Python and usability

You do not really understand Python until you understand something about usability as it appears in Python. Usability is the soul of "Pythonic."

It's not all about the computer!

There is something genuinely different about Python, and to explain it we would like to discuss the advantages of C.

If you want to nano-optimize every ounce of performance you can get, there is little serious competition to C. You can write assembler for different platforms, or write in C++ that is multi-paradigm like Python and have some parts of your program use high-level features like objects, templates, and operator overloading, while still writing almost unadulterated C for parts that are performance-critical. And the group of programmers that "vote with their keyboards" for using C this way, includes Guido van Rossum, who created Python. The first and canonical Python implementation is written in C, and a Pythonista underscoring the point that Python's switch statement is a very efficient dictionary will explain that Python's dictionary is implemented in tightly optimized C.

But this kind of advantage comes at a price. In the canonical list of ways to *shoot yourself in the foot* in different programming languages, C is "for people who want to load their own rounds before shooting themselves in the foot." In one Python forum, a wannabe 133t hax0r asked how to write a buffer overflow in Python, and a wry Pythonista replied apologetically: "We're sorry, but Python doesn't support that feature." But C does support the "feature" of buffer overflows. Its default string handling never leaves home without it. With manual memory management and manual handling of pointers, C also supports "features" including all kinds of memory leaks and subtle pointer errors that can be extremely difficult to debug. Python closes this Pandora's box, although Python is hardly the only language with the wisdom to do so. Python, PHP, Ruby, Perl, Tcl, and Java all close the Pandora's box that must be wide open if you are to have tightly optimized C.

C has been called a language that combines the power of using assembler with the ease of using assembler, and there may be no compiled language that surpasses C for power over bare metal, or for corresponding possibilities for tight optimization. However, this is not the only way to keep score. Python keeps score by another metric: programmer productivity.

The one overriding concern motivating decisions in Python is not how you can get the tightest control over the computer's productivity. It is how to let the programmer be most productive, and it has been said of this relentless pursuit of programmer productivity that capital sentences are passed with less thorough deliberation than obscure Python features. And if you have used Python, the difference you have experienced is precisely because of this one overriding concern, this relentless pursuit. The people in charge of Python have decided that Python is not about what to do to optimize the computer; it is about what you do to empower the programmer.

If you are interested in usability, you have a good working example of usability to look at. To put Python's strength a little differently, Python is a language where the one overriding concern and relentless pursuit is usability for you, the programmer. If you are working on usability, you are working to give end-users the same kind of thing that Python gives you. You are making a product more Pythonic to use, as opposed to giving the more C-like experience of an interface that lets users load their own rounds before shooting themselves in the foot.

Usability is about how to go from giving C user interfaces, to giving Pythonic user interfaces.

What to do in the concrete

We might take a cue from expert practice in solving problems updating Gentoo Linux. Gentoo is not an attempt to make the best "for the rest of us" Linux distribution; Gentoo is like a brand of car intended to be a favorite of amateur and professional mechanics. It allows very fine-grained control and tightly tuned systems. However, upgrades do not always work, and if we try to keep a Gentoo installation up to date, we may find that the upgrades break.

There may be a lot to Gentoo, but there is one basic, versatile, powerful technique that works for a wide variety of problems: copy the error message or salient parts, and make a well-crafted search to see where the problem has come up on the web. Most of the time deft searching is the primary skill to address breakage, and when things break, using this one skill well is often all you need even for very different problems.

There are a lot of usability methods, and a web search for "usability methods" will turn up as much information as you care to read. However, one or two basic methods, used well and used persistently, can deliver a lot of power. We suggest:

- Get five "average Joe" users who are not programmers or insiders, and ask them to do tasks with your system. NEVER help them, even by pointing out something very little and obvious. (If we help them, we have tainted our data.) Observe with a notebook; if you can videotape the interactions, that's great. Oftentimes they will have trouble in the "wrong" part of your system, not the part you're trying to focus on; that is still valuable data to heed.

- Observe people in their own "field environment," on their turf, doing their tasks, their ways. Once again they will do things that catch you off guard. Being caught off guard, and writing down what they are doing "wrong," is a good part of why such observations are desirable. This is an even more powerful setting to learn exactly how "The user is always right."

Furthermore, these should not be something tacked on at the end, as user acceptance testing is traditionally done by the waterfall method. They should feed into Agile iterations: *test early, test often*. An early, cheap, unsophisticated set of usability tests early on is more valuable than an expensive and in-depth test when things are set in stone. That the first attempt will be wrong is non-negotiable, and the user interface should be considered wrong until it tests as working—but this is another form of the basic observation in software development that untested code has defects and should be recognized to have defects until it has been tested and defects have been addressed.

Further reading

There are several resources available to expand your know-how on the topic:

- Academic anthropology texts, even though they usually do not mention usability. James Spradley's *Participant Observation* quoted earlier is one such text. The Wikipedia articles for "participant observation," "ethnography," or "cultural anthropology" provide a good nutshell summary and footnote texts that offer a helpful broadening of horizons.

- With Alertbox (http://useit.com/alertbox), Jakob Nielsen provides quick, five- or ten-minute nuggets of usability insight, and while some people complain he is stuck in the past, his work remains a basic primer about things that people still get wrong today.

- Edwin Tufte's works, such as *Envisioning Information*. His works often discuss the process of a makeover to deliver information with more accuracy and less distraction, and are a good reference point. They are not always related to computers, but they deal with usably solving difficult problems in presenting information visually.

- Plain Language (http://plainlanguage.gov) is a U.S. government website that deals with makeovers for usability in language. Like Tufte, they start with something that is painful to use and demonstrate how to transform it to something much easier.

- A List Apart, http://alistapart.com. Not all of their content is centered on usability; however, they discuss designing things well.

- Web searches for "usability" or related phrases. There's a lot of good stuff there. As mentioned earlier, there are several sites listing usability techniques. One such site was mentioned:
http://www.usabilityfirst.com/usability-methods/

Only half of these are directly about improving software or web usability, but the combination of direct and oblique references will help you pretty much as far as you have time and energy to dig.

Summary

We have covered a lot of material here; let us summarize some salient points:

- Most Python/Django types have some personal strengths that are relevant to usability testing, even if we do not realize we have them.
- Cultural anthropology is bedrock to the way of observing that helps with users.
- When you are testing, resist the temptation to help the user and taint the test.
- Waterfall placement of UAT as the last step is broken, but usability works well when it is integrated into Agile iterative processes from the beginning.
- Get it wrong the first time, and keep iterating until it is excellent.
- Test early, test often.
- A lot of unsophisticated tests are worth more than you might think.
- There are some very good resources out there that cover transforming from something terrible to something excellent.
- Focus groups and their whole approach is deprecated in usability work because the horse's mouth is a vastly overrated source of information.
- Observe with a notebook, and record things on camera if you can.
- Especially in usability and user interface, do not ask, "What can the computer do?" Ask instead, "How can the computer support the person using it?"
- Relevant interests that can help us range from history to cross-cultural encounters to martial arts; getting better at usability means stretching out into other areas besides programming.

This brings us to the end of our book. Let us turn to an appendix on debugging. We will look at debugging, and while we will cover tools such as Firebug, our work will not be about tools in the computer, but skills in the developer that wield different tools to cut to the heart of bugs.

Let's begin!

Debugging Hard JavaScript Bugs

In this section we are going to look at debugging hard bugs. (If there is a particular kind of bug that is old hat and is debugged easily, wonderful—but then you do not need this appendix's assistance.)

In this chapter we will cover:

- Some aspects of hard debugging in any context
- Using browser debugging tools, which will be considered as a group

Firefox (with Firebug), Chrome, IE 8, Opera, and Safari have something a bit like Firebug. Firefox, Chrome, IE8, and Opera all offer debugging facilities and all let you use `console.log()`.

"Just fiddling with Firebug" is considered harmful

With a tool like Firebug comes a temptation to offload the responsibility from our shoulders to the debugger's. Features like Firebug's `console.dir()`, which lets you explore an object interactively, can be very powerful. However, they can become a crutch.

Cargo cult debugging at your fingertips

Who is most effective in hand-to-hand combat: someone unskilled who is wielding a sword, someone unskilled wielding a mace, or a good blackbelt who is empty-handed?

Any, or depending on the martial art, all of these people may be more effective with a weapon than without. But weapons do not wield themselves: people, skilled or unskilled, wield them. And as impressive a tool as Firebug is, or Chrome's developer tools, a skilled developer using `alert()` well can and will debug better than a programmer who hopes that Firebug will provide a way out of the difficult work of understanding hard bugs.

Some people have raised concerns that expensive medical diagnostics make for worse physician diagnoses, not better. The reason for this is that a doctor relying on clinical observation is aware of the need for attentive vigilance in trying to make the best observations from what is available. With testing, there is a new temptation to try and let the test make the diagnosis, and a test that is asked to make a diagnosis is just not as good as a good physician's observation and reasoning. Nobody sets out for this to happen, but it does happen.

In the imagination of popular children's stories, detectives carry around magnifying glasses to look at things. Detectives today use more technology, not less, and can and do make magnified photographs. Perhaps the picturesque magnifying glass is a quaint image, and real police detectives may not use them as well-equipped soldiers do not have quaint flintlock muskets any more. But it is the martial artist, detective, doctor, *or developer*, who uses the tool. And that means that before we look at how good debugging can use Firebug or Google Chrome's developer tools, we should look at good debugging itself. Only after we have laid a foundation is it appropriate to ornament it with the virtues of good debugging weapons.

The scientific method of debugging

The core of the scientific method is not just something useful for explicitly labeled science. It can be used in several cases. In the scientific method, we do something like the following:

- Start with something you have observed but you don't understand
- Then you make hypotheses: educated guesses that might account for the phenomenon
- Think of an experiment, or experiments, where your hypotheses predict different results
- Perform the experiment(s) and try to narrow down which hypotheses account for all the data
- Repeat the cycle as desired

In science, this method is applied to understand how the natural world works. In scientific debugging, we use it to understand how our software does not work: we cannot solve the problem correctly until we understand what the problem is. And in debugging, band-aid solutions are just that: band-aids that leave the root cause unaddressed. The scientific method of debugging is not a tool for finding a band-aid that will mask a problem, but for finding the root cause so we can fix it there. We try first to duplicate a problem, then reproduce it consistently, then pin down when it does and does not happen. This is true whether or not we have debugging tools to use.

Exhausting yourself by barking up the wrong tree

Often when we are having trouble finding a bug, we are looking somewhere the bug cannot be found. You cannot find something by looking twice as hard in the wrong place.

Sometimes, *if we listen*, we will get subtle, easily overlooked clues that we are barking up the wrong tree. For instance, suppose we have the following code:

```
function init()
    {
    if (detect_feature())
        {
        initialize_with_feature();
        }
    else
        {
        initialize_without_feature();
        }
    }
```

And we can't tell which branch of the conditional is being executed. So we add `console.log()` calls (which work in either Firebug or Chrome):

```
function init()
    {
    if (detect_feature())
        {
        console.log("init 1");
        initialize_with_feature();
        }
    else
```

```
        {
        console.log("init 2");
        initialize_without_feature();
        }
    }
```

> We might suggest a naming convention for `console.log()` calls of the function's name, and then a space, and then a number or unique identifier for the call, and then any variable or other information which we might want to inspect. This is both easy and makes large amounts of logging material, *if we need it*, more navigable.

So we run this, and to our consternation nothing shows up in the log: neither `init 1` nor `init 2` is logged. The temptation is to say that the experiment was a complete failure. But if we are open to a surprise and a bit of serendipity, the experiment was a success: it showed that neither branch was being executed. That could be because `init()` was not being called at all, or because `detect_feature()` was hanging and not returning, or throwing an exception that is silenced later on. So to test that, we could add another `log` line:

```
    function init()
        {
    console.log("init 3");
    if (detect_feature())
        {
        console.log("init 1");
        initialize_with_feature();
        }
    else
        {
        console.log("init 2");
        initialize_without_feature();
        }
    }
```

And then we have evidence either that `init()` is not being called, or that it is being called but `detect_feature()` is not completing, quickly and successfully, and passing control to either branch of the conditional.

The humble debugger

Dijkstra's famous essay *The humble programmer* talked about how arrogance about one's programming abilities makes for a bad programmer. Humility can help us debug, and not only by letting us accept that our code has defects. Another side of programming humility, on a deeper level, lets us be open to surprises. Humility is an openness that can receive serendipity, and it is an openness that can receive what the code actually has instead of projecting its desires, reading into the code what it wants to see. More concretely, part of humble openness means that when you do something and the program doesn't do what you want, you are open, and choose to be open, to what the program is actually doing. What you avoid is doing the same thing a few more times in the hope that it will work correctly when you know you have seen a bug.

In concrete, this means unplugging a time sink that slowly nickels and dimes away time spent sticking one's head in the sand when we could cut to the chase and start real debugging the *first* time the bug shows itself, not reluctantly after it refuses to go away and yield to our wishful thinking. *If you are looking and looking for a bug and not finding it, the reason may well be that the bug you are looking for doesn't exist anywhere. What you need to do is recognize when you are searching and by accident stumble over a different problem that will let you address the issue.* Now part of debugging may involve legitimately doing things again to try to sound out the scope and what triggers a bug. But that does not make it helpful to consent to having our time nickeled and dimed away because we allow ourselves wishful thinking and the tacit hope that maybe the bug will go away without being fixed if only we try again a time or two.

Solving hard bugs is usually a matter of serendipity. It is like trying to find a needle in a haystack, and accidentally discovering that there are valuables that had been hidden in the haystack. It is tripping over the truth but not, *pace* Winston Churchill, picking yourself up and continuing on.

The value of taking a break

Taking a break can work. Asking an extra set of eyes can work. And pulling an all-nighter is working harder, not smarter: one hour of looking at code with fresh and well-rested eyes is worth a dozen hours of staring at the same code with blurry, sleepy eyes.

If humility matters more than you might think, persistence may be overrated. If you are locked into finding a bug one way, you may do well with a break. *A Whack on the Side of the Head* by *Roger von Oech, Business Plus*, available as an iPhone app, may be invaluable (see http://creativethink.com/). *Conceptual Blockbusting* by *James Adams, Perseus* is also invaluable. A bit of brainstorming may help you loosen up from being locked into searching where the problem may not be at all. And a bit of exercise can get blood flowing as well as loosening your thoughts.

Two major benefits to asking for help

There are two major benefits to asking for help. The first benefit is that the person you ask might be able to solve the problem. But there is another, less obvious benefit: when you ask another programmer for help, usually you do not just say "My program is not working"; you carefully explain what is going on so the other person has something to go on. And it happens more than you might expect that in the course of explaining what is going on, you realize what is causing the other bug, whether or not your dialogue partner spoke a word. "Confessional debugging" happens all the time.

Firebug and Chrome developer tools

Firebug set the standard for good debugging support, and Chrome web development tools are not a port of Firebug to Chrome, but are for Chrome what Firebug is for Firebox. Both are powerful; for CSS work, sometimes there may be things visible in Firebug that do not show up in Chrome.

The basics across browsers

Firebug's console displays the output of `console.log()`, and it also displays requests (`GET`, `POST`, and the like), which you can drill down and see their contents.

One helpful thing when something isn't working is to look at what the server is returning in response to requests. The basic question is whether the server is sending good data that the client is not handling properly, or whether the server is sending bad data: in terms of scientific debugging, this is a way to narrow down where the bug is hiding.

Appendix

The console, with the output of `console.log()` statements, looks like this:

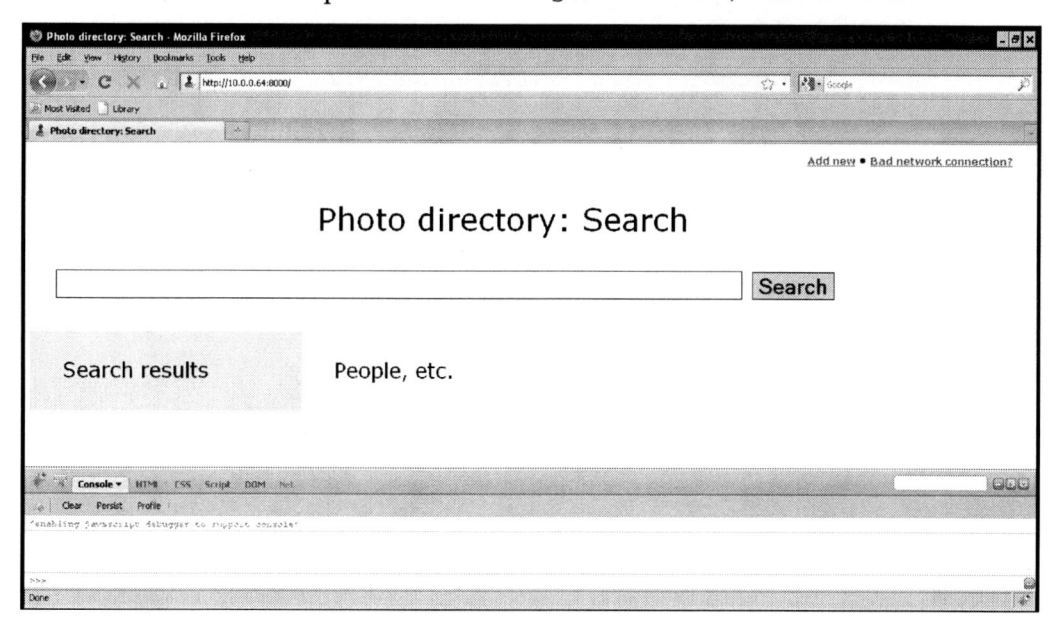

It is accessed by installing Firebug from `http://getfirebug.com/`, and then clicking the bug icon at the bottom-right of your window:

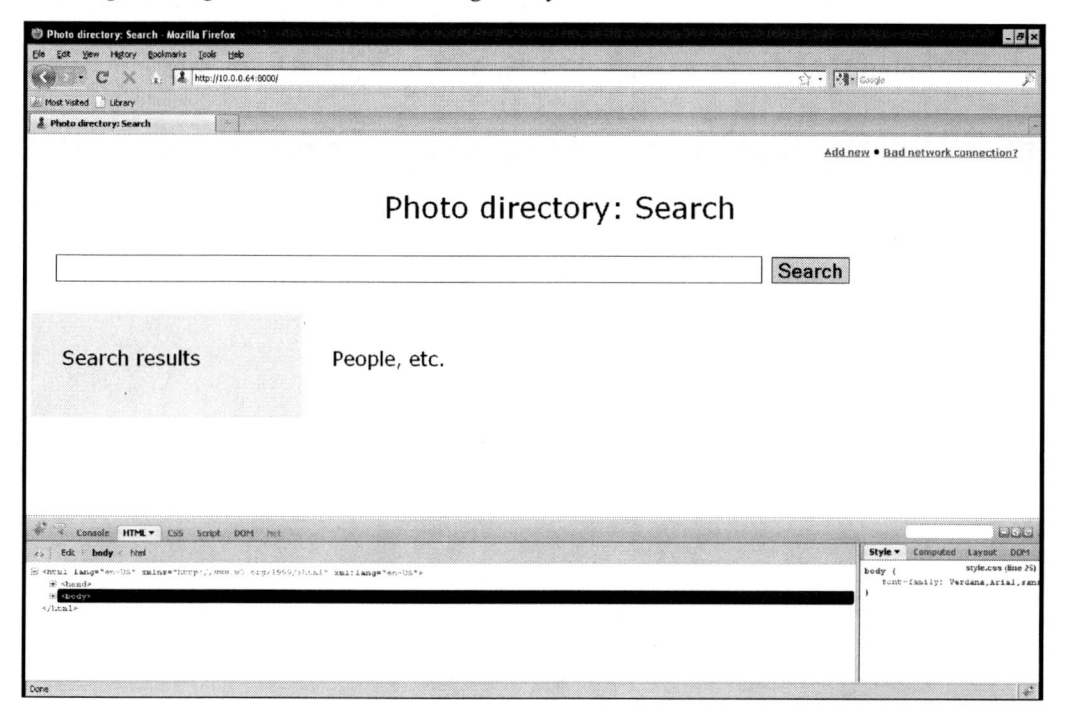

Debugging Hard JavaScript Bugs

Google Chrome has developer tools under its **View** menu, and lets you see the JavaScript console:

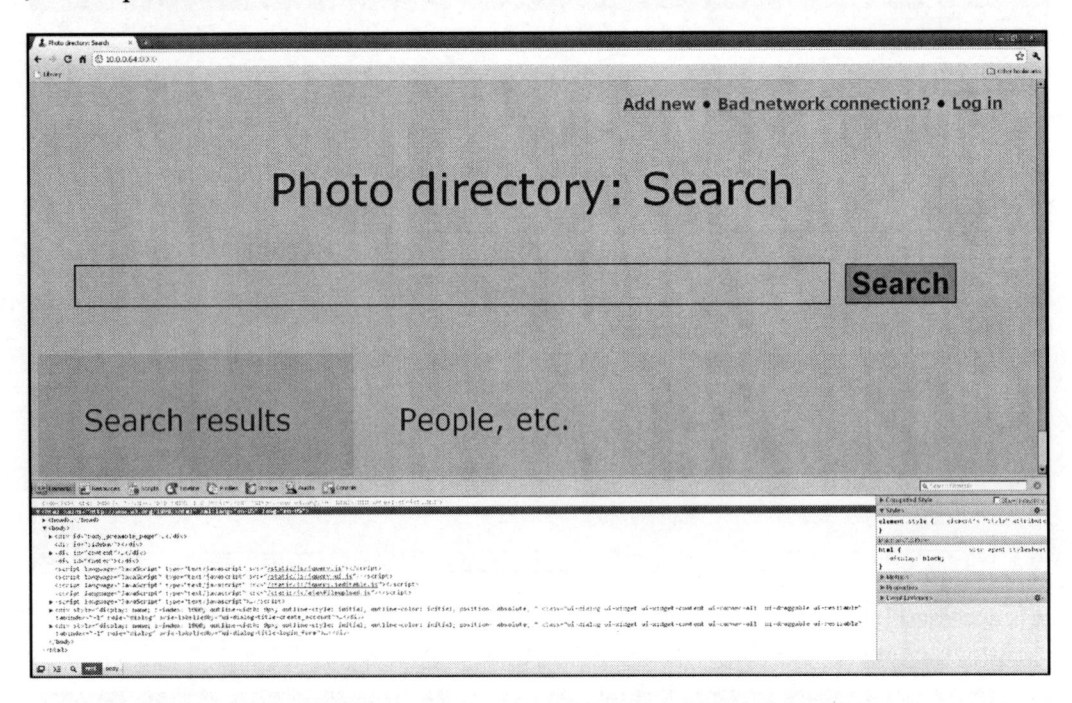

Internet Explorer has developer tools available as shown in the following:

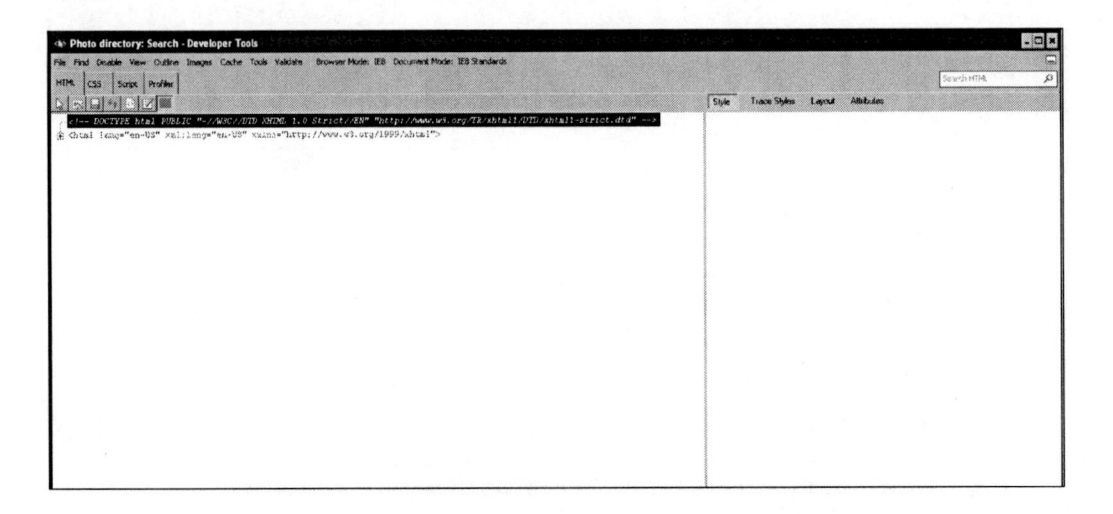

And in Opera, we have the following:

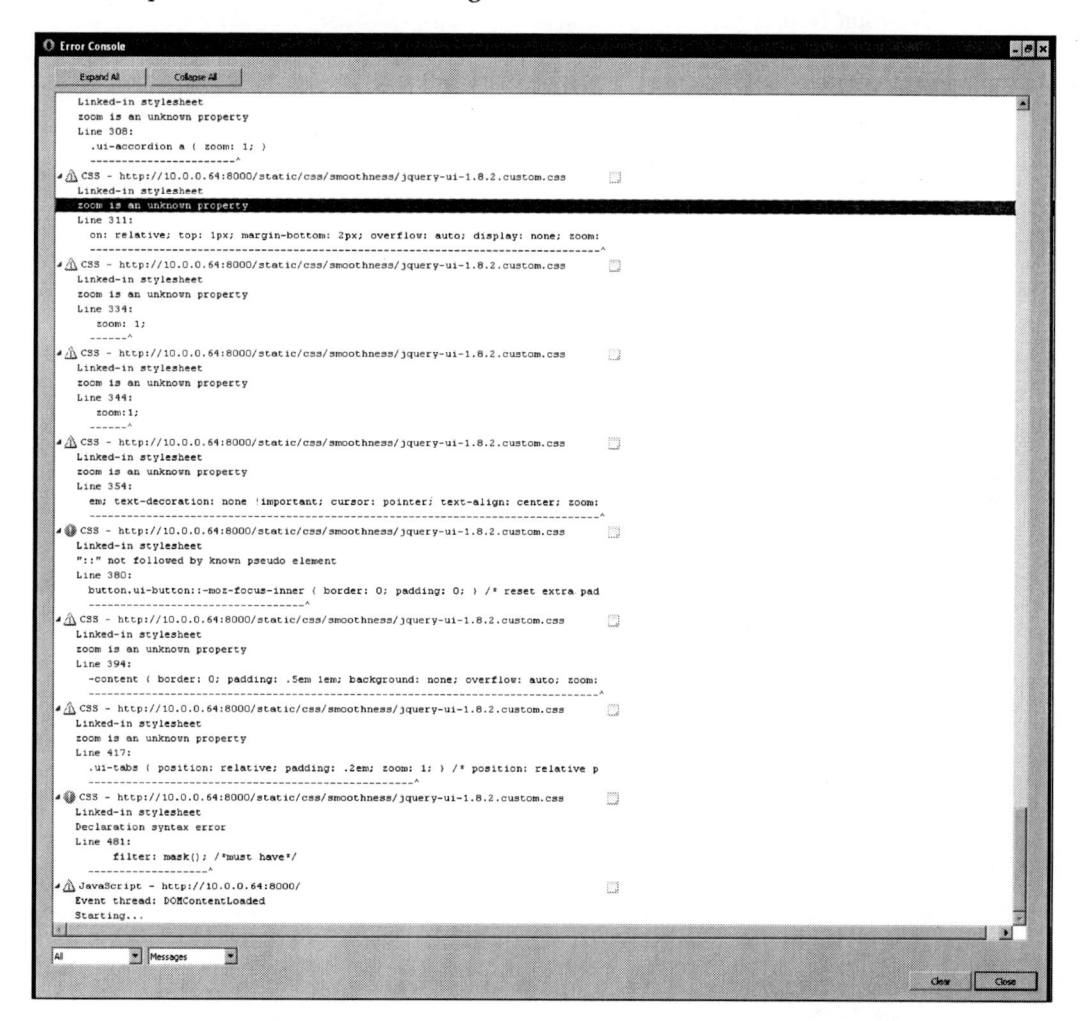

Zeroing in on Chrome

Chrome has the following tabs/buttons:

- **Elements**, which allows drilldown access to the live DOM.
- **Resources**, which is a dashboard for seeing what the delays were in a page being rendered.
- **Scripts**, which provides debugger services in the tradition of GDB for debugging JavaScript, including setting breakpoints, seeing the values of variables, and so on.

Debugging Hard JavaScript Bugs

- **Timelines**, which can be used to track resource usage for optimization. The bottom-left hand of the screen has record/stop and clear buttons:

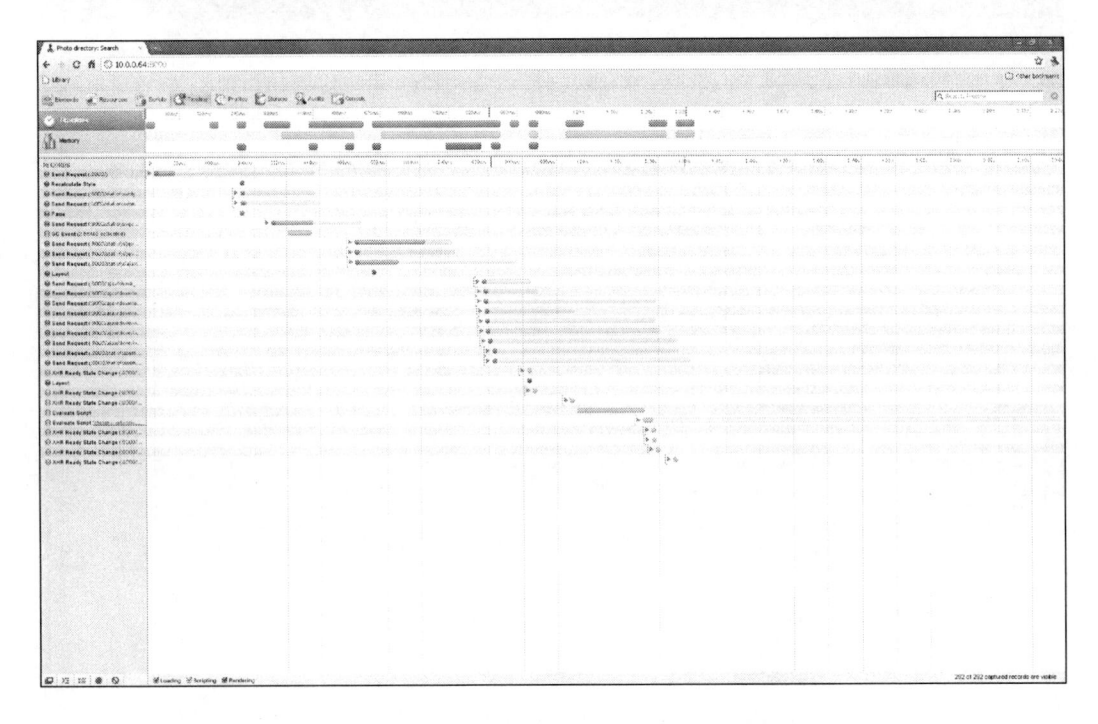

- **Profiles**, which allows CPU and memory usage profiling.
- **Storage**, which looks at cookies, sessions, HTML5 databases, and other local storage.
- **Audits**, which are meant to support third-party plugins to audit pretty much anything: mobile readiness, network optimization, and so on.
- **Console**, which provides a command-line console that includes but goes beyond Firebug's command line.

What you can see, in terms of the DOM, JavaScript, CSS, and so on, you can modify to allow surgical experiments rather than reloading a page and doing multiple things to keep track of state. In keeping with *"Where there is output, let there be input,"* clicking, double-clicking, or right-clicking on the live DOM model, JavaScript code, properties in CSS as well as the DOM or JavaScript, and the like, can be used to modify existing values.

Firebug got the game going and showed what it was to utilize a JavaScript debugger correctly. Internet Explorer has something vaguely in the same vein, but perhaps not a full-blooded replacement. Google in making Chrome tried to see how far they could push the envelope; as already mentioned, the developer tools are for Chrome what Firebug is for Firebox, but they are not a Firebug port. They are extremely deep and worth a book in their own right; Google's resources on the web can be found at http://www.chromium.org/devtools, with an in-depth video at http://tinyurl.com/GoogleChromeDevToolsInDepth, to which we refer the reader for further study. A dir(), for example, of our PHOTO_DIRECTORY namespace yields both a broad overview and deep possibilities for drilling down:

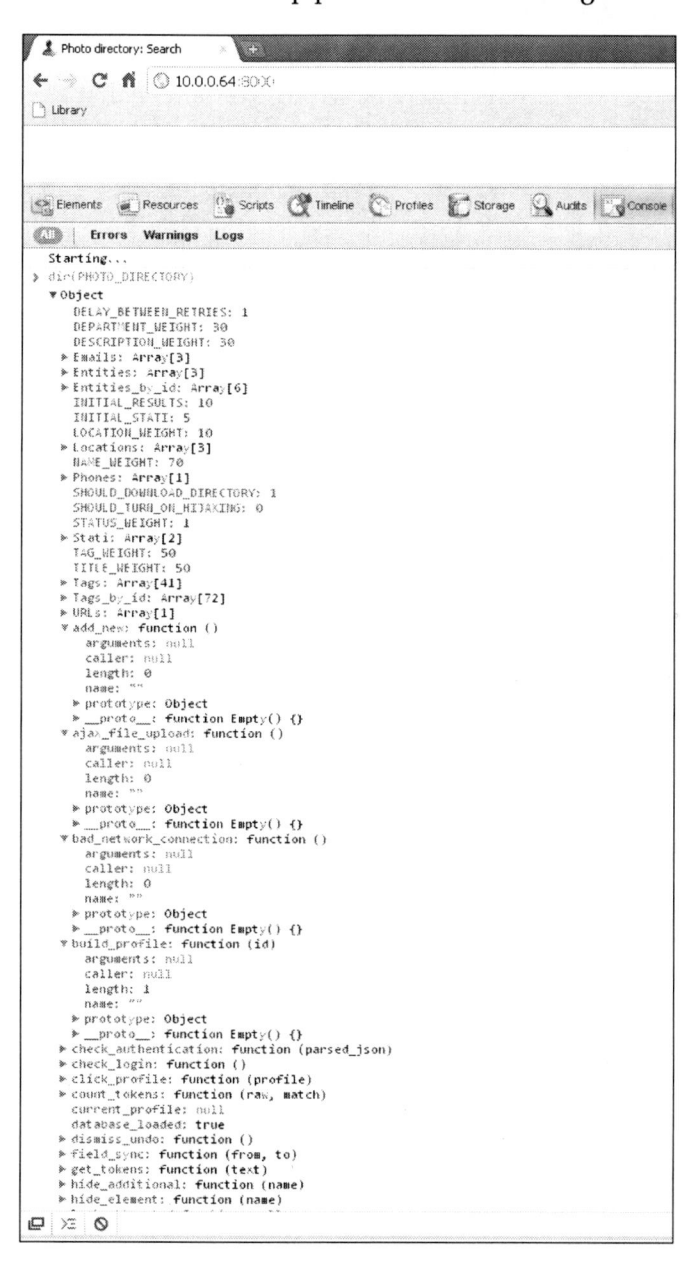

Debugging Hard JavaScript Bugs

Let's stop a minute and pause for a moment of, "That's funny..."

We are not now actively trying to solve a bug, but we may have stumbled on something odd: this screenshot shows three **Entities** and six **Entities_by_id**. Our off-the-cuff expectation may be that that the two counts should be the same. Even though we aren't actively trying to track down a bug, nor address symptoms, this may be the root cause of a bug.

Before we drill down it would help to think. There are at least two obvious expectations, one or both of which may be wrong. It could be that `Entities_by_id` are getting things twice; we observe that six **Entities_by_id** is exactly a multiple of three **Entities**. Or it could just be a few more. If there are `Entities` that have been deleted, it could be that `Entities_by_id` reflects deleted entries and `Entities` does not. With that in mind, let's drill down and see what we see, how well the system treats our hypotheses:

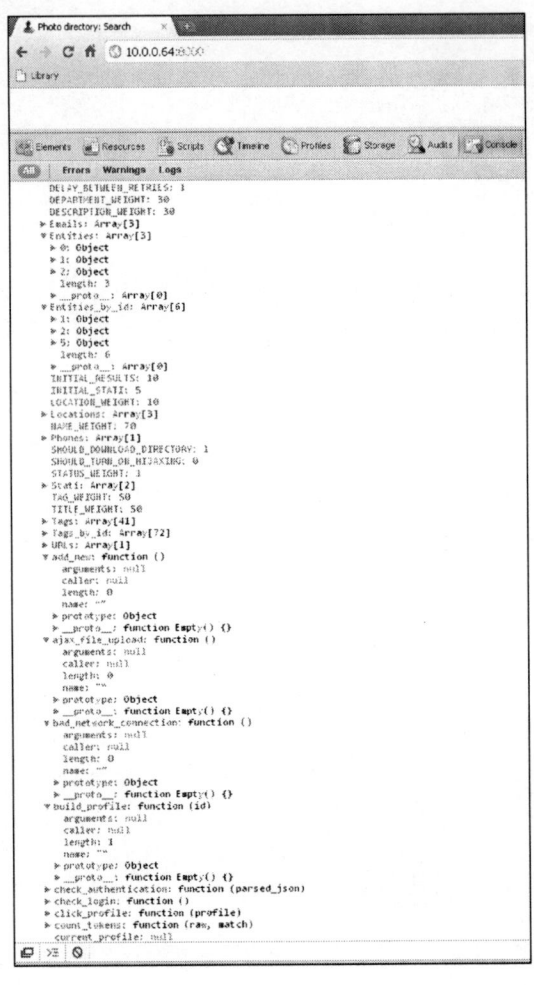

Appendix

This suggests another explanation, that despite Chrome leading us to believe we have a six-element array, we might have an array of length 6 from JavaScript's perspective, but the keys used to populate it max out at five. It has exactly three physical entries, just like the other. Let's go over to the **Scripts** page and select the **:8000/** entry (the one for JavaScript on the page, although we can see other source files too). That reads as follows:

```
PHOTO_DIRECTORY.load_database = function()
    {
    if (PHOTO_DIRECTORY.no_network ||
        !PHOTO_DIRECTORY.SHOULD_DOWNLOAD_DIRECTORY)
        {
        return;
        }
    $.ajax(
        {
        success: function(data, textStatus, XMLHttpRequest)
            {
            if (PHOTO_DIRECTORY.check_authentication(data))
                {
                if (PHOTO_DIRECTORY.Emails.length == 0)
                    {
                    PHOTO_DIRECTORY.tables_loaded += 1;
                    }
                PHOTO_DIRECTORY.Emails = data;
                if (PHOTO_DIRECTORY.tables_loaded >=
                    PHOTO_DIRECTORY.tables_available)
                    {
                    PHOTO_DIRECTORY.database_loaded = true;
                    }
                }
            },
        url: "/ajax/download/Email",
        });
    $.ajax(
        {
        success: function(data, textStatus, XMLHttpRequest)
            {
            if (PHOTO_DIRECTORY.check_authentication(data))
                {
                if (PHOTO_DIRECTORY.Entities.length == 0)
                    {
                    PHOTO_DIRECTORY.tables_loaded += 1;
                    }
                PHOTO_DIRECTORY.Entities = data;
                PHOTO_DIRECTORY.Locations = data;
                for(var index = 0; index < PHOTO_DIRECTORY.Entities.length;
                    ++index)
                    {
                    PHOTO_DIRECTORY.Entities_by_id[
                        PHOTO_DIRECTORY.Entities[index].pk] =
                        PHOTO_DIRECTORY.Entities[index];
                    }
                if (PHOTO_DIRECTORY.tables_loaded >=
                    PHOTO_DIRECTORY.tables_available)
                    {
                    PHOTO_DIRECTORY.database_loaded = true;
                    }
                }
            },
        url: "/ajax/download/Entity",
        });
    $.ajax(
        {
        success: function(data, textStatus, XMLHttpRequest)
            {
            if (PHOTO_DIRECTORY.check_authentication(data))
                {
                PHOTO_DIRECTORY.tables_loaded += 1;
                PHOTO_DIRECTORY.Phones = data;
                if (PHOTO_DIRECTORY.tables_loaded >=
                    PHOTO_DIRECTORY.tables_available)
                    {
                    PHOTO_DIRECTORY.database_loaded = true;
                    }
                }
            },
```

`load_database()` loads into `Entities_by_id` exactly what the name would suggest: it is being used as a hash with what turn out to be primary keys assigned by Django, and this installation has some entries that are deleted, leaving holes. It so happens that, for our implementation, the JavaScript interpreter treats this as a (slightly) sparse integer array.

This particular bug hunt was a lottery ticket that, like most lottery tickets, didn't pan out. However, it is an example of how to debug live, and live debugging isn't just when you use the tool optimally and pin down an annoying bug with seven symptoms. That may be the kind of story we prefer to tell our fellow programmers, but it isn't the only story in a debugging phase of programming. It is a live example of the exploratory process that sometimes finds the bugs being traced, sometimes stumbles on unrelated bugs, and sometimes doesn't turn up anything interesting. (Or it may turn up something else interesting, like a juicy hook for an improved feature offering.)

The point of debugging remains scientific debugging, even with tools at our fingertips that will do all this and more.

Summary

In this appendix, we have looked at the basic mindset for debugging and use of tools, tools available for different browsers, and Chrome's developer tools.

In this book, we have had a whirlwind tour of Django Ajax with jQuery, and paid attention to usability. We have covered the basics of Ajax with Django, jQuery as the most common JavaScript framework, server-side validation, especially in light of usability, server-side database search in Django, jQuery UI in-place editing, how to implement autocomplete functionality, Django's ModelForm as a powerful and easy tool, client-side processing, including a client-side database, customization and further development, tinkering to make a working system better, usability for hackers, and debugging JavaScript.

Where next?

Probably best a mixture of web searches, library trips, practical development, and a brainstorm or two about places to go!

Index

Symbols

$.aj0axSetup()
  $.get() 45, 46
  $.post() 45, 46
  .load() 46
  about 45
  sample invocation 45
$.ajax()
  about 39
  closures 40, 41
  context 40
  data 42
  dataFilter 43
  dataType 43
  error(XMLHttpRequest, textStatus, error-
     Thrown) 44
  prototypes and prototypal inheritance 42
  success(data, textStatus, XMLHttpRequest)
     44
  type 44
  url 44
(?u) 97
-cmp 99
.getJSON() 43
.load()
  about 46
  sample invocation 46, 47
@ajax_login_required decorator 107
@login_required decorator 107

A

admin.py 106, 107
AHAH solution
  about 189-192
  Django templates 192
Ajax
  about 8
  partial page updates 8
  technologies 9
ajax_profile() 244
Ajax technologies
  Comet 20
  CSS 19
  DOM 19
  HTML/XHTML 17
  iframes 20
  JavaScript 9
  JavaScript/Ajax libraries 21
  JSON 18
  server-side technologies 21
  XML 18
  XMLHttpRequest 14
**anthropological observation, usability 266,
    267**
anthropology
  about 262
  resources 283
anthropology-based techniques
  about 263
  card sorting 263, 264
assumptions
  making 76
  U.S.-based assumptions! 72, 74
Asynchronous JavaScript and XML. *See*
    Ajax
authenticate() function 110

B

body_main hook 116
boilerplate code
  inserting, for jQuery UI 154, 155
build_profile() 258

C

C
  advantages 280, 281
card sorting
  about 263
  example 263, 264
cargo cult research 265
Cascading Style Sheets. *See* CSS
Chrome
  developer tool 290, 292
  tabs/buttons 293-298
clean() method 65, 66
clean_<fieldname>() method 66
clean_serialnumber() method 66
client-side
  handling 209-232
client-side search 86
closure-based example
  about 52
  creating 52-55
Comet 20
console.dir() 285
console.log() 285
contains 101
CPR 267
cross-cultural encounters 272, 273
CSS
  about 19, 232
  for styling directory 232-240
culture shock 270

D

database
  handling, through Django models 86, 87
  searching for 95-100
day 101
Daylight Saving Time
  handling 252-258

decorator 105
detect_feature() 288
Django
  about 7, 21, 35
  AHAH solution 189-192
  kickstart example 22
Django admin interface 122, 123
Django models
  database, handling through 86, 87
  for intranet employee photo directory 87-94
Django templates
  workaround 146
Django templates, for AHAH
  about 192
  parent template 192
  profile drill-down template 192-201
  search results template 192-195
Django templates, workaround
  about 146
  Ajax behavior, turning on 156
  boilerplate code, from jQuery UI documentation 154, 155
  first workaround 148-153
  interest-based negotiation 146, 147
  refining 159-162
  server side code 156-159
Django templating engine
  about 23-30, 114
  benefits 24
  kickstart example 22
Document Object Model. *See* DOM
DOM 19
Domain Specific Languages. *See* DSLs
Don't Repeat Yourself (DRY) 43

E

else clause 139
endswith 101
Entity class 90
exact 101
eXtensible Markup Language. *See* XML
ExtensionField 88

F

Facebook 83
field_sync() 252

Firebug
  about 285
  barking up wrong tree 287, 288
  benefits, of asking for help 290
  cargo cult debugging 285, 286
  developer tool 290, 291
  humble debugger 289
  scientific method, of debugging 286
footer_javascript_page 116
functions.py
  about 106
  project-specific functions 107
  StackOverflow solution 107

G

Gentoo 282
gt 101
gte 101

H

Hello, World!
  customizing 168-170
  expanding 168-170
  ModelForm, using 165-167
hide_element() 252
hijaxing 120
homepage() 245
homepage field 91
HTML 17
human speech 8

I

icontains 101
iendswith 101
iexact 101
iframes 20
image field 94
in 101
instanceof keyword 12
Internet Explorer
  developer tool 292
intranet employee photo directory
  models for 87-94
iregex 101

isinstance() function 12
isnull 101
istartswith 101

J

jargon file
  about 279
  example 280
JavaScript
  about 9
  language decisions, limitations 10
  setting 32
  versus Python 12
JavaScript/Ajax libraries 21
JavaScript frameworks 35
Jeditable-enabled elements 248
jQuery
  about 125
  selectors 48
jQuery-powered Ajax 7
jQuery Ajax facilities
  $.aj0axSetup() 45
  $.ajax() 39
  about 39
jQuery UI
  boilerplate code, adding for 154, 155
jQuery UI autocomplete
  adding 142, 146
jQuery UI themeroller 142
JSON 8, 18
JSON.parse() method 43

L

language decisions, JavaScript
  limitations 10
LinkedIn 83
Location model 89, 135
Location object 89
login() function 110
low-level validation
  about 62
  malicious input, example 63, 64
  regular expressions, matching 62, 63
lt 101
lte 101

M

methods, XMLHttpRequest
  abort() 14
  getAllResponseHeaders() 14
  getResponseHeader() 14
  open() 15
  send() 15
Model 21
ModelForm
  page appearance, customizing 170-182
  using for Hello, World! 165-168
ModelForm hood
  customizing 182, 183
models
  for intranet employee photo directory 87-94
models.FileField() 94
Monster.com 262
month 101
MTV pattern 21, 108

N

name__icontains 101
notes field 89
notifications div 114

O

Object-relational Management (ORM) 100, 102
offer_login() 118, 249
OFFICE_CHOICES list 87
office field 89
onload event 119
onmouseover handler 247
onsole.log() function 216
overlaid function 8

P

page
  making responsive 127
  plugin, including 127
page-specific JavaScript 136, 137

page appearance, ModelForm
  customizing 170-182
partial page updates 8, 9
password input
  handling 250, 252
plugin
  including, on page 127
profile drill-down template 195-201
progressive enhancement 142-146
prototypes and prototypal inheritance 42
py-editdist package 97
Python
  versus JavaScript 12

R

regex 101
run_validators() 65

S

search.html 107, 114-121
search results template 192-195
selectors, jQuery 48, 51
send_notification() 117
server-side search 86
server-side technologies 21
server side views
  AHAH server-side search function 207, 208
  AHAH view 203
  entities, deleting 202
  helper functions, AHAH view 204, 206
  updated model 206
  user login status, verifying 202
setTimeout() 117
SGML 18
show_element() 252
sorl-thumbnail 99
Standard Generalized Markup Language.
    See SGML
startswith 101
static content
  setting 32
style.css 106, 113
success function 118

T

tagging.register() 93
technologies, Ajax
  Comet 20
  CSS 19
  DOM 19
  HTML/XHTML 17
  iframes 20
  JavaScript 9
  JavaScript/Ajax libraries 21
  JSON 18
  server-side technologies 21
  XML 18
  XMLHttpRequest 14
template
  about 21
  for client-side requirements 128, 129, 132
  page-specific JavaScript 136, 137
  profile bulk 132, 133
  server-side, support on 137-139
  whitespace and delivery 133-136
TextStatus tags 93
to_python() 65
traceback 271
TurboGears 35
tweaks and bugfixes
  Borg behavior, eliminating 244, 245
  default name, setting 244
  deleted instances display, preventing 246-249
  favicon.ico, adding 249
  jQuery's load(), confusing with html() 245

U

U.S.-based assumptions!
  conforming to 72, 74
Uniform Determination Of Death Act 268
update_autocomplete() event handler 156
updated urlpatterns 241
usability
  anthropological observation 265-268
  anthropology-based techniques 263
  cargo cult research 265
  debugging 271, 272
  history 273
  live cross-cultural encounters 272, 273
  methods 282
user
  optimization 278

V

validate() 65
validation 78
validation, Django way
  about 64
  approach 66, 67
  error messages, avoiding 71
  GPS coordinates, example 70, 71
  Pythonic way 68, 69
  steps 65, 66
  zero-one-infinity rule 68
View 21
views.py
  about 106
  functions, webpages rendering 108-112
Visual Basic .NET 262

W

Web 1.0 8
Web 2.0
  about 8
  features 9
Website class 91
week_day 101
Whitesmith brace style 209
workaround, Django templates
  about 146
  Ajax behavior, turning on 156
  boilerplate code, from jQuery UI documentation 154, 155
  first workaround 148-153
  interest-based negotiation 146, 147
  refining 159-162
  server side code 156-159

X

XHTML 17
XML 8, 18
XMLHttpRequest
  about 9, 11, 14
  methods 14
  properties 15
XMLHttpRequest methods
  abort() 14
  about 14
  getAllResponseHeaders() 14
  getResponseHeader() 14
  open() 15
  send() 15

Y

year 101

Z

zero-one-infinity rule 68

[PACKT] open source
PUBLISHING — community experience distilled

**Thank you for buying
Django JavaScript Integration: AJAX and jQuery**

About Packt Publishing

Packt, pronounced 'packed', published its first book "*Mastering phpMyAdmin for Effective MySQL Management*" in April 2004 and subsequently continued to specialize in publishing highly focused books on specific technologies and solutions.

Our books and publications share the experiences of your fellow IT professionals in adapting and customizing today's systems, applications, and frameworks. Our solution based books give you the knowledge and power to customize the software and technologies you're using to get the job done. Packt books are more specific and less general than the IT books you have seen in the past. Our unique business model allows us to bring you more focused information, giving you more of what you need to know, and less of what you don't.

Packt is a modern, yet unique publishing company, which focuses on producing quality, cutting-edge books for communities of developers, administrators, and newbies alike. For more information, please visit our website: `www.packtpub.com`.

About Packt Open Source

In 2010, Packt launched two new brands, Packt Open Source and Packt Enterprise, in order to continue its focus on specialization. This book is part of the Packt Open Source brand, home to books published on software built around Open Source licences, and offering information to anybody from advanced developers to budding web designers. The Open Source brand also runs Packt's Open Source Royalty Scheme, by which Packt gives a royalty to each Open Source project about whose software a book is sold.

Writing for Packt

We welcome all inquiries from people who are interested in authoring. Book proposals should be sent to author@packtpub.com. If your book idea is still at an early stage and you would like to discuss it first before writing a formal book proposal, contact us; one of our commissioning editors will get in touch with you.

We're not just looking for published authors; if you have strong technical skills but no writing experience, our experienced editors can help you develop a writing career, or simply get some additional reward for your expertise.

[PACKT] open source
community experience distilled
PUBLISHING

Django 1.0 Website Development

ISBN: 978-1-847196-78-1   Paperback: 272 pages

Build powerful web applications, quickly and cleanly, with the Django application framework

1. Teaches everything you need to create a complete Web 2.0-style web application with Django 1.0
2. Learn rapid development and clean, pragmatic design
3. No knowledge of Django required
4. Packed with examples and screenshots for better understanding

Learning jQuery 1.3

ISBN: 978-1-847196-70-5   Paperback: 444 pages

Better Interaction Design and Web Development with Simple JavaScript Techniques

1. An introduction to jQuery that requires minimal programming experience
2. Detailed solutions to specific client-side problems
3. For web designers to create interactive elements for their designs

Please check www.PacktPub.com for information on our titles

[PACKT] open source
community experience distilled

Django 1.1 Testing and Debugging
ISBN: 978-1-847197-56-6   Paperback: 436 pages

Building rigorously tested and bug-free Django applications

1. Develop Django applications quickly with fewer bugs through effective use of automated testing and debugging tools.
2. Ensure your code is accurate and stable throughout development and production by using Django's test framework.
3. Understand the working of code and its generated output with the help of debugging tools.

jQuery 1.4 Reference Guide
ISBN: 978-1-849510-04-2   Paperback: 336 pages

A comprehensive exploration of the popular JavaScript library

1. Quickly look up features of the jQuery library
2. Step through each function, method, and selector expression in the jQuery library with an easy-to-follow approach
3. Understand the anatomy of a jQuery script
4. Write your own plug-ins using jQuery's powerful plug-in architecture

Please check **www.PacktPub.com** for information on our titles

Lightning Source UK Ltd.
Milton Keynes UK
174218UK00002B/108/P